Voices of Drought

① Sun Sea and Sound by Rommen ed.
978-0199988860

② Funky Nassau by Rommen
978 0520265671

③ Musical Life in Guyana by Cambridge
978 14968 09766

④ Chocolate Surrealism by Njorogé
978-14968 06895

⑤ Music and Black Ethnicity
978-156QQ 07081

Voices of Drought

The Politics of Music and Environment
in Northeastern Brazil

MICHAEL B. SILVERS

UNIVERSITY OF
ILLINOIS PRESS
Urbana, Chicago, and Springfield

Library of Congress Cataloging-in-Publication Data
Names: Silvers, Michael B. author.
Title: Voices of drought: the politics of music
    and environment in Northeastern Brazil /
    Michael B. Silvers.
Description: Urbana: University of Illinois Press,
    [2018] | Includes bibliographical references
    and index.
Identifiers: LCCN 2018018121| ISBN 9780252042089
    (hardcover: alk. paper) | ISBN 9780252083778
    (pbk.: alk. paper)
Subjects: LCSH: Music—Political aspects—Brazil,
    Northeast. | Droughts—Brazil, Northeast. |
    Ecomusicology—Brazil, Northeast.
Classification: LCC ML3917.B6 S59 2018 | DDC 306.4
    /842098131—dc23
LC record available at https://lccn.loc.gov/2018018121

Ebook ISBN 978-0-252-05083-1

To Mom and Dad

Whence comes the *baião*?
It comes from beneath the clay of the earth.

. . . .

Whence comes hope, the sustenance that spreads the green
from your eyes across the plantation?
Oh, it comes from beneath the clay of the earth

—Gilberto Gil, "De onde vem o baião" (Whence comes the *baião*)

Contents

Acknowledgments

I AM INDEBTED TO the many wonderful and generous people who have helped me with the research and writing of this book over the past nine years. Various granting agencies and institutions supported this work throughout its many stages: the American Council of Learned Societies, the U.S. Department of State and MTVU, the Lemann Institute for Brazilian Studies at the University of Illinois, the John A. and Grace W. Nicholson Gift Fund via the UIUC Unit for Criticism and Interpretive Theory, the University of Illinois Campus Research Board, the UCLA Department of Ethnomusicology, and the UCLA International Institute, as well as the publication subventions from the American Musicological Society supported by the Dragan Plamenac Endowment and the UIUC College of Fine and Applied Arts.

Many thanks to those who offered me logistical support: Kimberley Johnson, Sabrina Bailey, Jennifer Gavel, Elis Artz, Nathan Mandel, Chad Wahls, Kirstin Dougan, Jeff Magee, Lori Melchi, Donna Armstrong, and the Office of the Vice Chancellor for Research at UIUC, specifically Nancy Abelmann, Maria Guillombardo, Craig Koslofsky, and Carol Symes.

Thank you to Susan Koshi and to Donna Buchanan, Jerry Dávila, Marc Hertzman, Alejandro Madrid, Gabriel Solis, and Deborah Wong for your thoughtful readings of my work and your helpful suggestions. Also a tremendous thanks to Jennifer Post and Daniel Sharp for insightful—crucial—comments.

Thank you to Anthony Seeger, who helped shape and sharpen this project. And many thanks to Steven Loza, Mitchell Morris, and Timothy D. Taylor.

Thanks to professors who planted the seeds for this research: two influential mentors in ethnomusicology, Gina Fatone and Janet Sturman, and anthropologist Lieba Faier, who first turned me on to posthumanist scholarship.

I am thankful for the exceptional mentorship of my ethnomusicology colleagues at Illinois—Donna Buchanan, Bruno Nettl, and Gabriel Solis—and for the support of my other colleagues in (ethno)musicology, past and present: Christina Bashford, Nili Belkind, Rick Deja, Lillie Gordon, Bill Kinderman, Chris Macklin, Gayle Magee, Ulrike Praeger, Katherine Syer, and Steve Wilson. Also thank you to the graduate students who took my Music and Ecology seminar in the spring of 2015: Maria Arrua, Emma Burrows, Lucas Henry, Jon Hollis, Jamil Jorge, Yi-Hung Ma, Gloria Mo, Elisa Moles, Andrew Somerville, and Nolan Vallier. And thanks to my own cohort from graduate school: Shannon Aridgides, Katie Stuffelbeam Blankenship, Rebecca Dirksen, Jennie Gubner, Michael Iyanaga, Andy Pettit, and Kathleen Wiens.

I am infinitely grateful to my writing partner, Catherine Appert, who read and commented on every word of this book at least two dozen times. Catherine, thank you.

Above all else, I owe an immense debt of gratitude for the profound kindness and generosity of the people I have met and come to know in Ceará.

This work is indebted to the research and ideas of many intellectuals and scholars in Ceará. Some of my preoccupations in this book were first theirs: to name but a few cited in the following pages, Márcio Mattos on the musical legacy of Luiz Gonzaga; Nirez on the significance of Lauro Maia; Oswald Barroso on "Asa branca" as a musical instance of the drought industry; and Danielle Maia Cruz, with Lea Carvalho Rodrigues, on the unique qualities of Ceará's Carnival and the holiday's articulation with cultural policy.

Many thanks are due to the immensely creative Ricardo Bezerra, who was my host father in Fortaleza when I was a college student and is now someone I consider family. Ricardo, a professor of landscape architecture, is also a composer/songwriter whose 1978 album *Maraponga* featured arrangements by the legendary Hermeto Pascoal and performances by Amelinha, Raimundo Fagner, Sivuca, and Jaques Morelenbaum. Ricardo also cowrote a couple of Fagner's earliest hits—most notably, the jangly "Cavalo ferro" and dreamy "Manera fru-fru manera." Ricardo helped inspire my research. He offered me not just guidance, friendship, and many research connections but also generous conversation and perspectives that inform this book. Ricardo, *obrigado*.

Ethnomusicologist Márcio Mattos has been another invaluable and generous mentor since I began this project. I am inspired by the applied work he, his students, and his colleagues do at the Universidade Federal do Cariri. Thanks also to Weber dos Anjos, Carmen Saenz Coopat, and the rest of the music faculty at UFCA.

Danielle Maia Cruz has been my anthropological sparring partner in Fortaleza for nearly a decade—she has brought me to the mat on too many occasions to count. I long for our debates.

Also thanks to DiFreitas, Elvis Matos, Descartes Gadelha, Flávio Paiva, Pingo de Fortaleza, Adelson Viana, Simone Castro, Patrícia Soares Holanda, João Soares, Heriberto Porto, Raimundo Fagner, Izaira Silvino, Nirez, Oswald Barroso, Lea Carvalho Rodrigues, Mary Pimentel, Sulamita Vieira, and Tarcísio de Lima, among many others who shared their time and their wisdom with me.

I have nothing but gratitude and *saudades* for my talented friends who helped me with this project: Nathália Cardoso, Tarcísio Martins Bezerra Filho, Priscila Lima, Lorena Nunes, Caio Castelo, Diego Pontes, Uirá dos Reis, Cátia Riehl, Sâmia Maluf, and Toinha Santos.

Thanks to my sister-in-law Janett and her wonderful family, especially Seu Platão, for their assistance with this project in so many ways.

Thank you to my editor, Laurie Matheson, for her sage guidance, and to Julie Laut, Mary M. Hill, Jennifer Clark, and the rest of the staff at the University of Illinois Press who helped me realize this project. And thanks to UIP for allowing me to reprint a significant portion of "Birdsong and a Song about a Bird: Popular Music and the Mediation of Traditional Ecological Knowledge in Northeastern Brazil" *Ethnomusicology* Vol. 59, No. 3 (2015): 380-397, here in chapter 3.

Thank you, Saxon, for you and for your editorial ear, for your willingness to learn to love the *sertão* with me, and for putting up with me as I worked on this.

Thank you to my mom and dad, who have supported this project and my academic path in countless ways. This book was born in the little apartment on Peace Street.

A little over a decade ago, my father, a social scientist who relied on quantitative methods throughout his career, began to advocate mixed-methods research in the years surrounding his retirement. I run no regressions here, but I hope to have carried the spirit of interdisciplinarity into this project.

Although this project has benefited from the knowledge and labor of others, its shortcomings are entirely my own.

Voices of Drought

Introduction

June 21, 2009
Orós, Ceará, Brazil

A wooden motorboat took us across the Orós Reservoir, a man-made oasis in the land of drought, on the day of my brother's wedding. We traveled around a small island owned by Raimundo Fagner, a balladeer with a string of hits between the 1970s and 1990s. His "Borbulhas de amor" (Love bubbles), a 1991 Portuguese-language cover of Dominican Juan Luis Guerra's love song, is now a *brega* (which literally means "tacky" and is the name of a genre of romantic pop) classic: "I wish I were a fish / so I could dive into your limpid aquarium / to make love bubbles to enchant you." Before sundown, we gathered for the event at the Fagner Foundation, a community center supported by the famous singer. We were in the height of the St. John's Day season, also known as the June Festivals, the biggest holiday in the Northeast of Brazil. For the wedding, the space had been festooned with typical St. John's Day decorations meant to recall a rural idyll: multicolored bunting, a bonfire, and scarecrow-like figures in hillbilly garb.

Orós, a small city in the *sertão* (backlands) of the northeastern Brazilian state of Ceará, is my sister-in-law's hometown. Her father, Seu Platão (Mr. Plato—he has a brother named Aristoteles), and two of her sisters still live there. Her other siblings and their families traveled six hours for the wedding from Fortaleza, the state capital, in a van with my family. The ceremony was short and heartfelt, with a moment of humor resulting from my brother's mangled Portuguese ("I promise to be unfaithful," he said after mishearing the priest). After the ceremony, the local quadrille troupe performed a choreographed square dance that, as is standard for St. John's Day quadrilles, involved a reenactment of what is called a "hillbilly wedding." We applauded, ate dinner, and spent the rest of the night dancing to a local trio playing the classic *forró* repertoire, mostly songs by Luiz Gonzaga, a recording star who sang about the *sertão* throughout the mid-twentieth century. There was the blind accordionist, whose cigarette dangled impossibly from his bottom lip as he shook the bellows to produce *forró's* characteristic accordion tremolo. There was the triangle player, who clacked the music's relentless pulses: one-e-AND-a-two-e-AND-a. And there was the *zabumba* drummer, who was also the vocalist and who let my father and Seu Platão suspend his drum over their shoulders to attempt the jumpy beat of the *baião, forró's* original rhythm, played with a mallet on the drumhead and a stick to strike the offbeat on the underside: ONE and *two AND* THREE and *four* and.

December, circa 1991
Tucson, Arizona

I remember buying a CD called *Brazil: Forró: Music for Maids and Taxi Drivers* as a gift for my mother. I gave it to her not because of the music but because it had a woodprint of a *forró* trio on the cover, and she collects Brazilian folk art. For three years in the early 1970s, my father, now a retired professor of public administration, taught and conducted research in Belo Horizonte, a city in southeastern Brazil. It was in Belo Horizonte where my sister learned to speak (my parents used to say Portuguese was her first language) and where my brother was born. My mother fell in love with Brazil and its language, literature, food, and art, and she kept the album I gave her among her large collection of Brazilian CDs. I remember listening to it; it is my first memory of *forró*.

I grew up in a family of Brazilophiles. My mother's Brazil is one of escape, of tropical paradise, beach, musicians Caetano Veloso and Maria Bethânia, and the infectious samba rhythms of Rio's Carnival, of *feijoada* black-bean-and-pork stew with glistening slices of orange on the side, and of family lore and memories of happiness. In my childhood, Brazil was ever present, often in the abstract.

June 2000
Serra do Doutor, Rio Grande do Norte, Brazil

The summer after graduating high school, I spent almost a month living in the home of a corn farmer in the interior of Rio Grande do Norte, a northeastern Brazilian state southeast of Ceará. I was there with two other American teenagers to help build latrines in the town where we were living. Karen, Betsy, and I spent our days wandering the endless hillsides of Serra do Doutor (Hills of the Doctor), more a smattering of homes along a stretch of highway than a stereotypical town, trying to select the nine neediest families to receive the latrines. Many homes had walls made of mud and sticks and often had no more than one room. Some had little more than a pile of straw as a mattress. We saw malnourished children with distended abdomens. We were told about years of drought in which livestock perished and there was little water to drink. By summer's end we had chosen our nine families, taking into consideration whether they could help with the construction and complete the work after we left. But our efforts were in vain. Before we had even arrived, the mayor hid our construction materials in the back of a schoolhouse. It was an election year, and he intended to redistribute them in exchange for votes after we returned to the United States. We happened to be there during the June Festivals, and for the first time I saw a St. John's Day quadrille, I met *forró* accordionists, and I learned to dance the northeastern two-to-the-right-two-to-the-left shuffle, my biggest accomplishment of the summer.

The Brazil I encountered in Serra do Doutor was unlike my mother's Brazil. It was a Brazil characterized by corruption, drought, and starvation. In the home where I stayed, I remember watching not Brazilian *novelas* or the great films of Glauber Rocha, which I had learned about growing up, but reruns of *Alf* and *Blossom* (with Joey Lawrence's iconic "whoa" dubbed seamlessly into Portuguese) on a television powered by a car battery and attached to a satellite dish on the tile roof. Parties, held in dusty fields, were accompanied by the sounds of *forró* and *baião*, not samba or Brazilian popular music (*música popular brasileira*, or MPB), as I had expected.

Two Brazils

I came to believe I had seen two contradictory Brazils: my mother's Brazil and the Brazil I experienced in Serra do Doutor. But these two poles—fantasy and reality, paradise and purgatory—are less contradictory than they seemed to my young mind. Each inflects the other. The economy and cultures of the Southeast developed in tandem with (and not in spite of) the Northeast's abjection and its steady flow of migrants. And the Northeast developed in response to legislation and media generated in and by the country's Southeast. Intellectuals have long argued that there are two distinct Brazils: the industrially advanced, modern, globally connected Brazil to the south and the underdeveloped, archaic, isolated Brazil to the north (e.g., Lambert 1959). It is a vision of

Brazil rooted in the work of Brazilian writer Euclides da Cunha, whose book *Os sertões* (Rebellion in the backlands) (1902) described a violent conflict between the nascent Brazilian republic and a group of millenarian *sertanejos* (literally, people from the *sertão*) in the backlands of Bahia. The turn-of-the-century work examined the boundaries between modernity and tradition, civilization and barbarism, the coast and the interior, and the South and the North.

While in terms of indicators of development, such as literacy and infant mortality, the states of the Northeast have long lagged behind those of the Southeast, broader realities complicate this two-Brazil model. Since the 1960s scholars have clarified that the disparate economies and cultures of Brazil are interrelated (e.g., Freyre 1961; Frank [1967] 2009). The regional binary also erases Brazilian diversity. Since 1940 the Brazilian Institute for Geography and Statistics (IBGE) has recognized five (for a brief period, six) regions, including the North, Center-West, and South, in addition to the Northeast and Southeast, each with its own geographical and cultural attributes. Furthermore, the Northeast itself is heterogeneous, and its cultural and environmental imaginary has long been in flux. In the early to mid-twentieth century there were two dominant "Northeasts": one characterized by opulent coffee plantations and a coastal Afro-Brazilian middle class, and another characterized by the *sertão*, an economy driven by cattle and cotton, and visions of rusticity, poverty, and drought (de Oliveira 1977; McCann 2004). Both of these Northeasts slowly replaced a third Northeast characterized by sugar plantations, with a much more expansive geographical reach, from the nineteenth into the early twentieth century (see Abreu and Brakel 1997 for the region's earlier colonial history). Moreover, for many onlookers, the Northeast of the turn of the twenty-first century might look like a place of metalhead culture or of beaches, shopping malls, and conspicuous consumption. In short, the northeastern imaginary, like the northeastern experience, is fragmented.

In Ceará I came to know two dominant, nostalgic imaginaries. One is characterized by Ceará's coast, with images of bobbin lace, anglers, and *jangada* fishing rafts (see Almeida 2003). The other, which is more prevalent throughout the state, is characterized by Luiz Gonzaga's *sertão* and is rooted in the political and economic conditions that produced what Francisco de Oliveira calls "the Northeast of drought" (1977, 35; also see de Carvalho 2003). Many of my interlocutors often employed the term "Northeast" as a synonym for the *sertão* or for the state of Ceará itself, despite the plurality of experiences and images within the state and the region as a whole. From such a perspective, to describe something as northeastern is to invoke the connotations and images of "the Northeast of drought."

In this book I explore the intersection of two Brazils, not the Northeast and Southeast but imagined and material Northeasts: the Northeast made through popular music and the Northeast where that music resounds. I focus on the places where caricature lends its form to truth, where the quotidian appropriates elements of the imaginary, rearticulates them, and gives them new meaning. At my brother's wedding, the singing of popular songs about the backlands in the backlands, the dramatized wedding at the wedding, and the decorations of a parodied rurality in a small northeastern city were elements of the performance of a Northeast shaped by mass mediation. Seu Platão's world is made of images of itself that have been elaborated by Brazilian culture industries and then projected back.

"The Northeast is a fiction / The Northeast never was," sang Belchior (1946–2017), a musician from Ceará whose poetic, earthy lyrics often draw comparisons to Bob Dylan, in "Conheço o meu lugar" (I know my place) from 1979. The discursive construction of the region as geographically and culturally distinct from the rest of the nation (see Albuquerque Júnior 1999) has affected it in material ways. By representing the *sertão*, filling its soundscapes, and becoming a part of the experience of northeastern life, *forró* has transformed into tradition. It is now understood as an element of the region's folklore and cultural heritage. How does the imagined *sertão* and its perpetuation through music align with the real *sertão* and the needs of its people? What are the sociocultural and material consequences of a discursively invented Northeast? Do drought songs effect change, and if so, are they a social good? While music has indeed influenced perceptions and experiences of the *sertão*, efforts to support music as heritage and as a means for social justice are sometimes at odds with the demands of environmental justice and related changes in society. Musical meaning is made in power-differentiated contexts, and music industries are subject to the same systems of inequality and corruption that aggravate drought. Indeed, the story of music and drought is inherently a story of structural inequality—between nations, regions, knowledge-bearers, social classes, and sectors of society.

There are five key concepts that run throughout this book: vulnerability, materiality, listening, nostalgia, and policy. The first two concepts (vulnerability and materiality) pertain to this book's key arguments, while the second two (listening and nostalgia) involve the book's subject matter and methodological foci. The final concept (policy) is central to the book's justification and its potential implications. These five topics animate and unite the book's six interlocking but geographically and contextually distinct case studies.

Vulnerability: Music and Environmental Justice

My primary argument in this book is that environmental crisis affects music and music making via politics and social difference, and thus environmental justice is germane to many key questions pertaining to the study of music and the environment. I echo the call of social ecologist Murray Bookchin, who seeks (in musical terms, no less) "a reharmonization of nature and humanity through a reharmonization of human with human" (1982, 11). In addition to assessing the effects of ecological change on music making and musical traditions, the impact of anthropogenic sound and sound making on nonhumans such as wildlife and natural resources, and music's ability to raise environmental awareness, students of ecomusicology (see Allen 2013) must also study the consequences, both musical and nonmusical, of environmental crisis for vulnerable populations. Ethnomusicologists have long understood music as constitutive and reflective of social categories and related processes of marginalization and resistance. Just as environmental crises threaten ecologies, they also result in forced migration, poverty, and limited access to water and other resources for the poor, three factors intrinsic to the case studies in this book. And prejudice, corruption, unfettered capitalism, and expanding neoliberalism, themes that also run throughout this text, intensify these realities.

Drought in the Brazilian Northeast should be understood as both a natural phenomenon and a complex social problem involving religious belief, politics, landownership, and, above all else, structural inequality (see Castro Neves 2007; Nelson and Finan 2009; Andrade 1985; Hall 1978; Taddei 2017). Although drought is naturally occurring (albeit worsened by anthropogenic climate change), corruption, rural beliefs about weather, and economic precarity result in increased vulnerability to drought for certain populations (Lemos et al. 2002; Kenny 2002). Some suffer from drought, while others do not, and this is not a consequence of nature but one of culture; or, as an adage attributed to Lord Charles Bowen (1835–1894) puts it:

> The rain it raineth on the just
> And also on the unjust fella:
> But chiefly on the just, because
> The unjust steals the just's umbrella.

A common critique of Brazilian drought policy has been that solutions tend to focus on water storage and delivery rather than on mending social inequality (see, e.g., Kenny 2002). An exclusively technological or environmental approach to drought relief misunderstands the realities of the people who suffer most by assuming that drought aid, new reservoirs and roads, and more irrigation can effectively help those who will likely be denied access to these resources by corrupt officials and businesspeople who care little about structural change. One study in the early 1990s found that for every $1,000 in drought aid sent to the Northeast, only $40 ever reached the intended recipients (Calvert and Calvert 1999).

Such a technocratic approach also disregards common feelings of suspicion toward scientists, meteorologists, and others sent by the government to help farmers in the backlands, and suggests that some northeasterners are naive to place their faith in religion and traditional knowledge instead. Fatalist notions that drought is caused and cured by the divine remain commonplace. Responding to a newspaper article in late November 2015 that claimed drought conditions would worsen in Ceará in December, January, and February due to El Niño, Cearense readers commented on the newspaper's Facebook feed that "God can reverse the forecast, you just need faith," that "there will be much rain if God wants it, and he does," and that "man's evil is his wanting to predict God's actions." Father Cícero Romão (1844–1934), a beloved priest who was the first mayor of the city of Juazeiro do Norte and is considered a local saint, once told his followers they could save themselves from drought if they followed ten steps (see Della Cava 1970 on Padre Cícero as a political figure). He advised them to practice rotational grazing of their livestock to allow pastures to regrow, to store rainwater, to make dams, and to plant trees, among other tips. "If the sertanejo obeys these precepts," he said, "drought will slowly come to an end, cattle will improve, and the people will always have something to eat; but if you do not obey, before long the whole of the backlands will become a desert." His words are painted on a wall not far from a statue of him visited each November by pilgrims who travel far distances to pray and leave votive offerings for the late priest. Many people in the Northeast value traditional wisdom about natural phenomena, and they trust sources such as Padre Cícero and musicians like Luiz Gonzaga, whose songs about drought now comprise many of forró's classic songs (on the significance of Gonzaga and Padre Cícero, see Greenfield 2009).

At the start of the second decade of the twenty-first century, tens of millions of Brazilians rose out of poverty and into a growing middle class. These changes came via leftist social programs and widening access to credit, expanding the reach of consumer capitalism. With new conditions came new tastes, new forms of performing distinction, and the capacity to purchase new consumer electronics, including flat-screen televisions and mobile sound systems. Economic changes—entailing a decline in vulnerability to drought in Ceará's *sertão*—brought changes to expressive culture and mass media. The seeming contradiction of a leftist social paradigm and elements of neoliberal capitalism came to a head with the eventual impeachment of president Dilma Rousseff of the Workers' Party (Partido dos Trabalhadores, PT) in 2016 in the midst of a far-reaching corruption scandal. I conducted my research for this book before the impeachment and during the optimistic Workers' Party era, during which two consecutive presidents, Luiz Inácio "Lula" da Silva and Rousseff, brought vast social reform, particularly to the Northeast. In the final two chapters of this book (chapter 5 was researched between 2009 and 2012; chapter 6 involves 2012 through early 2016), my observations pertaining to popular music, cultural policy, and government foreshadow the coming political and economic instability.

I understand ecological, economic, and cultural processes to be interrelated (see Latour 2005; Greenough and Tsing 2009; Escobar 1999, 2006). In particular, drought in northeastern Brazil entails local and regional social identities, as drought disproportionately affects nonwhites, the poor, and women (see de Melo Branco 2000), just as anthropogenic climate change disproportionately affects vulnerable populations more generally (Baer and Singer 2016; Ribot 2014). Nancy Guy (2009) has called on ethnomusicologists to add environmental concerns to the race/class/gender "trinity" that we often pursue in our scholarship. The categories of race, class, gender, and nature are in many ways coconstructed, with overlapping and interlacing histories and meanings. Thus, to be concerned about drought is to be concerned about the politics of the environment, the politics of class, and the politics of culture.

Materiality: The Dynamic between Drought and Popular Music

My secondary argument, a corollary to the previous argument, is that drought has indeed affected music making, but music making has in turn affected drought—in all the cultural, political, and socioenvironmental senses outlined above. Drought has been responsible for the existence of natural resources used in sound recording (chapter 1). It has spurred migrations that gave rise to *forró* (chapter 2). It has inspired songwriters (chapters 2 and 3). It has resulted in birds vocalizing in particular ways, which musicians have sung about and mimicked (chapter 3). It has entailed and contributed to certain ways of listening (chapters 3 and 4). It has participated in the social construction of social categories, particularly certain regional identities and socioeconomic structures (chapters 4 and 5). It has served as a justification for upholding certain notions of tradition (chapters 5 and 6). And it led to the withdrawal of public Carnival financing (chapter 6). Music, on the other hand, has contributed to the cultivation of (and demand for) drought-resistant natural materials (chapter 1). It has been a vehicle through which people could combat drought: musicians have protested specific policies and circumstances related to drought and raised money and awareness (chapters 2 and 4). It has helped some individuals understand certain ways of listening for rain and drought as locally significant (chapters 3 and 4). It has upheld and challenged beliefs about drought and social categories that correlate with drought vulnerability (chapters 2, 3, and 4). And it has filled drought-plagued landscapes with sound (chapters 4, 5, and 6).

In *The Man Who Bottled Clouds*, a documentary film about Humberto Teixeira (one of Gonzaga's primary songwriting partners), Gilberto Gil said, "The music is full of landscape, and the landscape is full of music." The renowned musician and former Brazilian minister of culture's reference to hearing the *sertão* in *forró* and hearing *forró* in the *sertão* is more than a poetic turn of phrase; it is a description of the interplay between sound and environment. Gil's quote employs chiasmus, a rhetorical device involving repeated words or phrases that trade places and that can involve a recognition that multiple elements reciprocally act upon each other. Such chiastic structures might be a helpful way of conceptualizing the mutual constitution of nature and culture as described in new materialist scholarship (e.g., Fausto-Sterling 2000; Haraway 2004; Ahmed 2008; Barad 2003; Frost 2016).[1] Music and drought are at once social and material phenomena (music involves sound waves, as well as aesthetics; drought involves a lack of precipitation, as well as vulnerability), and these factors interact.

Furthermore, the relationship between music and drought—and its articulation with social life—is complex, not directly causal. Social behavior, self and group identity, social mobility, vulnerability, and taste do not simply emerge in the interplay between structure and agency (see Giddens [1984] 2013) but are the effects of a complex network of interactions between human and nonhuman, as well as material and abstract, entities (see Latour 2005). Individuals, institutions, regions and nations, social categories, media, climate, and plants and animals, among other factors, shape expectations and experiences via the interactions among them and in concordance with their own inherent or constructed properties. That is, material things such as rain, wax, and sound come into contact with—and shape—abstract things produced through art and mass mediation, such as regional imaginaries. These imaginaries clash against or conspire with abstract things produced through practice, such as racial and class identities, which themselves come up against institutions such as industries, governments, and traditions. These in turn regulate and exploit material things such as rain, wax, and sound while restricting, financing, and promoting social things such as imaginaries, relationships, and music.

Each case study in this book entails the workings of popular music. Mass mediation has been a means through which drought is experienced by audiences and expressed by musicians. Jesús Martín-Barbero argues that mediation in Latin America generates inequality and vice versa: "Inequality fragments society and weakens the means and mechanisms of communication," while, conversely, the fragmented means and mechanisms of communication limit the "possibilities for political and cultural cohesion" (2006, 280). Ana María Ochoa Gautier extends this observation to sound, arguing that the aural "has been a sphere of crucial constitution of Latin America's highly unequal modernity" (2006, 804). Forró and drought interact as they do precisely because forró is a recorded, mass-mediated, and broadcasted music associated with certain hierarchies and populations, certain technologies, certain seasons, and certain places. In addition, music industries interact with local, state, and national politics in ways that affect the soundscape and the social production of musical meaning.

As I mention above, I have observed music—as a social activity and a kind of sound—transform under expanding neoliberalism. In the case of forró, I have heard musicians, cultural activists, and scholars routinely complain about diminishing state funding for expressive culture. These concerns surprised me at first, because Brazilian infrastructure for expressive culture impressed me in comparison to ours in the United States. Most notably, in the period I conducted my research, the federal government had a Ministry of Culture, something we do not have in the United States. The Brazilian government also offered prominent, substantial tax write-offs to individuals and corporations who support the arts and culture, resulting in book publications, concerts and concert festivals, CDs, and countless other objects and experiences. Over time, I came to understand that the complaints were responding to a broad cultural shift in which mainstream society was beginning to view music primarily as a product. By this, I do not mean that music was not a product in earlier eras— on the contrary, this book's first chapter concerns the establishment of the modern music industry in Brazil, and professional musicianship is hardly a recent phenomenon. Moreover, forró, in all its major forms, has always been a commercial genre, despite musical borrowings from noncommercial practices. What has changed are the ways in which and the extent to which it has been a product. Most visibly, a lack of regulation within a regional music industry (chapter 5) and the privatization of cultural events that were once publicly sponsored (chapter 6) have shown neoliberalism to encompass government, the music industry, and the soundscape.

Listening: Reception and the Laboring Soundscape

This is a book about listening as culture. It concerns the reception of nostalgic northeastern music; the ways it is remembered and referred to by farmers and others in the backlands; the means by which it fills rural and urban soundscapes, thus articulating local senses of belonging; and the fraught ways it continues to signify northeasternness and Ceará in changing economic circumstances. These differing stories about the reception of this music, which reveal constructions of identity and emerge from national and local political flows and economic circumstances, dovetail with stories about drought's effect on music and music making.

How we listen is a product of culture (Feld [1982] 2012). Through auditory culture—our shared habits of listening—we define the terms and boundaries of modernity, democracy, citizenship, and personhood (e.g., McCann 2004; Erlmann 2004; Ochoa Gautier 2014; Thompson 2002). We practice and articulate moral and sacred selfhoods (e.g., Hirschkind 2006; Oosterbaan 2008). We negotiate social categories such as race, class, and gender (e.g., Sakakeeny 2010). And we enforce or resist paradigms of power more generally (e.g., Attali [1985] 1992).

What we hear—the soundscape itself—is also a product of culture (Schafer 1977). We construct soundscapes with our voices and bodies (e.g., Eidsheim 2015), our musical performance (e.g., Buchanan 2016), our built environments (e.g., Peterson 2012; Sterne 1997), and our machines, broadcast technologies, and reproductive media (e.g., Schafer [1977] 1994; Katz 2004; Bull 2004; Bijsterveld 2008; Greene and Porcello 2010). We regulate soundscapes through policy (e.g., Bijsterveld 2008; Cardoso 2016). We silence nonhuman elements of our soundscapes with our own noise, species extinction, and other interferences (e.g., Schafer 1977; Krause 2012). The making of the northeastern soundscape entails legislation and aesthetics, power and resistance, and technologies, birds, and bodies of water, factors that also shape ways of hearing the soundscape.

To be more specific, the soundscape is a product of labor. Industries and markets, professional musicians, their unions and professional societies, and workers in the commodity chains that produce music technologies work with and against each other in the production of the sonorous contemporary world. Expanding on the work of Raymond Williams (1973, [1977] 2009), Thomas Rogers, in his book *The Deepest Wounds: A Labor and Environmental History of*

Sugar in Northeastern Brazil, calls the northeastern landscape a "laboring land-scape": "Land and people were bound together in their minds, not just by the ties of culture, law, and belief" but also "by coercion, the sense of entitlement and control passed down across generations by those in power, and a history of slavery and plantation agriculture" (2010, 8). The northeastern soundscape, by that same token, is a *laboring soundscape*: sound and people are bound together in the minds of northeasterners not just by the ties of culture, the rules of aesthetics and musical genre, and belief but also by the histories of labor, place, and control as they pertain to musicians and the general population alike.

Sound is an especially potent field of cultural production in modern Latin America (Ochoa Gautier 2006; Bronfman and Wood 2012). In Ceará music is often present in public soundscapes, where it mediates aspects of local culture: commerce, religion, class, understandings of nature, notions of public and private spheres, and articulations of local and cosmopolitan desires. In my experience, wherever I have encountered people, I have often encountered music. A vendor routinely walks through Fortaleza's streets chanting, "Ô chegadinho-chegadinho-chega-di-nhô" while clacking a triangle to the rhythm used in the *baião* as he sells *chegadinhos,* a kind of baked snack.[2] The downtown square in the city of Iguatu has speakers mounted to the telephone poles that surround the plaza, emitting a broadcast from a local radio station. During one visit, I heard a crowded sacred pilgrimage site in Canindé bounce with the sound of secular music blasting from speakers in a car's trunk. Music routinely plays from cars, kitchens, and shops, bringing private auditions into public spaces. I offer other examples of music in the quotidian soundscape throughout this book. Much of this music is *forró,* or is related to *forró,* and it sometimes has lyrics that describe romanticized visions of places very much like those where the music resounds.

Nostalgia: Ecological Longings

This book is also about music and the nostalgic sounds and lyrics of *forró.* Mass-mediated *forró* and related northeastern genres often describe landscapes of the *sertão* in their lyrics and recall the backlands in their music via instrumentation, timbres, modes, vocal techniques, and rhythms. By representing landscapes, musicians can express and produce visions of modernity and urbanization, class identities and national politics, and the understanding of nature itself (much as in Williams 1973; Schama 1995). Musicians, and not just those in Brazil, express anxieties about changing environments and construct senses of place in a variety of ways. Music reflects changing attitudes about environmental features as they become polluted (Guy 2009), changing relationships with, and notions of, landscape (e.g., Post 2007; Impey 2013; Morcom 2015), and changing approaches to the conservation or preservation of wilderness (Toliver 2004). Even genre names can imply concerns about environmental and cultural change (Rees 2016). Music can also serve a deliberate, communicative purpose to protest and address environmental concerns and crises (e.g., Morris 1998; Dibben 2009; Ramnerine 2009; Ingram 2008; Pedelty 2012, 2016; Stimeling 2012; Mark 2014). More generally, songs and the act of singing about and in specific places help groups and individuals construct senses of place and corresponding senses of identity (e.g., Wrazen 2007; Solomon 2000; Stokes 1997; Fox 2004; Feld [1982] 2012), as well as mediate relationships between music, place, and cosmology (e.g., Feld [1982] 2012; Levin 2006; Roseman 1991; Seeger 2004).

With nostalgic music about the landscape, composers and musicians explore cultural attachments to places and environments that might be threatened or have already been lost to cultural and ecological change (Rehding 2011). Nostalgia pervades much northeastern Brazilian music, particularly songs that concern the region's landscape. A longing for home and loved ones inspired drought refugees to compose and consume this music in the mid-twentieth century, and today these same nostalgic songs and their musical qualities represent the northeastern region and its landscape and people. Since the nineteenth century, expressions of nostalgia have been employed in other contexts for nation building (Boym 2002), to mark and lament changing social and economic systems (Williams 1973), to cope with urban migration and changing kinship structures (Dent 2009), and for cultural critique and cultural preservation in a postauthoritarian era of expanding neoliberalism (Sharp 2014), among other things. Nostalgia calls attention to what has been lost to industrialization, changing relationships with the land, and environmental degradation. Forró's nostalgia called attention to the landscapes, places, and people left behind due to ecological crisis.

Nostalgia involves a longing for both an irredeemable past and a distant home (Tester 2002). The former aspect of nostalgia reifies the past, that is, time. The latter reifies the homeland, that is, place. Keith Tester writes that nostalgia "is not just a repudiation of where I am" but "also a way of coming to terms with my present position" (2002, 66) and thus entails the reconciliation of both the passage of time and the experience of exile. It is this dialectic within forró's saudade (longing) that seems to interest forró scholars most. In what ways is forró a neotraditional music of modernity, bringing the past into the present? And how is it an artifact of the contemporaneous, distant backlands, bringing the country into the city?

Nostalgia, I should note, has particular relevance in many Lusophone musical contexts: a great number of scholars have explored the significance of *saudade*, a Portuguese word that describes an intense longing for another person, time, place, or thing (similar to nostalgia but more closely related to "homesickness," with a wider range of settings and objects and sometimes implying the impossibility of its satisfaction).[3] *Saudade* is a theme in the lyrics of a number of musics in Portugal, Lusophone Africa, and Brazil, and it figures prominently in the music of northeastern Brazil, in which it often expresses a desire to return home once the social and environmental conditions of drought improve.[4]

Policy: Climate and Cultural Sustainability

What is at stake in an ethnomusicological study of climate? If music truly is a meaningful element of the construction of group identity, the formation of regional geographies, the practice of citizenship, and the understanding of natural phenomena, as I claim here and as countless ethnomusicologists and others have argued elsewhere, can climate's effect on music and musical practice disrupt these crucial processes? Although drought in the Brazilian Northeast is not a direct result of climate change, there is evidence that climate change is causing drought cycles to increase in frequency and is resulting in longer and more severe droughts. Ceará experienced its fourth consecutive year of drought in 2015. Reservoirs throughout the state ran dry. Crops failed. The typically verdant Cariri Valley in the south of Ceará became desert-like. And state Carnival funds were cut once again as a result. Yet the parties carried on, mostly funded by private companies instead of public coffers. Climate change, cultural policy, and culture industries worked in tandem to rearticulate notions of traditional culture and heritage.

An old cliché claims that northeasterners have withstood drought due to their valorization of strength, resilience, and perseverance. Yet for *sertanejos* to adapt to drought, they have needed more than a strong will. Even the management of cloud seeding, reservoirs, and agricultural practices has been inadequate to ameliorate the severe and ongoing lack of rain in a place with so much poverty and corruption. Drought adaptation involves—and has involved—a holistic set of variables that demand careful balancing: social welfare with increasing neoliberalism, cultural policy with mass mediation, and the tensions among the ludic, the identitarian, and the most basic needs for survival.

Ethnomusicologists in Brazil have theorized connections between social needs and the survival of musical heritage and musical practices in the face of environmental, economic, and cultural change. Manuel Veiga (2013) observes that scholarly discussions about the so-called sustainability of music might inspire renewed attention to the basic human need for music, as well as to music's ability to shape culture. Angela Lühning (2013) aptly notes that music exists within broader "cultural ecosystems," an idea that resonates with my own understanding of music in Ceará (on music and cultural ecologies, also see Titon 2009; Archer 1964; Neuman 1990; Schippers and Grant 2016). Lühning suggests that, given the complexity of cultural ecosystems, we must advocate social justice in a general sense to maintain meaningful musical practices: "Sustainability lies in ensuring favorable social structures, our 'cultural ecosystems,' that make people want to continue making music" (2013, 55). Preservationist and traditionalist efforts, including some in Ceará, on the other hand, tend to overlook the coconstructing processes of environmental, economic, and cultural change. Environmental policy, economic policy, and cultural policy can each affect the other in unexpected and meaningful ways.

A document released by the World Health Organization, written by a group of nongovernmental organizations to educate policy makers about the social dimensions of climate change, says that "the interplay between climate as a phenomenon, its related policy, and society—including the role of *people* as victims to and agents of climate change—are critical to climate policy" (2011, 5, italics in original). I do not presume to have insights into climate policy, but this story of music and drought in northeastern Brazil can offer an example of the interaction between climate and social life across the span of over more than a century in a place where a warming climate is now aggravating a long-standing environmental problem.

Geographical Setting

I conducted the research for this book between 2008 and 2016 in Ceará, which shares cultural and environmental characteristics with neighboring states yet also possesses many unique qualities. It is, most significantly, the state that has been the most predominantly characterized by drought by the mass media, even when compared to others in the drought-prone area referred to by politicians and scholars as the Drought Polygon, which includes most of the northeastern states and parts of Minas Gerais in the Southeast.

Northeastern Brazil is divided into three primary geographical subregions: the *zona da mata* (literally, the "forest zone"), the *agreste* (a subhumid hilly region inland from the *zona da mata*), and the *sertão* (the backlands, but also the term for a semiarid region comprising the bulk of the interior of northeastern Brazil, whose scrubby biome is known as *caatinga*).[5] The *zona da mata* near the coast is fertile and suitable for the growth of sugarcane, while the *agreste* and *sertão* often suffer from drought and therefore lack arable land. In popular discourse in Ceará, people refer to the state's three geographical settings: the coast, the hills (the *serra*), and the *sertão*.

Although much of Ceará can be lush in years of rain, the vast majority of the state is semiarid (see map 1), which in dry years resembles the landscape of the American Southwest. Prickly pear cacti, wooly *xique-xique* cacti, and *mandacarus*, which look similar to organ-pipe cacti and are often drawn to look like saguaros in advertisements and artwork, are commonplace. Regional fauna includes guinea pigs, anteaters, and a considerable variety of birds, such as guineafowl and the *asa branca* (picazuro pigeon). But the animals most prevalent in and around the region's small towns are donkeys (called *jegues* and *jumentos*) and (frequently emaciated) cows, which graze withered foliage beside the cracked earth of dry reservoirs and riverbeds. On a desolate stretch of road in Ceará leading to the border of Pernambuco, a lonely gas station had a billboard displaying the business's fitting name: Arizona of the *Sertão*.

In contrast, Fortaleza, the state capital, is a coastal city of high-rise apartments, suburban sprawl, and some 3.5 million residents in its metropolitan area. It is one of the biggest vacation destinations for Brazilian tourists, especially during the Christmas / New Year season, who travel to Ceará for its beaches and a large waterpark aptly named Beach Park. From the mid-1990s to the mid-2000s, Fortaleza was also a destination for European sex tourists, although that has been curbed significantly in recent years to attract more Brazilian families looking for an inexpensive getaway from the bustle of the Southeast. The protracted construction of a world-class aquarium and development of beachfront communities with golf courses that smother dunes with grassy turf brazenly ignore the region's recurring droughts. Although Fortaleza sits on the coast, drought is as present there as it is elsewhere in the state, evident in daily conversations, in the local geographical and cultural imaginary, in radio and television news programs, in in-migration patterns, and in the city's own water resources.

A Brief History of Drought in Ceará, circa 1500–circa 1900

There are records of drought in the Brazilian Northeast since shortly after the arrival of the Portuguese on Brazil's shores. In 1552, a mere fifty-two years after Pedro Álvarez Cabral landed in Porto Seguro, a Jesuit missionary named Antônio Pires wrote that in the Pernambuco Captaincy "there have been four or five years in which it has not rained" (Pires 1988, 123).[6] Writings left by missionaries suggest that much of the area's indigenous population also suffered

MAP 1. The semiarid region of Ceará. The darker shaded area, covering all but a narrow strip near the coast, is semiarid. Source: Ceará em mapas, available on the site of the Instituto de Pesquisa e Estratégia Econônica do Ceará (IPECE), Governo do Estado do Ceará © 2007, http://www2.ipece. ce.gov.br/atlas/capitulo1/12/images3x/Regiao_Semi_Arida.jpg

from drought (see Cardim 1939). There were at least four notable droughts recorded in the seventeenth century, eleven in the eighteenth, and eleven more in the nineteenth (see Guerra 1981; Aguiar 1983).

Following a drought in 1845, waves of *flagelados* (drought victims; literally, the "scourged") fled to Fortaleza, resulting in new laws intended to "discipline" and "civilize" these migrants (Vieira 2002, 18). From 1865 to 1877 Fortaleza flourished. The period of growth, marking the start of the city's belle époque, came as a result of drought-relief aid and from trading cotton with Europe, especially England, bringing "characteristics of capitalism" to Fortaleza's economy (Olivenor 2002, 49–50). The nation as a whole was in its first industrial era, and much of the Brazilian bourgeoisie looked to Europe and Argentina for refined musical culture (Santos 2002). The most popular song form of the time, the *modinha*, was inspired by eighteenth-century ballads from Portugal, and many nineteenth-century Brazilian *modinhas* drew stylistically from Italian art songs and operatic arias. Waltzes, polkas, mazurkas, schottisches, and quadrilles, all imported from France, were the period's popular dance rhythms.

The economic expansion slowed with the onset of the 1877–79 drought (commonly referred to as the Great Drought), killing half of Ceará's population and causing tens of thousands of migrants to flee from the interior to Fortaleza, disrupting the recent progress and bringing disease, crime, and starvation. In response, local officials sent the migrants to live in concentration camps on the outskirts of the city. "The relationship between the urban population and the rural poor," historian Frederico Castro Neves writes, "would never be the same" (2002, 76). Emperor Dom Pedro II, who disingenuously vowed to sell every last jewel from his crown to help the drought victims, sent Gaston d'Orléans, the count of Eu and husband of Pedro's daughter Princess Isabel, to lead a commission to assess the situation in 1879. Prince Gaston traveled the Northeast and made a number of suggestions, all involving technological and agricultural solutions rather than social ones: the construction of dams and reservoirs, the digging of irrigation canals, and the transposition of the São Francisco River, a project that remains in progress and a source of controversy.

There were seven droughts between 1888, the year Brazil abolished slavery and the year before it became a federal republic, and 1913. Some lasted as long as two years. This was not a twenty-year cycle but something unpredictable, frequent, and often devastating for the region's population. In 1902 Euclides da Cunha published *Os sertões* (Rebellion in the backlands), which, via an essentialist depiction of the northeastern character, raised national consciousness about the region's climate and people. As the northeastern problem became increasingly visible at the turn of the century, the young nation began efforts in earnest to ameliorate suffering. The construction of the Cedro Reservoir in Quixadá, which had begun under Pedro II in 1884 and finished in 1906, provided work for a small number of drought victims. In 1909 the government established the Inspectorate for Works against Drought (IOCS), which undertook more civil engineering projects, including new roads and wells.

Yet these efforts proved inadequate. A prescient newspaper article from January 8, 1889, noted, "The flow of migrants into the capital has become gigantic," and "public works, reservoirs and railroads, which have been planned by the government, as many as there are, will still never be sufficient to provide work for all those in need" (qtd. in Castro Neves 2002, 78).[7] Many people left the region altogether, as out-migration was (and remains) often the best option. Those who moved to Rio de Janeiro, Brazil's capital from 1763 to 1960 and the center of the nation's radio and recording industries through much of the twentieth century, helped transform the vision—musical and otherwise—of the Northeast and northeasterners. Their music eventually came to be known as *forró*.

On *Forró*

Forró is a musical genre that permeates the questions and topics I explore in this book. By this I mean that although *forró* is not the subject of the book, it is nevertheless the fabric from which it is fashioned. You might say this is a book about drought in the key of *forró*. I am ultimately less concerned with *forró* as a genre category (although I take up genre as a process in chapter 5) than I am with all the performative—cultural and sonic—elements surrounding *forró* (Madrid and Moore 2013), as well as the material components of the music (e.g., the phonographs, loudspeakers, sound systems, and markets). *Forró* is but one matrix of sounds in a vast soundscape and one component of a complex cultural ecosystem.

The word *forró*, which originally meant "party," is itself polysemous: it refers to a type of party, a type of venue, a type of dance, a type of ensemble, a type of rhythm, and a genre—actually a set of three genres, discussed below.[8] It is also an industry, an affect, a feeling of time, and an archive of nostalgic artifacts, both aural and visual. To many listeners in Ceará, the sounds of *forró* signify the "Northeast of drought."

Forró has a number of key musical attributes. Its typical ensemble—conceived by Luiz Gonzaga in the radio era—includes a piano accordion, a zabumba bass drum, and a large steel triangle. Its rural predecessors include *violas caipiras* (ten-string guitars, sometimes resophonic, also sometimes known as *violas nordestinas*), *pífanos* (fifes), *rabecas* (fiddles), and other percussion instruments such as the *pandeiro*, the snare drum, and cymbals—the latter two instruments are associated with fife bands (*bandas cabaçais*, or *bandas de pífanos*).[9] Recent iterations of *forró* include the instruments of cosmopolitan popular music, such as electric guitars, electric bass guitars, keyboards and synthesizers, drum sets, and saxophones. Its melodies, especially the classic songs from the past century, are typically modal, performed in Mixolydian, Dorian, or dominant Lydian (or acoustic) scales. *Forró* musicians and those knowledgeable about the genre's musical qualities tend to call these scales "modes" and refer to them by their Greek names, excluding the latter scale (the dominant Lydian), which is often referred to as the *modo nordestino*, the northeastern mode. Tiago de Oliveira Pinto (2001) has observed that performances of northeastern traditional musics are characterized by a neutral third scale degree, a phenomenon he has measured in cents. He argues that consequently there can be neither major nor minor, and thus no functional harmony, in traditional practices. He writes that "the northeastern *bandas de pífanos* [fife bands], the *aboios* [herding calls], the ballads of the *repentistas* [improvising vocalists], the songs of the *caboclinhos* [practitioners of a Carnival tradition from Recife], the *pé-de-serra* [foothills] *forrós*, this entire vast repertory is characterized by the neutral third" (2001, 242). He goes on to say that when accompanied by a tempered piano accordion in *forró*, a genre that does employ functional harmony, vocalists, *pífeiros* [fifers], and other musicians maintain the characteristic neutral third, an observation with which I agree. *Forró* also entails a collection of dance rhythms, primarily the *baião*, *xote*, *xaxado*, *arrasta-pé*, and *forró*.

Above all, *forró* is a dance, experienced through rocking hips, shuffling feet, and the warmth of another person. Each *forró* rhythm has its own feel, its own movements, and its own tempo. The (very popular) *xote* is a couple's dance in which your cheeks are pressed together, or the tops of the sides of your scalps are touching, or you can smell your partner's hair as their head rests gently on your shoulder, or yours on theirs. (In the Northeast, a *cheiro*—a sniff—of the scalp is as tender as a kiss.) You rock and shuffle together to the slow bounce of the *zabumba* drum (ONE rest THREE FOUR), the moderate, often swung pulse of the triangle (*one*-e-*AND*-a), and the accordion triads chirped over each e-*AND*-a. You rotate gracefully as you drag your feet together, two steps there, two steps here. The *baião* is a little quicker—your feet come off the ground a bit more, and you hold each other tight. The *arrasta-pé* is the fastest and is like a *xote* played in double time and danced as a quick two-step. The *xaxado*, traditionally performed by men to imitate the toe taps and shuffles of the legendary bandit Lampião and his gang, is performed by men and women alike on dance floors, sometimes in groups, sometimes independently (for more on Lampião, see Greenfield 2009; Chandler 2000). In the quadrille (*quadrilha*), danced in large groups to brisk *marcha* and *arrasta-pé* rhythms and generally only during St. John's Day, you jog in place and clap in pairs, then twirl and do-si-do. You and your partner, elbows linked and heads ducked low, make a conspiratorial and carefree dash through a tunnel of raised arms. Regardless of where you dance *forró*, its movements are explicitly northeastern. Each dragged foot kicks up dust, imagined and desired, back home in the *sertão*.

Forró is associated with a population known as *caboclo*, people of mixed Portuguese and Indigenous ancestry. *Caboclo* identity is linked to the *sertão*, and the term is sometimes synonymous with *nordestino* or *sertanejo*, even though the Northeast and *sertão* have populations characterized by miscegenation, like much of the rest of Brazil, with roots particularly in West and Central Africa, the Netherlands, and Syria/Lebanon, in addition to Portugal and local Indigenous populations. Many of *forró's* musical attributes carry this heritage of miscegenation. People often describe *forró* as containing elements of Brazil's so-called three races—Portuguese, African, and Indigenous—although its origins, which are not of particular interest to me here, are certainly more complex. For example, the quadrille and many of these couple's dances have French roots. The piano accordion was introduced to Brazil by Italian immigrants. The *pandeiro* and *rabeca* have Moorish roots.

One of *forró's* defining features is that it emerged as a genre of popular music in the context of diaspora among impoverished, racially othered workers. The often-maligned Cearense population is stereotyped by southeastern Brazilians as being short in stature and having flat heads (*cabeças chatas*). Cearenses are recognized as migrants. On multiple occasions, I have heard Cearenses called "Brazilian Jews," a term that (I have been told) is primarily intended to refer to their diasporic spread throughout Brazil. I have also heard middle-class southeastern Brazilians refer to working-class northeastern Brazilians of unknown origin as Cearenses or Baianos (from Bahia), as if the state demonyms are themselves slurs.

At the turn of the twenty-first century, there were three genres described as *forró*: university *forró*, electronic *forró*, and foothills *forró*. University *forró* (*forró universitário*) is a genre of *forró* from São Paulo in the 1990s that mostly employed the *xote* rhythm and was popular among college students (see Fernandes 2005). In Ceará, the word *forró* typically refers to a genre of popular dance music often called electronic *forró* (*forró eletrônico*) that was first popularized in the 1990s and is now associated with enormous parties, consumable, mass-produced dance music, extravagant stage shows with lighting displays, dancers performing choreographed routines, lyrics that many consider vulgar, and bands with rock instruments (see Pedroza 2001; Trotta 2009). *Forró pé-de-serra,* often translated into English as "traditional *forró*" or "roots *forró*" but which literally translates to "foothills *forró*," refers to the *forró* and *baião* of the mid-twentieth century, created and popularized by Luiz Gonzaga and his ilk. Other northeastern musics, including mainstream popular music and regionalist rock genres, as well as northeastern jazz and art music (not discussed here), have borrowed musical elements from *forró* and related traditional genres, including rhythms, scales, and instruments, as well as subjects for lyrics.

Forró can be a musical shorthand for the Northeast, for the *sertão,* and for drought. Today, if Brazilian musicians want to index the Northeast, rurality, or the hardships of drought, they can quote one of Gonzaga's canonical songs or employ one of the *forró* rhythms, the timbre of one of the *forró* instruments, the typical scales, the visual imagery associated with *forró* parties or *forró* venues, or the shuffling two-to-the-left, two-to-the-right dance step. The landscape is embedded directly into the traditional genre's name, foothills *forró.*

Ceará has many qualities that distinguish its musical context from the more frequently studied nearby state of Pernambuco, which is recognized for its valorization of traditional musical culture and its role in the Brazilian music industry, having produced Luiz Gonzaga and the internationally recognized Manguebeat movement of the 1990s. Pernambuco is also home to the city of Caruaru, known for its St. John's Day celebrations—a holiday closely associated with *forró* music.

Many of the traditions in Pernambuco that are marketed and commemorated by the media and by large tourist festivals also exist (often in distinct forms) in Ceará, but without as much recognition. Ceará's Cariri region is known as a center of religious practice in the Northeast, and individuals and neighborhood groups continue to practice many older musical and cultural traditions. Cultural heritage is highly valued in Cariri (see Coopat and Mattos 2012 on traditional music in Cariri). Not insignificantly, Luiz Gonzaga was born and raised in Exu, a Pernambucan town near the border of Ceará that is essentially a part of the Cariri region. When Gonzaga's family went to the nearest city, they went to Crato, in Ceará. He often referred to Crato and Juazeiro do Norte in songs and interviews. That is, the traditions from the Northeast that Gonzaga grew up with and the places he sang about were from Cariri, a region that also influenced notions of state identity in Ceará.

Fortaleza's (and Ceará's) relationship with *forró* is unique. Fortaleza is the birthplace of the electronic *forró* industry, responsible for touring *forró* stage shows that draw enormous crowds all over the Northeast. While many intellectuals and musicians will argue that electronic *forró* has little musical value, they will also point out that the *forró* industry is extremely powerful and dominates the radio waves. During the St. John's Day season in 2017, traditional *forró* musicians across the Northeast launched a campaign protesting the presence of electronic *forró* and other genres—including electronic dance music and *música sertaneja*, a rural "country" genre from South-Central Brazil—at northeastern St. John's Day parties with the slogan "Devolva meu São João" (Give back my St. John's Day).

Forró is a historically and musically significant element of the northeastern soundscape. It is integral to a broader sound ecology that entails more than the sounds of the genres called *forró* and the many musical practices that preceded and surround them. It also includes other sounds—birds, water, machines, and voices—that comingle with live and broadcasted music. Quite literally, the soundscape can be heard in *forró*, just as *forró* can be heard in the soundscape.

Chapter Outline

I began this research as an effort to answer a question: Given that drought is so prevalent in the scholarship on Ceará—in history, poetry, biology, anthropology, social psychology, and agricultural economics, to name but a few disciplines—and that the description of drought and the *sertão* is a defining feature of the lyrics of classic *forró*, might there be connections between drought and this music that exceed the lyrics and extend into the genre's broader musical and material culture? It was after undertaking a significant portion of my dissertation field research that I learned of a new field of study being called ecomusicology. I consider this book a musical ethnography and cultural history in the methodological and theoretical tradition of ethnomusicology, but I put my research in dialogue with several questions and themes of contemporary ecomusicology: the materials of musical instruments, music as environmental protest, acoustemologies and traditional ecological knowledge, soundscapes, cultural sustainability, and the environmental cost of music events. This research, like much ethnomusicological research, was methodologically diverse, entailing a combination of ethnography, archival research, the analysis of lyrics and music, and soundscape study. I cast a wide net and studied many situations, objects, and songs that linked music to drought.

The six case studies I write about here offer distinct examples of drought's relationship to commercial popular music as it pertains to social inequality and structural hierarchies at various levels. I have organized the cases chronologically, beginning in 1877 in chapter 1 and ending in 2016 in chapter 6, although chapters 3, 4, and 5 juxtapose historical recordings in their early, mid-, and late twentieth-century contexts (respectively) with the contexts of their present-day receptions. Each chapter cumulatively builds upon the argument or context of the previous chapters, demonstrating how certain material realities contribute to the musical constitution of the northeastern imaginary and how the imaginary contributes to the making of the material—and musical—world. In this sense, each case study facilitates or explains the conditions of the next: (1) drought-derived natural resources enabled the recording of popular music onto 78 rpm records → (2) drought refugees recorded protest songs about the climate onto those records → (3) audiences learned and celebrated particular ways of understanding drought by listening to those very songs → (4) recorded songs about drought also filled local soundscapes through broadcasting, and the control of broadcasted sound upholds, constructs, and contests structures of inequality →(5) structures of inequality, themselves related to the legacy and management of drought, articulate with cultural policy and music industries to determine which music, some that still describes local landscapes, is now representative of local senses of place, while commercial dance music has largely supplanted traditional music as the prime local genre →(6) many parties featuring this locally significant commercial dance music have been suspended due to the cost of drought.

In each of these cases, drought and music work together via changing social and economic contexts, from twentieth-century urbanization through present-day unbound neoliberal capitalism. These articulations of music and drought are contingent upon markets and nested and overlapping power structures at the local, regional, national, and hemispheric levels. Music and sound, along with music technologies, industries, and spatiotemporal contexts, are vehicles through which these systems are enacted, reproduced, and challenged.

In chapter 1 I explore the materials of sound recording. Through a case study of the use of carnauba wax from northeastern Brazil in the fabrication of wax cylinders and 78 rpm records in the early years of sound reproduction, the chapter shows that the exploitation of natural resources for mass-produced music technologies is also a story of labor and trade relationships within the Northeast and, mostly, between the Global North and the Global South.

In chapter 2 I examine foothills *forró* as a form of environmental protest voiced through the strategic use of nostalgia, through dancing bodies and occupied spaces, and through explicit requests aimed at the government and the Brazilian populace alike. Much scholarship on foothills *forró* understands the genre as either a kitschy regional caricature or an authentic channel from the city to the backlands. Instead, I consider it a deliberate effort to generate sympathy and aid for northeasterners, for whom it also offered comfort and a musical space-time of their own.

Chapter 3 concerns the process through which Luiz Gonzaga's voice—recorded, disseminated, and popularized by a national music industry—became a vehicle for the transmission of ecological knowledge about rain, drought, and the meaning of birdsong. Into the twenty-first century, rain prophets, who announce their observation-based forecasts at a public event in the backlands each January, take inspiration from Gonzaga's mass-mediated songs, sometimes referring to a song's lyrics when discussing knowledge about the weather. In doing so, they assert their trust in local ecological knowledge over other kinds of institutionally sanctioned knowledge about the local ecology.

Chapter 4 explores the construction and management of the soundscape of Orós as it relates to Raimundo Fagner and his music. Fagner, who is closely associated with the city, often names it in his songs and in public, employing it as a metonym for the drought-ridden backlands and a source of northeastern authenticity. But in the actual soundscape of Orós, Fagner's rendering of the city and his own habits of listening collide with the aural aesthetics and needs of the local population. As both an icon and a sometime resident of Orós, he expresses, contributes to, and disrupts the city's soundscape.

In chapter 5 I dialogue with ideas about the sustainability of musical culture by offering a case study in which robust cultural policy, which has been helpful in supporting foothills *forró*, was implemented by the same leftist government that brought millions of Brazilians out of poverty at the start of the second decade of the twenty-first century. The new consumer class amplified the success of electronic *forró*, which is often considered a threat to foothills *forró*. It is this paradox—that the leftist goals of ameliorating poverty and of bolstering a cultural policy that can sustain vibrant music ecologies might be at odds—that I wish to bring to the debate over musical sustainability.

Chapter 6 looks at the cost of Carnival celebrations in an era of economic austerity due to drought and an economic crisis. In 2014, 2015, and 2016 an ongoing drought of historic magnitude led the governor to redirect state monies intended for Carnival and other music-related celebrations to more urgent drought-relief efforts. Is music as vital as water? In the context of a national economic crisis and a massive drought, I claim that electronic *forró*'s continued dominance points to the increasing neoliberalization of culture in Brazil in the wake of the social successes of the Workers' Party and a period of optimistic and ambitious cultural policy.

I have written this book with ethnomusicologists, ecomusicologists, and Brazilianists in mind. I aim to show ethnomusicologists that the ethnographic and historical study of music's relationship to climate can entail the same methodologies, theories, and intellectual histories as other issue-, critique-, and crisis-based paradigms prevalent in present-day ethnomusicological scholarship (see Rice 2014). The primary factors here that link climate to music are social: vulnerability, material and cultural webs, auditory culture, nostalgia, and policy. To ecomusicologists, I contend that the politics of environment have inflected the politics of music and sound, and vice versa, and I respond to the ecomusicological questions and themes I address by arguing that many ecomusicological concerns are matters of social life as much as they are matters of humanity's relationship to the environment.

To Brazilianists, these case studies show that drought has been and remains an element of *forró* in terms not only of its origins and lyrics but also of its sound, its reception via practices of listening and the ways in which it is understood, and its relationship to broad changes to the Brazilian political economy and the consequences for cultural policy and music industries. In other words, the changing experience of drought and the changing relevance of popular music result from and contribute to changing experiences of capitalism in the Northeast. Furthermore, drought does not provide a metanarrative for this northeastern context, but it is integral to it, as it is connected to senses of place, social identities, and aesthetic values, as well as to natural resources used in media, patterns of migration, inequality, and state and municipal budgets.

The common myth of drought in the Northeast says that the region is its climate, that geography is destiny. Such deterministic thinking is, of course, outmoded and problematic. But, more important, it is simplistic and inaccurate. Throughout this book, I insist that (1) drought is a matter of politics more than climate, and that (2) drought is an ongoing narrative about the Northeast constructed in large part by the southeastern culture industry. In short, drought in the Northeast is a matter of unequal and complex relationships: between the Global South and Global North, the Northeast and Southeast, the private sector and the government, and the socioeconomic strata within the Northeast itself.

A final note: I use English translations (my own, except where noted) of the original Portuguese wherever possible. There are only a few Portuguese words that run throughout this text: *forró, baião, sertão, sertanejo, nordestino* (person or thing from the Northeast), and Cearense are the most common.

MAP 2. Ceará and the Northeast in the context of Brazil and South America

MAP 3. Relevant cities in Ceará and Pernambuco

CHAPTER 1

Hills, Dales, and the Jaguaribe Valley

Carnauba Wax at the Dawn of Recorded Sound

THE YEAR 1877 IS MARKED by two notable events that might at first glance appear unrelated. In Ceará the Great Drought began. Over the next two years, it killed half the state's population (some five hundred thousand people) and decimated herds of cattle, the engine of the state's economy. Meanwhile in New Jersey, Thomas Edison invented the phonograph, creating a tin-foil-covered cylinder onto which sound could be recorded and played back. Over the next ten years, Edison's contemporaries began experimenting with the composition of the cylinders. Chief among the substances they tried was a wax from the carnauba palm, a commodity that Brazil had recently begun exporting to the United States, primarily from Ceará, where the wax was transforming into one of the key industries to ease economic dependence on cattle. Carnauba wax, produced by the tree as an adaptation to drought, enabled the mass reproduction of sound and ultimately became a standard element of sound recording into the 1940s in both the United States and Brazil.

The wax remains a significant cash crop for Ceará. By 2012 the state's export of carnauba wax was valued at nearly $67 million, with myriad uses, including polish for shoes and floors, coating for gummy bears and batteries, and an ingredient in soap, matches, lipstick, microchips, and other household and industrial items. Although it no longer plays a role in sound reproduction, its former use in phonograph cylinders and discs is noted in the vast majority of encyclopedia and trade-publication descriptions of the vegetable wax.

Archival documents—primarily industry periodicals, diplomatic publications, print advertisements, and newspaper articles—show that the story of carnauba and the materials of early sound recording is one of global trade, labor, resource extraction, and the environmental adaptation of both trees and people to a semiarid climate. These factors allowed a wax to form on a palm tree in Ceará, to be harvested by Brazilian workers and then sold to American corporations, to become a surface onto which sound was recorded and thus a significant element of the nascent music industry, and then to return to Brazil as a medium for the transmission of musical sound.

What this history tells us is that the recording industry has always been transnational. Recording technologies have always involved natural resources. And the exploitation of natural resources always entails human relationships. Moreover, the capacities to record sound and to mass-reproduce recordings owe a debt to living beings scattered across our globe, among them, insects, donkeys, trees, and workers, most of whom never imagined their hands were touching materials that might someday carry someone's voice.

Ethnomusicologists have long taken note of access to materials used for musical instruments. For example, scholars have shown that the woods and bamboo needed for two of the most iconic instruments of northeastern Brazil—the *rabeca* (fiddle) and *pífano* (fife)—were expensive and increasingly rare at the turn of the twenty-first century (Murphy 1997; Crook 2009). Since the early 2010s, a growing number of music scholars have written about the materials of musical instruments as an ecocritical intervention to organology.[1] Other related works have emphasized the significance of and interaction between the materials themselves via actor-network theory and object-oriented ontology.[2]

I extend these conversations in two ways. First, following the work of Kyle Devine (2015), I write about the materials—and material histories—of sound reproduction technologies as ethnomusicologists and organologists have written about the materials and materiality of musical instruments. I consider this a single conversation about the physical objects of musical sound. Second, my analysis of these instruments, in this case wax cylinders and phonograph records, considers not just environmental conditions and the significance of a tree and its wax but also histories of colonial trade and circulation; hierarchies and networks of global, regional, and local inequality; and the systems and circumstances of labor. These systems and circumstances include the legacy of slavery, the practices of peonage, and the working conditions of carnauba groves in Brazil and recording studios in Brazil and the United States.

Natural resources have long been extracted from the Global South to meet the aesthetic and technical demands of musicians and sound engineers from the Global North. Writing about colonialism, slavery, and brutality to elephants in piano manufacturing in the nineteenth century, Sean Murray writes, "Every time a musician sits at an ivory keyboard, she situates herself, consciously or not, in relation to the exotic material she touches to sound the notes" (2009, 4). So too with every listener who put a phonograph record on an Edison Diamond Disc Machine in the early twentieth century. The diamond stylus, with a notable colonial history of its own, comes into contact with shellac, a resin produced by an insect and imported from South and Southeast Asia (see Devine 2015 on shellac in sound reproduction). The grooves that carry the sound were transferred onto the shellac record from a master disc likely made from Brazilian wax. Carnauba wax, as peripheral as it may seem in the production process, links drought and the ecology of northeastern Brazil to the early music industry.

Moreover, the wax involves Brazil's position in the Global South and implicates the conditions, values, needs, and desires of workers involved in carnauba forestry, commodity trading, and sound recording, as every step in the commodity chain is an arena of cultural production (Tsing 2011). As carnauba trees entered the world of agriculture and global trade, the local significance and use of the trees, which provided shade in the backlands, materials for building and maintaining typical rural homes, and straw for handmade hats, gave way to the needs of the export market, and the tree's wax took on new meaning.

In this chapter, I first describe the tree's ability to thrive during drought and the related production of its profitable wax. I then discuss the tree's many uses in the rural Northeast and the relationships among its uses, labor, and land tenure in the nineteenth century. Next, I examine the export of the wax to Europe and the United States at the turn of the twentieth century and explore the attitudes of merchants, importers, and industrialists toward the wax and the Brazilian workers responsible for harvesting it. I then turn to its use in sound recording, looking at how the wax and its properties affected the recording process and the working conditions of sound engineers and musicians. Finally, I discuss the wax's return to Brazil in the early years of the Brazilian recording industry and its role in creating Brazilian popular music, which traveled on wax discs between Brazil and Germany before ever reaching Brazilian ears.

The Tree of Life

"The air was filled," wrote folklorist Luís da Câmara Cascudo, recalling carnauba trees in the *sertão*, "with the dull sound of the rough palms fanning themselves, slowly, in the midday heat. The carnauba explained everything" (1964, 50). An official symbol of Ceará since 2004, the tree is significant as a practical resource, a key element of the economy, and an icon of the state.

The carnauba palm grows throughout the *caatinga* along river valleys, particularly the Jaguaribe River in Ceará, the Parnaíba River and its tributaries in Maranhão and Piauí, the Piranhas-Açu River in Rio Grande do Norte, and the famed São Francisco River in northern Bahia and Pernambuco. Its name in Portuguese is both *carnaúba* and *carnaubeira*, and its scientific names are *Copernicia prunifera*, *Coryphe cerifera*, *Copernicia cerifera*, and *Arrudaria cerifera*. Its Portuguese name derives from its indigenous name in Tupi, *carana-iba*: *caraná* means "scratchy," and *iba* means "wood." An earlier name, given by the Cariri people, was *ananachi* (Cascudo 1964). The wax of this tree, which is also known as the wax-palm and has been called the Tree of Life, has been referred to as Brazil wax, Ceará wax, jungle wax, Johnson Wax, and food additive E 903.

In 1955 a twelve-year-old girl named Pattie Bussom from Williamsport, Pennsylvania, wrote into "Ask Andy," a syndicated newspaper column for children, to inquire about carnauba wax. Andy responded to Pattie:

> The story of carnauba is a story of hardship, endurance and final success. It begins in the cruel climate of northern Brazil. There the fierce winds blow hot and dry. The hero of the story is a proud palm tree called Copernicia Cerifera. Early naturalists called this tree that could grow in an impossible climate the Tree of Life. The Brazilians call it the carnauba—or the wax palm.
>
> No one would dispute the sturdy palm's claim to the title King of the Wax Trees. Most plants produce a certain amount of wax to shield their leaves from the drying air. Some produce enough to make it worth our while to take this plant wax. But no plant's wax can compare with the wax of the carnauba, either in quantity or in quality. (*Spokane Daily Chronicle*, July 11, 1955)

Andy's explanation that the tree produces wax as an adaptation to drought is widely but not universally accepted. The hardy tree has been planted in a range of contexts with varying success: most notably, in Ceylon, Tanzania, Hawaii, Florida, and the Brazilian state of Pará along the Amazon River. In most cases, the tree thrived but failed to produce wax. In Pará it produced wax, but only on isolated trees and in diminished quantities to those produced in the Northeast (Taube 1952). In Florida the tree was killed by frost in the winter (see Johnson 1972). The plant's ability to grow while failing to produce wax in humid environments, coupled with the facts that it can grow partially submerged in water during periods of flooding and that it produces excess wax during periods of extreme drought, has led botanists and others to conclude the wax is an adaptation to the drought-flood cycle of the Brazilian Northeast. The waxy secretion prevents evaporation and protects the leaves against the heat. Skeptics of this hypothesis have attributed the wax to properties of the soil or the tree's genetic

FIGURE 1. Carnaubal, Marco, CE. Instituto Brasileiro de Geografia e Estatística. Date unknown.

makeup (Taube 1952; Johnson 1972). Yet the drought hypothesis prevails. The understanding of the wax as an adaptation to drought has become part of the tree's mythology and an element of its marketing. An essay from 1944 from *Chemical and Engineering News* emphasizes drought's role in the production of this "useful" wax:

> It is not altogether strange that some of the most unusual and useful plants thrive in fantastic climates and places on the face of the earth. . . .
>
> It is in one of these strange climatic areas of the earth that a most useful tree species thrives and survives the unusual combination of too much and too little rainfall. . . .
>
> Nature has trained the palm to form a protective coating of wax on its fronds to prevent excessive evaporation during the long droughts. (Knaggs 1944, 1564–1565)

During an expedition to Ceará in 1935, Herbert Fisk Johnson, then president of S. C. Johnson and Son, Inc., and grandson of the founder of the floor wax company, came to the same conclusion: "Nature has seen fit to coat all of its delicate plant structures with a thin cutinous layer of wax. The blossoms, fruit, leaves, and young shoots of all plants are protected with wax. In addition to the protection which this layer of wax affords against the destructive action of the atmosphere, the waxy coating aids in the conservation of moisture within the plant by preventing evaporation from the enormous expanse of exposed surface" (1936, 1005–1006).

The wax has long been known to be a good material for candle wax, and its sale within Brazil has been profitable for the Northeast, especially for the economies of Ceará, Piauí, and Maranhão. Referring to the wax's significance for the "people of the dry *sertão*," American poet Elizabeth Bishop, who lived in Rio de Janeiro between 1944 and 1958, called the wax "the compensation given them by God for the scourge of drought—since when there is rain the palm produces no wax" (2011, 208).

The carnauba tree was valuable for northeasterners not only for its wax but for all its elements: its roots, its leaves, its fruit, and its wood. A communiqué from a newspaper in Ceará in 1850 called the trees "the most profitable of our province," "a special treat of Divine Providence," and "a favor like manna, which God made fall in the desert every day to nourish his chosen people."[3] A U.S. consul to Brazil wrote in 1939, "To the average person carnauba connotes merely an exotic wax, but to the *sertanejo* of the Brazilian Northeast the carnauba palm is perhaps even more valuable than the camel to the Bedouin."[4] In 1837 French traveler Jean Ferdinand Denis described the carnauba as a "tree of life," echoing Alexander von Humboldt's description of the moriche palm as such due to its multifarious and far-reaching uses among Venezuelans (e.g., see Cascudo 1964; Denis and Famin 1837). Despite subsequent misunderstandings to the contrary, Denis's description of the tree as a "tree of life" referred to its many uses by the local population and not to its ability to survive in a harsh climate. Many writers have romanticized carnauba as the only resource needed for constructing a rural home. Augusto Tavares de Lyra wrote about the tree's many uses in 1911:

> The carnauba alone can make a *sertanejo* house.
> The trunk forms the timber, the buttresses, the platforms, the purlins, the rafters, the slats—the overall skeleton of the construction—and the straw provides coverage for the roof and lining for the walls. There's more. All the furniture and all the utensils are made of carnauba. The shelves, tables, benches, and the cabinet are made of carnauba planks. (1912, 298)

The list goes on: floor mats, sieves, brooms, fans, hammocks, and hats could be made from its durable fibers. Its sap could be used as an insect repellent or as a drink, sometimes fermented. Its core and buds could be eaten as hearts of palm. Its fruit could be eaten raw, especially during times of drought, or crushed into cooking oil. Its seeds could be ground, roasted, and consumed as is or with coffee. Its roots could be pulverized and used as seasoning or made into medicine for skin diseases and rheumatism, among other ailments (see Johnson 1972). It was a noted source of shade in the backlands, and its wax was commonly used for candles to illuminate rural northeastern homes.

The carnauba's usefulness aligned with the system of land tenure in northeastern Brazil present since the early colonial era. Workers would squat on vast plantations, where they would satisfy their basic needs with available natural resources, including those offered by the tree. In 1944 sociologist T. Lynn Smith, writing about land tenure and the living conditions of northeastern workers, wrote, "Through long practice the *caboclos, matutos,* and *sertanejos* feel free to squat or 'intrude' where they please. They establish temporary quarters, help themselves to the carnauba . . . and other things to be had for the taking" (1944, 198).

The use and sale of products made from the tree can also be considered a kind of climate adaptation. Before the Brazilian government began to address drought through aid, research, infrastructure, and other approaches at the turn of the twentieth century (see chapter 2), rural northeasterners had developed a number of their own methods for survival. Anthropologist Bernard Siegel (1971, 241) lists four that were common in the nineteenth century: making small dams to catch rainwater, digging wells, practicing agriculture in dry riverbeds and along the rims of dams, and deriving cash income from xerophytic (surviving on little water) plants. The carnauba was among the most profitable of the xerophytic plants. In the mid-nineteenth century its most valuable products were hats and floor mats made from its fibers, as noted by James Wetherell (1860, 90–91), a British vice-consul to Bahia and later to Paraíba who described the profitability of the handmade straw mats and hats in 1854.

The Carnauba Wax Industry

By the end of the nineteenth century, the carnauba no longer primarily provided for the local population with its wood, its fibers, and its fruits; instead, it became useful for its economic yields, becoming a valuable export commodity grown for its wax and joining a long history of agricultural trade that dates to the start of the colonial era. Brazilwood was the nation's first major export, extracted for a vivid red textile dye made from its heartwood. Sugar came next. Large northeastern sugarcane plantations produced enough sugar to make it Brazil's leading export into the mid-seventeenth century. The sugar trade paved the way for three key formative elements of northeastern life: large sugarcane plantations resulted in the latifundium system of land tenure; its intensive demands contributed to the cruel process of forced labor through the enslavement first of indigenous peoples and then of Africans; and its success led to Brazil becoming a plantation economy, trading its commodity crops on the global market, for the next five centuries (see Skidmore 2010). In other words, enduring, unequal systems of landownership and class, of race and racial prejudice, and of Brazil's position in the hemisphere had roots in agricultural trade primarily from the Northeast. The production of carnauba wax comfortably slid into the social and economic grooves carved out by earlier commodities.

Carnauba wax's value has been known outside of Brazil since the early nineteenth century: the first shipment from Brazil (twenty-six tons) went to the Netherlands in 1845. In an essay from 1811, an English chemist named William T. Brande described his experiments with the wax to see if "it might prove an useful substitute for bees wax, and constitute, in due time, a new article of commerce between the Brazils and this country" (1811, 261). His results were positive, and he concluded that carnauba wax, when combined with beeswax, made a good material for candles.

The sale of the wax grew steadily through the second half of the nineteenth century. It was featured at the Paris Exhibition in 1867 and at Brazil's National Exposition in 1875. By then, it was already a profitable export, sold for candle-making and as a coating for parquet floors. An English-language publication titled "Agricultural Instructions for Those Who May Emigrate to Brazil" from 1875, in trying to attract foreigners to buy land, claimed that "the carnauba palm is so plentiful" that Brazil was already exporting a substantial amount of the material (Moreira 1875, 56).[5] By 1887 the wax had reached the laboratories of American inventors and engineers who had been experimenting with the material as a surface onto which they could record sound, a technology that was still in its infancy.

Brazil began exporting carnauba wax in truly large quantities in 1894, first to England and then to the United States. The United States imported some $260,000 of carnauba wax from Ceará in 1896, accounting for nearly a third of the state's earnings from exports to the United States, second only to skins from goats and sheep. Prices for the wax began to rise, and foreign markets took note of the tree's expanding range of applications. A document published by the U.S. secretary of state in 1897 said, "There are many . . . woods of great value, but the most wonderful of all . . . is the carnauba palm" (1897, 659).

The timing of the commodity's entry into the global marketplace was critical. Following each major drought in Ceará in the nineteenth century, each one further destroying the cattle industry, something—a cultural shift—would seemingly rescue Ceará's economy. The drought of 1824–26 spurred migration within the backlands, sending Cearenses from the dry *caatinga* to the verdant hills (the *serra*), where they could grow subsistence crops, manioc, cereals, sugarcane, and coffee. After the drought of 1845, Ceará saw the expansion of commercial agriculture, including carnauba wax, as well as coffee and tobacco (Santos 2012). A newspaper article from Ceará in 1853 calls the carnauba wax industry a result of "the neediness and the hunger of 1845, by sheltering the inhabitants of the banks of the Jaguaribe and rescuing them from it" (*O Cearense*, March 5, 2). Another article from 1863 ("Noticiario," *Pedro II*, January 6, 3), credits one man, Manoel Antônio de Macedo, with creating the carnauba wax industry in Ceará as a remedy for the devastation left by the drought of 1845: "[In] the calamitous era in which Ceará found itself grappling with a devastating and calamitous drought, [the people of Ceará] were encouraged by his example to the poor by making resources available that converted it into a permanent industry, and which today constitutes one of the most precious sources of wealth in the province." The drought of 1877–79, the most severe, and the abolition of slavery in 1888 were met with intensified commercial agriculture, thus concentrating land and wealth among a smaller portion of the population than before and altering labor practices (Santos 2012).

By the early twentieth century, carnauba groves were worked by sharecroppers or tenant farmers who were forced to rent not only the land but also their tools, clothes, and other needs on credit directly from the landowners, creating, in effect, a system of debt servitude. A scientist for S. C. Johnson and Son, Inc., wrote, "Whether the worker delivers one-third of the carnauba yield, or pays a fixed rental, or hires out as a day laborer, the result is always the same: the landowner gets most of the money and all the wax" (Taube 1952, 391).

The wax was typically harvested in the dry season, generally in two annual cuttings, sometimes three. A worker, handling a long-armed pruning hook, would remove fronds selectively from the trees. The fronds would fall and would then be gathered by two workers, who bundled and carried the leaves or loaded them onto the backs of donkeys, which were led by a driver (see figure 2). The workers would bring the bundles to a yard, trim the moisture-retaining stalks, and lay the fronds side by side, leaving them to dry for several days. Workers would then take the dried leaves to a small enclosed shed, protected from the wind, or to an open space, where they would slice the leaves into segments and beat the wax powder from the fronds. Luís da Câmara Cascudo observed the musicality of the wax-removal process: "Once the straw has reached the desired grade of dryness, in which percussion will make the thin polish of wax come off, they will begin the 'beating' [*batida*], the 'batting' [*batedura*], and the 'banging' [*batimento*]" (1964, 55). These workers performed the most difficult step in the process, as they typically worked in very hot, poorly ven-

FIGURE 2. Colheita de Carnaúa (Carnauba harvest), Fortaleza, CE. IBGE. Date unknown.

tilated spaces, in which they would inhale the wax particles. The final stages involved passing the wax through a screen before melting it over an open fire, then straining the molten wax to remove dirt and other impurities, and finally pouring it into pans and leaving it to solidify. The solid wax would be broken into chunks and bagged for sale.

According to one study from the early 1950s, although carnauba workers were typically men, women and children were also often involved in harvesting the wax (see figure 3). Furthermore, unsafe and illegal conditions, including the presence of an open flame and the use of oxalic acid, were also common (Taube 1952). Machines called the Guarany and the Cyclone, which shredded the leaves to remove the powder, ultimately obviated the most labor-intensive jobs on many of the plantations.

The export market for the wax expanded greatly over the first three decades of the twentieth century. New applications were being discovered on a regular basis, and traders and lobbyists lauded it as a versatile and strong substance. A British trade journal in 1915 promoted it, writing about an "opportunity for diverting trade in this valuable commodity" to Britain and claiming that its uses were many: "It is, for example, used for imparting a gloss to linen and a lustre to leather. It serves as a basis for boot polish. It is used in the manufacture of high-grade candles and discs for gramaphones [*sic*]" (*Board of Trade Journal*, March 11, 660).

FIGURE 3. Beneficiamento de carnaúba em Cabeceiras do Piauí (PI) (Processing of carnauba in Cabaceiras, Piauí). IBGE. 1957.

But as its popularity grew, so did the demands of the industry, thus placing increased pressure on Brazilian workers. Some members of the American
chemical industry saw Brazil and Brazilians as inefficient and inept at managing the growth of the trees, at providing access to adequate trade ports, and
at collecting and properly grading the wax, causing "considerable dissatisfac-
tion both among dealers and consumers" (*Trade Information Bulletin* 1932, 20).
Echoing foreign complaints levied against Brazilian workers during the rubber
boom, which resulted in the British and Dutch relocating the rubber industry
from the Amazon to the East Indies in the 1910s, concerns about the carnauba
industry were similarly tinged with prejudice against Brazilian workers who
failed to meet the expectations of the growing industry. A publication from
1918 called the carnauba wax industry "undeveloped," saying that "any very extensive expansion will require a more efficient and up-to-date procedure under
the direction of large-scale enterprise." It continued, "In the past the industry
has been in the hands of small native growers who have sold their output to
exporting houses on the seacoast" (U.S. Government Printing Office 1932,
23). A trade publication from 1932 expressed frustration at the tree's failure to
produce the wax outside of Brazil, given what it saw as the shortcomings of
the Brazilian wax industry. It goes on, claiming that conditions in Brazil slowed

potential growth: "There is room for considerable expansion in the Brazilian carnauba-wax industry, as a large part of the carnauba-palm tracts are at present unexploited. Lack of transportation and systematic development, however, has considerably retarded progress" (U.S. Government Bureau of Foreign and Domestic Commerce 1932, 21).

By 1936 some 4,800 tons of the wax had been imported into the United States, primarily by S. C. Johnson, whose headquarters in Racine, Wisconsin, now house a building called Fortaleza Hall, named in honor of the Fortaleza-based Carnauba Expedition taken by employees of the company in 1935. In the years following the expedition, S. C. Johnson acquired two carnauba plantations near Fortaleza, where the company could experiment with its own growing and harvesting techniques, bringing American agricultural, scientific, and labor practices, along with expanded mechanization, to Brazil to increase the quality and size of yields (Taube 1952). Although it is best known today as a floor and car polish, the wax was recognized in the 1920s primarily for its use in audio recording and other reproductive media such as carbon paper and a coating on film.

Talking Wax

About seventy-five years after the English chemist William Brande experimented with carnauba wax's suitability for candle wax, an American inventor named Charles Sumner Tainter discovered that a similar mixture—carnauba and beeswax—made an excellent surface for sound recording. Tainter's earlier beeswax-coated cylinders for his graphophone machine were an improvement over Thomas Edison's tinfoil ones, but the material was still too soft. In 1887, in a race against Edison and his phonograph, Tainter filed a patent with the U.S. Patent Office for his "new and useful improvement in tablets for use in graphophones." In his patent application, he asserted that beeswax, which by then Edison had been mixing with paraffin, was too "soft and sticky" for a recording surface. "Very few substances" he wrote, "are found suitable for this purpose, as properties or characteristics of a peculiar kind are essential to the production of an accurate record, one that will not be impaired by lapse of time and which will give loud and clear reproduction" (U.S. Patent 393,190, 1887). It was an era of discovery and experimentation in sound reproduction. The following year, Emile Berliner, working in Washington, D.C., began recording on discs rather than cylinders. And Tainter quickly moved on to coating his cylinders with other substances, as did Edison and his team, whose early cylinders were solid wax.

The nascent industry's single most consequential advancement at the end of the nineteenth century was mass reproduction. Rather than recording each cylinder individually, which required musicians and speakers to perform each selection multiple times, employees for Edison found that if they plated the original cylinders with metal, they could mold new wax cylinders from the metal impressions (see Sutton 2010). It took over a decade before molded cylinders became commonplace, as the process was one of a couple of mass reproduction techniques tested at the time, and there was uncertainty about the best way to create the molds. Early trials involved pouring molten wax into the mold; later efforts involved pressing preformed wax blanks into the mold. Ultimately, a molten blend of waxes was found most suitable for mass reproduction, facilitating the creation of multiple copies of a single recording (between 120 and 150 copies per day) and forever changing understandings of music and experiences of sound.

The key ingredient in the new mold was the hard and brittle wax of the car-nauba, with its high melting point and its tendency to shrink as it cooled (see figure 4). A newspaper article in 1902 argued that prior materials had one of two limitations: With very hard recording surfaces, only the loudest sounds could be recorded. On the other hand, very soft materials, which could record quieter sounds, deteriorated quickly during playback. Carnauba wax was soft enough to capture acoustic and musical nuances and hard enough to withstand repeated uses:

What is described as an important improvement in phonograph records has been made. Until very recently the wax records have been made of soft materials. . . .

This new record is composed of several kinds of wax. . . .

The principal ingredient is a vegetable wax that comes from the Province of Ceara, in Brazil. It is a secretion of a certain palm tree and is known in the trade as Carnauba wax. Two of its peculiar properties are its hardness and the way it shrinks in cooling. Both of these qualities made it valuable in casting the high speed hard wax records.

Briefly the manufacture is as follows: A master record is made on the soft mineral soap cylinder, in the same manner as always has been done. Then a mold is made by electroplating this master; first gold and then with copper.

Then the original record is melted out and the mold is ready to have the Carnauba wax composition poured into it. This wax contracts very much in cooling; and as the depth of the groove is only two-thousandths of an inch, the shrinkage is enough to let the cast record drop out of the mold when it is cool. (*Weekly Republican-Traveler* [Arkansas City, KS], July 17, 1902, 8)

41

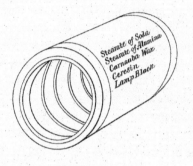

No. 782,375.   PATENTED FEB. 14, 1905.
J. W. AYLSWORTH.
COMPOSITION FOR MAKING DUPLICATE PHONOGRAPH RECORDS.
APPLICATION FILED NOV. 3, 1903.

Attest: Inventor:

by   Atty.

FIGURE 4. "Composition for making duplicate phonograph records." 1905.

By 1903 Edison was marketing the two-minute cylinders as "Gold Moulded" records, and for a handful of years, the wax remained the industry standard. A note from a weekly pharmaceutical periodical in 1905 says the following about "gramophone wax": "Much secrecy is observed by makers as to the composition of wax for gramophone records, but carnauba wax is used largely" (1905, 542). By 1907 the use of the Brazilian wax in audio recording was significant enough to have increased demand for the substance, resulting in higher prices, described in a consular report from that year from the Foreign Office of Great Britain: "Quite recently, it appears, the discovery has been made that carnauba wax is the substance most suitable for the manufacture of records for phonographs and gramophones, and the additional demand thus created has had the effect of materially increasing the value of the wax in question" (Diplomatic 1907, 178).

The wax's suitability (and ensuing popularity) for audio recording helped quickly bring about its demise. Rising costs, along with Edison's desire to create cylinders that could hold four-minute recordings, led to the phasing out of carnauba wax, which was replaced by ebonite, an inexpensive waxy substance made from coal. By 1912, facing competition from Columbia, which had acquired the Indestructible Phonograph Company and its celluloid cylinders, Edison stopped producing wax cylinders altogether in the United States, producing his new cylinders out of celluloid instead (Sutton 2010).

In the first years of the twentieth century, engineers realized that Emile Berliner's shellac discs, which were easily and inexpensively reproduced, could be recorded on both sides, a significant improvement over the cylinders. The International Zon-O-Phone Company (later a subsidiary of Victor's Universal Talking Machine Company) sold its very first double-sided records in 1902—in Brazil to a man named Fred Figner, who sought to release albums with Brazilian recordings on one side and American or European recordings on the other. By 1908 discs were already outpacing cylinders. Columbia stopped producing new cylinders in 1909; the United States Phonograph Company did so in 1913. That same year Edison introduced his Diamond Discs, which were superior in fidelity to Victor's and Columbia's discs. After 1915 new recordings were almost exclusively made on discs rather than cylinders, which were no longer produced at all after 1929.

Whereas cylinder recordings for phonographs were etched onto soft mineral soap, transferred to metal molds, and then reproduced in hard wax or celluloid, the disc recordings for gramophones were cut onto wax masters, transferred to metal pressers, and then stamped into shellac reproductions. Carnauba wax reemerged as a useful substance, as it became the primary ingredient in the new wax masters. A headline from *Business Digest and Investment Weekly* from 1918 reads: "Wax in commerce and industry: Its uses now range from electrical insulation to the water-proofing of shells and cartridges—*and the gramophone industry must have its share*" (22, no. 11, emphasis added). The article goes on to say, "Even before the [First World War], carnauba wax found a ready use in the manufacture of phonograph and gramophone records" (389).

By the start of the 1920s, the American recording industry had become the largest importer of carnauba wax.[6] Although masters were also sometimes cut into blanks made from distilled coal, the recording process came to be associated with the wax and vice versa. In the 1920s the word "wax" became a slang term for a record. Recording a record was often colloquially referred to as "waxing a record," a phrase that first appeared in print in 1935 (see the *Oxford English Dictionary*).

Waxing a Record

Carnauba wax was responsible for some of the logistical attributes of the recording process. Specifically, working conditions of audio engineers and musicians were tied to the properties of the wax itself. The recording process began by shaping a cake of carnauba wax into a very thick disc. A recording engineer for Capitol Records described the preparation of the wax discs: "We had to shave the wax blocks down so they were absolutely smooth, and then polish them with a diamond stone. When they were ready to be used, they looked like a mirror: you could see yourself in them, they were so highly polished and shiny. If you had to cut and polish those waxes, they would sometimes break, and since the machine revolved at about 1,800 rpm, it could be very dangerous!" (Carson Taylor, quoted in Granata 2004, 26).

Improbable workplace hazards aside, the wax also required a very hot recording studio for engineers and musicians. After polishing the discs and placing them on a recording lathe with a stylus, engineers would adjust the room temperature. The carnauba wax was full of impurities. To prevent errors in the production process, engineers had to keep recording studios hot enough for the wax to stay soft. Accounts of early jazz recording sessions in the 1920s describe studios as unventilated, humid, and "uncomfortably hot," which writers have attributed to the qualities and constraints of the wax (Kennedy and Gioia 2013, 33). Some photographs of these recording sessions show musicians dripping in sweat (Lion 2005; Kennedy and Gioia 2013).

Once the recording was made, with the sound etched onto the wax, the fragile wax disc, not intended for playback, would be electroplated—coated with silver nitrate—then dipped in a hot bath to coat it with copper. Engineers would then separate the copper from the wax master, and the new copper disc would become the stamper from which the shellac discs would be pressed. The wax was then shaved down, polished, and used in subsequent recording sessions until it was too thin to be used, at which point it would be melted down into new cakes of wax.

Carnuaba Returns to Brazil

The Brazilian recording industry, nearly as old as the American recording industry, acquired the wax secondhand. Fred Figner, a Czech businessman who had immigrated to the United States and later to Brazil to make a fortune selling the new technology, imported both blank and prerecorded wax cylinders from the United States to Brazil. Before settling in Rio de Janeiro, Figner first landed in the northern city of Belém in 1891, carrying with him a battery-powered electric phonograph, blank cylinders, and tubes, batteries, and other accessories to delight the Brazilian public with the new technology (on Figner, see Franceschi 1984, 2002; Hertzman 2013). Within a year he left Belém. His first stop on his southward voyage was Fortaleza, followed by other state capitals en route to Rio de Janeiro, making recordings along the way. The wax cylinders he showcased in Fortaleza were, of course, made from the stuff of nearby palm trees, having traveled overseas before returning home.

Once in Rio, Figner opened a music store and recording studio in the city's downtown on a street called Rua do Ouvidor (Street of the Listener). Figner, who imported more recordings than blank discs, made substantial use of machines—first hand-cranked and later motorized—that could shave and polish prerecorded wax cylinders so they could be reused. Figner would stay up until midnight to prepare the cylinders. "Sometimes," he wrote, "I would shave the cylinders until midnight, and I would take the ferry to Niterói [a city near Rio de Janeiro]; and at eight a.m. I would already be back in the shop to make the recording" (quoted in Franceschi 1984, 24). Imported cylinders were fragile, and they often broke while being transported to Brazil, so reusable cylinders were necessary.

In the first few years of the twentieth century, Figner became the largest seller of Columbia's single-sided gramophone discs. He initially had no way to reproduce the recordings in his small studio. Artists would record onto wax at Figner's studio, Casa Edison, and Figner would send the masters to Germany, where Zon-O-Phone would electroplate them and press them into the shellac discs. The peripatetic wax traveled the Western world, from Brazil to the United States or to Europe, where it would be mixed and prepared as a cake that would become a master disc; then back to Brazil, where music would be recorded onto it; and then to Germany, where it would be stamped into the final discs; which were returned to Brazil. It was only in 1913 that Figner opened Brazil's first record factory, Fábrica Odeon, with the equipment to press records.

Figner began selling records and devices throughout Brazil as early as 1903 via mail order. A gramophone appeared in 1905 at an upper-class celebration in Ceará. The inaugural ball of the Clube Athlêtico in Fortaleza featured one of the machines, which brought "candid, sincere, and cordial smiles" to those who heard it (*Jornal do Ceará*, May 2, 1905). In the following decade, Brazil became one of the largest markets worldwide for the recording industry. The growth of the Brazilian recording industry paralleled and intertwined with that of the carnauba wax industry. The profitability of the wax benefited people in Ceará by improving the economy, which enabled them to purchase the very same mass-media technologies that employed the wax. The skyrocketing price of carnauba wax brought new wealth to places such as Limoeiro do Norte in Ceará. The Jaguaribe Valley region acquired its first radio in 1936, telephone in 1939, and cinema in 1940 as a result of the carnauba boom (Garfield 2010).

Wax and the Soundscape

In 1947 Brazil's commercial attaché to Canada gave a speech at a trade meeting in which he encouraged Canadian importers to do more business with Brazil. "Remember," he told a crowd that included mayors and presidents of trade boards, "that when you use carbon paper at your office or listen to a phonograph record, it is thanks to the carnauba wax" ("Urges Development of Brazil-Canadian Trade," *Ottawa Citizen*, February 28, 1947). For two moments surrounding the turn of the twentieth century, profitable and sustainable carnauba wax helped enable the recording and mass production of sound. More generally, the record industry—and the very capacity to record sound—owes a debt to the natural formation of wax and other materials, to commercial agriculture, and to the markets for such materials that connect the Global South to the Global North. And these materials are significant in their local contexts, to local senses of place, local systems of inequality, and local webs of meaning. After being traded abroad and then returning home in new forms, the materials take on new meanings as new significance gets etched onto the material. By shaving clean and then recording Brazilian music onto prerecorded American cylinders, which were made from the Brazilian wax, Fred Figner made manifest this process of layering meaning onto exported and reimported materials.[7]

The poetic symbolism of the wax leaving Ceará's backlands and returning in the form of records carrying music that would fill local soundscapes with audible meaning has not been lost on musicians in present-day Ceará. Musician and journalist Flávio Paiva writes that singer-songwriter Eugênio Leandro (b. 1958), born and raised in Limoeiro do Norte, where he was surrounded by the production of carnauba wax, has acknowledged the significance of the wax's journey on his own musical production: "Eugênio's music is rooted in the vision of a boy who played around in the markets and saw the production of carnauba wax in the Jaguaribe Valley. Wax that, according to him, ended up going to RCA Victor in the United States, where they made the old records, and it would return in the form of black grooved platters for the needles of the radio broadcasters from the [Jaguaribe] Valley to fill the backlands with music" (2014, 75).

Sounds from these 78s filled the soundscapes of Ceará through the mid-twentieth century and reverberated into the twenty-first. As I will explore through much of the rest of this book, *forró* recordings held sounds that were inflected with local and national senses of place and local knowledge, they established a northeastern musical (and socioenvironmental) lexicon, and they were heard in local ways by northeastern audiences. But what cannot be heard in the music or seen on the discs is the distance the wax traveled—and the underlying stories of drought adaptation, labor, social hierarchies, and global trade—between the moment it formed on the leaves of a Cearense tree and the time it reached Cearense ears in the form of musical sound.

CHAPTER 2

"Help Your Brother"

Drought Songs as Protest

FORRÓ WAS BORN OF DROUGHT. As explained in this book's introduction, a series of severe droughts led to an exodus from the rural Northeast that lasted from the late nineteenth century through the first half of the twentieth century.[1] Drought refugees, most of them men, found themselves in new, unfamiliar circumstances in the metropolises of the Southeast and in the Amazon to the north. Urban songwriters in the Southeast composed music inspired by the influx of migrants and a growing awareness of drought. The migrant workers themselves, from diverse parts of the Northeast, consolidated a regional identity that included a shared musical aesthetic. Their music combined a variety of northeastern musical rhythms, timbres, modes, and other elements with urban musical practices. One such genre came to be known as *baião* and, ultimately, *forró*.

At the same time, due to the flood of northeastern migrants into southeastern cities and increasing media and political attention on drought, the notion of a Northeast region, characterized by its semiarid climate, began to replace the previous regional binary of North and South, making the Northeast a unique place in the Brazilian imaginary. Musicians and record companies took advantage of the new regional designation, segmenting the audience by region and producing music that could be marketed as northeastern to the growing class of northeastern migrants and to those who remained in the Northeast itself. The first half of the twentieth century also saw vast efforts for nation building that exploited notions of rural authenticity, thus bolstering demand for northeastern rural music. It is in this sense, wherein drought victims and refugees inspired, made, and consumed new music, that *forró* was born of drought.

Forró and its forerunners were also, in many ways, political responses to drought. Northeastern popular music was a form of drought protest in three distinct ways. First, through its nostalgic recollection of the backlands, the music called attention to the cultural and environmental consequences of drought. Alexander Rehding has written that nostalgic music can be read through the lens of ecocriticism: "[In] marveling at landscapes as an integral part of our cultural identities, we begin to understand how much else we stand to lose if those landscapes disappear" (2011, 413). In the case of the *sertão*, concerns have involved not cultural loss related to the loss or degradation of the landscape but the sociocultural implications of the failure to combat periodic droughts. Second, Adriana Fernandes (2005) has argued that northeastern dance music created spaces, movements, and feelings of time for northeastern bodies—many of them drought refugees—to occupy while in the marginal position of exile. I emphasize that their exile was often ecological in nature. Third, in song lyrics, stage banter, and interviews, northeastern musicians made direct appeals to government officials, the Brazilian population, and religious figures (priests, saints, and the Roman Catholic God) for aid. Music was a symptom of and a remedy for the imbalance of power between the Northeast and the Southeast as it affected drought, drought migration, drought exploitation, drought mismanagement, and drought inaction.

Northeastern popular songs made specific demands: for the recognition of the Northeast, its people, and their plight; for donations to be sent to drought victims; for government assistance in the form of loans, money transfers, public works, and drought-proof employment; for divine intervention; for rain. This music took a stance on drought as both a social and an ecological concern and expressed it through lyrics, musical sound, and the physical occupation of space and time. Like music elsewhere in the world that protests environmental change (e.g., Stimeling 2012; Guy 2009; Ramnarine 2009; Pedelty 2012; Ingram 2010), *forró* was a form of environmental protest.

I do not mean to say that northeastern popular music was or is primarily protest music. It has always been primarily dance music and even played into hegemonic desires involved in the process of nation building. Rather, my aim is to understand how and why composers, performers, and listeners of this music created and experienced it for practical and political reasons related to the conditions of drought, involving ecological exile, resource allocation, public works, and prejudice. In addition, the reverse argument, that this music could not have entailed political motivations, discounts actions and statements made by northeastern performers. As I discuss at the end of this chapter, some scholarly and popular writings on northeastern music, particularly *baião* and *forró*, have considered it essentially commercial and in poor taste. By insisting on the music's political facets, I am also insisting on a recognition of northeastern agency.

I begin this history approximately five decades before Luiz Gonzaga popularized the *baião* to explore various ways northeastern popular music can be linked to environmental protest, a process I periodize and narrate (more or less) chronologically. And I expand beyond Gonzaga to explore other musicians who were working in related ways, often with similar goals. I first examine northeastern traditional celebrations with roots in medieval Europe and in Roman Catholicism that were, in their own ways, demands for rain and expressions of weather as a social, cosmological, and temporal phenomenon. I then turn to pastoral art songs at the turn of the twentieth century, which were often nostalgic responses to urbanization and alienation from the rural world. From there, I explore Brazilian popular music's articulation with nation building, folklore research, and the early Brazilian music industry in an era of growing awareness of drought in the Northeast. Not all music about drought and the Northeast, however, was intended as protest or implicated in some larger project; some was exploitative of the concern surrounding drought. I then discuss efforts by Luiz Gonzaga and his contemporaries to invent northeastern dance genres with nostalgic lyrics and sounds. Next, I introduce Gonzaga's direct efforts and appeals to authorities, southeasterners, and religious figures for drought aid. I conclude by exploring some of the musical and symbolic legacy of *forró*'s nostalgia, movements, and entreaties. Throughout this chapter, I emphasize the music of exiled northeasterners and Cearenses in particular, as the story of northeastern music has too often been told from the perspective of the Southeast, as a national phenomenon.

The Salvation of Rain

There are records of praying for rain in northeastern Brazil since the colonial era. Luís da Câmara Cascudo (2012) writes of northeasterners singing Roman Catholic *ad petendam pluviam* (to beg for rain) votive masses during periods of drought: "Da nobis, quaésumus Dómine, plúviam salutárem: et áridam terrae fáciem fluéntis caeléstibus dignánter infúnde (Give to us, we beseech you, Lord, health-giving rain: and graciously infuse the dry face of the land with heavenly streams)" (Catholic Church 1961, 1301, translation by Anna Andresian).

In his 1888 book *Festas e tradições populares,* José Alexandre Melo Morais Filho writes about devotional processions to pray for rain: "In times of drought, when the sun, which revives nature, kills the plants and the living; when dusk resembles a red-hot copper oven that scorches the roads and the fields; and hunger and death rise from plantations that roast, from wells without water like hollowed-out sockets, from smoke that curls into fantastic spirals from the burning forests, the priests and the people take refuge in God" ([1888] 2002, 219). The penitents, he writes, would walk through the streets en masse, singing *benditos* (prayers) for rain, accompanied by the sounds of birds, frogs, and insects. In one such *bendito,* they ask Mary for rain and sustenance: "Queen of eternal glory, / mother of God, sweet and merciful, / give us water that wets us, / give us bread that sustains us" (223). In another, they ask her for mercy: "Have mercy, Lady / on our tears and pain. / We die from thirst / because we are sinners" (223). (According to Cascudo [1986], a folktale blamed drought on the ingratitude of the people of Ceará to their god.)

The two holidays most closely associated with northeastern traditional culture, Epiphany and St. John's Day, are both related to water, as both involve baptism. St. John's Day, the feast day of John the Baptist and celebration of the June solstice, came to Brazil with Jesuit missionaries who employed the holiday to convert Amerindians. The Jesuits brought elements of St. John's Day that have persisted: bonfires and the association of the holiday with marriage, fertility, and the harvest season (Chianca 2007; Cascudo 2012). Although practices more directly associated with water in Europe, such as wading into bodies of water for their curative properties, are associated less with St. John's Day in Brazil (and perhaps more with New Year's Eve and the Feast of Yemanjá), the connections between the agricultural season, the weather, and St. John's Day have persisted in the New World. In 1808, when the Portuguese throne moved to Brazil, with the royal family came fireworks and dances associated with the holiday, most notably, quadrilles. The holiday only became associated with rurality (and urban stereotypes of rurality) in the early twentieth century (see Chianca 2007).

Epiphany, or Kings' Day (Dia de Reis), commemorates the adoration of the Magi. The dance-drama performances between Christmas and Kings' Day are called *reisados* in Ceará.[2] A French traveler named Pierre Denis noted that rainfall was associated with commemorations of Epiphany in Ceará in the first decade of the twentieth century. The celebrations he witnessed involved the performance of a mumming practice known as *bumba meu boi* (or sometimes *boi* or *boi-bumbá* in Ceará, where it is performed within the *reisado*). He wrote that *bumba meu boi,* when practiced in rainy years on the day before Epiphany, celebrated "the time when the rains are heralded by the first showers, and there is gaiety everywhere" (Denis 1911, 343–344). Denis also notated the lyrics to a song he learned during his travels: "When the months of *fêtes* are over . . . when January nears—then folk begin to listen, each hoping to hear the first growling of the thunder. . . . Nowhere is life so gladdened—as ours in the bush—when the year gives a goodly winter, and the thunder rumbles in the sky" (333).[3] Denis's observations suggest a connection between habits of listening (for "the first growling of the thunder"), the rainy season, and the performance of songs and musical dance-dramas.

Northeasterners who traveled south to Rio de Janeiro brought their music and calendrical celebrations, including *reisados* (and the similar *lapinha, pastoril*, and *bumba meu boi*) that were performed on Epiphany along with the pre-Lenten street carnivals that were yet to characterize the southeastern city. These laborers, from various states in the Northeast with distinct celebrations and musical practices, transformed fin-de-siècle Rio de Janeiro into a melting pot of rural northeastern practices. In celebrating the various northeastern calendrical practices, migrants revived northeastern experiences of time, weather, and sound and celebrated the memory of the joy and pain of the desire for water.

Pastoral Nostalgia and Urbanization

Many of the first mass-mediated portrayals of the backlands focused less on drought than on generalized rurality. A number of popular *modinhas* (Brazilian art songs with roots in Portugal and influences from Italy) from the nineteenth through the early twentieth century, which were sold as sheet music and performed in urban parlors, described rural landscapes and alluded to the backlands. This was a period of industrialization and urbanization, and many of these songs exhibited a yearning for a simpler time symbolized by rurality and the innocent sounds of birdsong. Such nostalgic recollections of rural life expressed a certain kind of resistance to the experience of urbanization. Notable *modinhas* with pastoral themes include Cândido Inácio da Silva's (1800–1838) "Busco a campina serena" (I seek the serene meadow) and Melo Moraes Filho (1844–1919) and Miguel Emídio Pestana's (1845–1885) "O bem-te-vi" (The great kiskadee). One of the most enduring *modinhas*, "Azulão (Opus 21)" (Bluebird), by composer Jaime Ovalle (1894–1955) and poet Manuel Bandeira (1886–1968), begins "Go bluebird . . . Go see my ungrateful. / Tell her that without her the *sertão* is no longer the *sertão*."[4] Birds—the great kiskadee, the bluebird, and others—connect the city to the backlands and link song to the natural soundscape, what Bernie Krause (2012) would call the "biophony."

As *modinhas* traveled from the parlor into the recording studio in the second decade of the twentieth century, pastoral lyrics remained popular. In 1914 the eminent singer, actor, and circus performer Eduardo das Neves released a recording of "O luar do sertão" (The moonlight of the backlands), a nostalgic song that expresses a longing for the beauty of the moonlight in the backlands, which shines brightly compared to that in the city. The song, written earlier that year, was credited to the equally renowned northeastern poet and *modinha* composer Catulo da Paixão Cearense (1863–1946), who penned the song's lyrics (and plagiarized the melody from a tune he learned from his friend João Pernambuco). Catulo, who belonged to the cultural elite of Rio de Janeiro, performed it regularly in theaters and salons around the city; the composition became his greatest achievement.

The success of "Luar do sertão" could be attributed to its description of the countryside in an era of urban growth. Although data on migration and urbanization in Brazil prior to 1940 are incomplete, there is incontrovertible evidence of the expansion of urban areas between 1872 and the first decades of the twentieth century due to abolition, international immigration, and internal migration. Rural-urban migrants from around Brazil could find meaning in the song, as its lyrics make no overt reference to the Northeast, where Catulo and Pernambuco were raised, and there are no obvious allusions to drought. Its melody, an adaptation of a northeastern folksong (a *coco*) called "Meu engenho é de Humaitá" (Mine is the Humaitá sugarcane mill) is also simple and easy to sing: the refrain begins with a leap from dominant to tonic and then moves in predictable yet sweet stepwise motion. Since its first recording in 1914, the song has been routinely covered by many of Brazil's biggest stars.

Musicians of the early twentieth century also introduced urban audiences to the *sertão* through musical sound. For example, Pernambuco regularly performed rural northeastern musics around Rio de Janeiro.[5] He had left the northeastern interior for the coast to flee drought in 1895 at the age of twelve (see Crook 2009) and then moved in 1904 to Rio de Janeiro, where he built a reputation for his knowledge of northeastern music. His improvisatory skills on the guitar and as a singer helped popularize northeastern styles like the *embolada*, a fast-paced singing style characterized by wordplay. He was a central figure in Rio de Janeiro's music scene in the early twentieth century and played in many of the era's most significant groups, including the Turunas Pernambucanos and the Oito Batutas, who were once described as a "Jazz-Band sertanejo," a backlands jazz band (see Hertzman 2013, 108). In 1912 Pernambuco and his Grupo do Caxangá paraded through Rio's carnival in caricatured northeastern costumes, carrying a banner that read "The Embolada of the North" while playing northeastern music. The ensemble included not only the legendary flutist, saxophonist, and composer Pixinguinha (Alfredo da Rocha Vianna Filho) and guitarist and songwriter Donga (Ernesto Joaquim Maria dos Santos), but also Jaime Ovalle, composer of "Azulão," mentioned earlier, and other prominent *choro* (a genre of urban instrumental music) musicians of the era.

The trajectories of João Pernambuco and Catulo da Paixão Cearense date the beginning of northeastern regionalism in Brazilian popular music to the earliest years of the Brazilian music industry. The two men expressed a longing for the Northeast in distinct ways, and their approaches to musical nostalgia persisted in Brazilian popular music: one textual, the other musical. Musicians like Catulo sang about the pastoral landscapes migrants left behind, while musicians like Pernambuco sought Brazilian musical authenticity in the styles, timbres, melodies, and rhythms of the Northeast. Both approaches to northeastern regionalist music making were inherently nostalgic. Catulo painted his northeastern landscape with lyrics; João Pernambuco conjured his with sound.

Northeastern Nostalgia, Nationalism, and the Invention of the Northeast

Since the time of the earliest nostalgic recordings, urban Brazilian musicians have also sung about drought's relationship to poverty and inequality and about the demand for charity to send north. During the drought of 1915, people around Brazil, especially in Rio de Janeiro, took to the streets to ask for donations to send to the victims (Azevedo 2012). That same year, Eduardo das Neves recorded a song called "Pobres flagelados" (Poor drought victims), which described beggars and vendors on the streets of Rio de Janeiro collecting contributions. The upbeat song, accompanied by guitar and *cavaquinho* (a small string instrument of Portuguese origin), paints a picture of a grassroots effort: speeches made on city streets, the wealthy filling briefcases with coins, and young migrant women selling carnations, lilies, and roses to raise money to send home to their families. "Never have you seen the nobles . . . so compassionate for the poor," Neves sang.

Yet most songs were less explicit about the needs of the Northeast. Rather, the Northeast and its traditional practices were often fodder for political and artistic efforts to craft a Brazilian national identity. In 1913 and again in 1921 Pernambuco, Pixinguinha, and Donga traveled to the Northeast to "collect" northeastern music to bring back to Rio. These trips occurred on the cusp of a broader trend in Brazilian modernism of the 1920s in which poets, authors, musicians, and others began efforts to fabricate a national voice; for some, this voice was rooted in rural folkloric practices (Andrade [1928] 2008).[6] In line with the modernist call to create Brazilian artistic idioms, ensembles like Turunas Pernambucanos continued to popularize *coco* (a northeastern dance rhythm), *embolada*, and other northeastern rhythms and styles, bringing these sounds into the radio era. Jararaca, a leader of Turunas Pernambucanos and eventually half of the regional music/comedy duo Jararaca and Ratinho, combined samba and rural northeastern sounds into a genre he called *samba sertanejo* (backlands samba). Although his best-known songs like "Mamãe eu quero" (Mommy I want, composed with Vicente Paiva) were playful Carnival marches with little connection to the Northeast, much of Jararaca's output alluded in both lyrics and sound to the region he left as a young man.[7] Other performers like Augusto Calheiros and his Turunas da Mauricéia performed *emboladas* and *cocos* alongside sambas while wearing stereotypical northeastern garb, with upturned hat brims, bandanas, and leather sandals.

For Dominique Dreyfus, the northeastern music of the 1920s and into the 1930s was increasingly characterized by a "tendency to present the Northeast as a *matuto* [a derogatory word meaning "hillbilly"] thing and by associating the *matuto* with the grotesque," thus making it into a caricature of ignorance and poverty (1996, 106). Racialized regional bias against northeasterners, along with concomitant accusations of indolence and backwardness, seemingly contributed to a federal response that tended to address drought through construction projects rather than lasting social programs. Such bias was perpetuated through song lyrics and musical clichés.

Northeastern music became a tool of propaganda in the 1930s. A coup in 1930 led to the deposition of President Washington Luís, and the Brazilian military installed Getúlio Vargas as the nation's president. Throughout the decade, Vargas sought to consolidate power by breaking up the long-held oligarchic system of landownership in the Northeast and other regional power structures throughout Brazil. To strengthen his vision, he took steps to promote elements of regional folklore as national symbols. The music of the Northeast figured prominently in these nationalist efforts: propagandistic government radio included programs of regional music, and new government agencies sponsored research into the nation's folklore, spurring scholarly interest in northeastern music. The 1930s were also a decade of literary regionalism, and the northeastern backlands were the setting of several high-profile works, including Graciliano Ramos's *Vidas secas* (Barren lives) (1938) and Raquel de Queiroz's *O quinze* (The year 15) (1930), which takes place on a farm near Quixadá during the drought of 1915.[8] Musicians like Manezinho Araújo continued performing urbanized *emboladas* and *cocos* on the radio and onstage through the decade. The folkloric revival of rural traditional musics continued to appear alongside literary and lyrical imaginings of the *sertão* and its people. The nationalism fostered by this music also raised awareness about the northeastern context.

Popular Music and the Exploitation of Drought

Not all musical treatments of drought can be understood as serving some greater project such as nationalism, urbanization, or drought protest. Some musicians exploited concern about drought for their own benefit. Unscrupulous individuals have, since the Great Drought of 1877–79, taken advantage of drought and the discourses surrounding tragedy in the Northeast for financial and political gain. This form of corruption, known as the "drought industry," is most evident in the misuse of drought relief funds or the granting of government contracts for projects that were never intended to be completed. But as folklorist, poet, and anthropologist Oswald Barroso expressed to me, it is also apparent, perhaps in a less odious sense, in Brazilian popular music.[9]

A drought from 1930 to 1932, for example, inspired one musician to write a song about drought to ingratiate himself with the Vargas government. Joubert de Carvalho (1900–1977), born in Uberaba, Minas Gerais, was a physician and songwriter who desired a medical position in Vargas's administration. According to popular legend, Carvalho sought advice from Rui Carneiro, an official in the Ministry of Transport and Public Works who was born in the northeastern state of Paraíba. Carneiro suggested the composer write a song about the current drought in the Northeast to curry favor with José Américo de Almeida, the minister of transport and public works, who was also from Paraíba (Azevedo 2012). The resulting song, "Maringá," told the story of a migrant who left her husband in a town in the interior of the state of Paraíba, where the only remaining water were the tears he cried for her. In the original 1932 recording, Gastão Formenti's theatrical rubato and the sense of urgency and pathos in his voice, accompanied by the Orquestra Victor Brasileira, dramatize the saga of the drought refugee.

Carvalho's efforts evidently prevailed: shortly after the release of the recording, which referred to Rui Carneiro's hometown, Carvalho earned a position as a doctor with the Maritime Institute, an organization he would ultimately direct. The song is more than a mere footnote in the history of popular songs inspired by drought in the Northeast; it was a major hit that was recorded by many of Brazil's crooners through the late 1950s and so beloved it became the namesake for a city in the southern state of Paraná in 1947.[10]

There remained, of course, more earnest motives for depicting drought in the Northeast that nevertheless transformed the narratives of drought victims into radio-era hits. Also in 1932 songwriter and civil engineer Sá Róris helped the Federal Inspectorate for Works against Drought (IFOCS) build a highway between Icó and Iguatu, two cities in the interior of Ceará. Later that year, Róris, who was inspired by the situation he witnessed, composed a song called "Vou deixar meu Ceará" (I'm going to leave my Ceará) (Azevedo 2012). Five years later, radio host and samba musician Almirante, perhaps better known for recordings like the Carnival hit "Yes, nós temos bananas" (Yes, we do have bananas, a response to "Yes! We Have No Bananas"), recorded the song with the Conjunto Regional de Benedito Lacerda: "I'm going to leave my Ceará / but I'll return once the weather improves." The lyrics also describe the silence of drought: "The grey-necked wood rail no longer sings. / The rufous-bellied thrush no longer sings. / My reservoir has run dry."

Between 1934 and 1936 Brazil experienced one of its worst droughts on record; it extended south into the states of São Paulo and Minas Gerais. With this crisis, the government began to address drought as a national problem, allocating 4 percent of federal tax revenue to drought relief (Hall 1978). Indeed, by the end of the 1930s the issues and symbols of the Northeast had achieved national relevance, as the problems were no longer limited to that region. The 1930s and 1940s were also an era of vast growth in the radio and recording industries, and many of the period's popular vocal ensembles had members originally from Ceará, including Quinteto Lupar, Trio Cearense, Trio Guarani, Trovadores do Luar, Trio Nagô, and Vocalistas Tropicais (see Paiva 2014; Severiano 2013). Bando da Lua, which performed and recorded with Carmen Miranda, had three Cearenses, and all five original members of Quatro Ases & Um Coringa (Four Aces and a Joker), one of the biggest groups of Brazil's "golden age of radio," were from Fortaleza. As more northeasterners entered the recording industry, as radio expanded, and as the Northeast region became an increasingly common image in Brazilian popular music, new forms of so-called northeastern music coalesced in the recording studios of Rio de Janeiro.

Northeastern Dance Music and Embodied Protest

Throughout the 1940s songwriters invented new dance genres aimed at northeastern migrants longing for home. One such artist was an aspiring composer and pianist from Fortaleza named Lauro Maia, a minor figure in the history of *forró* but a musician whose career exemplified the regionalist musical trend to create dance music with nostalgic lyrics about the Northeast, best known in the figure of Luiz Gonzaga. Their resulting music gave drought refugees a reason to move their bodies and the Brazilian population a motive to empathize. Although it was generally not intended to be protest music, this dance music was nevertheless a potent form of resistance.

In 1940 Lauro Maia mailed a letter addressed to Almirante to Rio de Janeiro in an attempt to break into the mainstream Brazilian music industry. Maia had achieved considerable fame in his hometown in the 1930s and had, among other accomplishments, won two prizes (judged by Ary Barroso) in 1936 for the best samba and best Carnival march in anticipation of the following season's Carnival. As a young composer, Maia was ambitious and made repeated efforts to invent—or at least unearth and popularize—the next big dance craze. In the letter to Almirante he referred to some of his new rhythms: the *miudinho*, the *galope*, and the *catolé*, which he described as "creations that will mark the era." Hoping to attract Almirante's attention, he enclosed the lyrics of two songs written for those rhythms: one, a *miudinho*, with lyrics that describe the accompanying dance moves; the other, a *catolé* called "Ôi jia," about a toad. The song's last verse begins, "When it rains the toad sings / gladdening my backlands." "A colossus!" Maia wrote about "Ôi jia." He continued, "The last strophe, the psyche of the Cearense. They say, and it is true, that the Cearense emigrates when there is drought in Ceará. Far away, his thoughts remain here. And even if he is living in good conditions, he returns from wherever he may be, even having to sacrifice everything, once he learns that it is raining in his backlands!" (Azevedo 1999, 110). Summarizing what had already become a cliché about the Cearense drought refugee, Maia's attempt at marketing his regional music to a national tastemaker foreshadowed his own future.

In 1942 the Brazilian Institute of Geography and Statistics officially recognized the Northeast as a distinct region, largely to facilitate drought relief efforts. In 1945, the year of yet another drought, the Brazilian government established the National Department for Works against Drought (DNOCS), moving the primary national agency for drought relief from Rio de Janeiro to Fortaleza. The nation's awareness of drought in the Northeast had grown again, and the region and its climate had reached a new level of prominence in national discourse.

Lauro Maia, who had written several songs that alluded to the backlands, including 1942's "Praga de urubu" (Plague of vultures) and the instrumental "Saudades do Cariri" (Longings for Cariri, the region in the interior of Ceará), moved from Fortaleza to Rio de Janeiro in 1945 with his wife, Djanira Teixeira, emigrating like the Cearenses described in his letter. Maia quickly found work as a song plugger for the Vitale Brothers, a sheet music publisher. He wasted little time promoting the *balanceio* (swing), a rhythm he learned in 1941 from Orlando Silva and Dorival Caymmi, two legendary musicians who helped Maia develop a more northeastern sound by suggesting the new rhythm. Maia's song "Eu vou até de manhã" (I'll go until morning), recorded by Quatro Ases & Um Coringa in 1945, became the first *balanceio* to reach a national audience (Azevedo 1999). The rhythm became Maia's calling card: ONE and two AND THREE and four and / ONE AND two AND THREE and FOUR and.

Shortly after arriving in Rio, he met and began collaborating with his brother-in-law, Humberto Teixeira, who, like Maia, attended law school before becoming a songwriter. Teixeira was familiar with Maia's compositions, a couple of which had been recorded by Quatro Ases & Um Coringa before Maia's departure from Fortaleza. Maia and Teixeira's first collaboration was a song written by Teixeira called "Terra da luz" (Land of light), a *samba-exaltação* (Teixeira described it as a "semisymphonic poem") in the style of "Aquarela do Brasil" (Watercolor of Brazil) about the beauty of Ceará's landscapes.[11] In the song's ambling and lushly orchestrated introduction, the lyrics refer to palm trees along Ceará's coast and the iconic *jangada* fishing rafts. The second half of the song, a samba, contrasts the heat of the sun in the drought-prone *sertão* with the joy and optimism brought by rain, which is celebrated by "strong and virile" Brazilians, *embolada* singers, and *viola* (ten-string guitar) players who, at rodeos, during singing duels, and in the streets, "sing the soul of the *sertão*." Maia wrote the orchestral arrangement and conducted the orchestra during the studio recording session for the first release of the song.

About the song, Teixeira said, "'Terra da Luz,' for me, is really my first musical expression of my *saudade* for the far-away land where I used to live."[12] Teixeira had lived through droughts as a child. "I was born in Iguatu, in the Cariri region," he said, "and at two years old I had my first debut as a drought refugee in the famous drought that Raquel de Queiroz immortalized in one of her books. The drought made my family leave Iguatu for more amenable lands. But we returned two years later, and I experienced other droughts."[13] In this collaboration with Maia, Teixeira began to explore the Northeast in his lyrics. The two eventually signed their names to some twenty-one songs together, including a *catolé* and at least four *balanceios*, including one called "Vamos balancear" (Let's dance the *balanceio*).

During his first year in Rio de Janeiro, Lauro Maia was approached by another young musician trying to make a career performing northeastern dance music. Luiz Gonzaga, an accordionist from Pernambuco, was playing new rhythms, the *chamego* and the *calango*, around Rio and on the radio, but he had begun looking for a songwriting partner to help him find greater success. He recorded instrumental accordion pieces—mostly waltzes, polkas, and *choros*, with an occasional northeastern *embolada* or his own *chamego*—between 1941 and 1945 and found modest success in early 1946 teaming up with a few lyricists from Rio, but Gonzaga felt their influence was too Carioca, too Rio de Janeiro. He said, "What really interested me was giving form to those songs from 'up there in the foothills,' songs that I knew to be pregnant with flavor, with soul, just lacking a hand to chisel them, to give them life" (Dreyfus 1996, 81). He knew Lauro Maia's work from the recordings of Quatro Ases & Um Coringa, and he suspected Maia could be his partner and his key to translating the Northeast into a new rhythm and style for a national audience.

Maia declined Gonzaga's invitation, claiming to be incapable of keeping pace with Gonzaga's ambitions. In Teixeira's words, Maia said the following to Gonzaga: "Look, guy. This whole campaign business, it terrifies me. I'm an undisciplined man, and I don't keep things or commitments from one day to the next. I think it probably makes more sense for you to get in touch with my brother-in-law, Humberto Teixeira. He's also a composer. He's better organized."[14] Gonzaga and Teixeira teamed up to become one of Brazil's greatest songwriting duos.

In October 1946 Quatro Ases & Um Coringa, accompanied by Gonzaga on accordion, recorded Gonzaga and Teixeira's second song, "Baião," which introduced a new dance rhythm to Brazilian audiences. "I'm going to show you how you dance the *baião*," the song begins. In the third verse, Teixeira's lyrics refer to the earlier rhythms of his brother-in-law and Gonzaga: "I've already danced the *balanceio, chamego,* samba . . ." Rhythmically, the *baião* and the *balanceio* are similar; the beat played by the bass drum is virtually identical at first, but the *balanceio* includes an additional bar that Humberto Teixeira, music researcher Nirez, and others have described as "stolen time." Dancers and musicians found the *balanceio* rhythm confusing, possibly prompting Maia's protestations in his song "Tão fácil, tão bom" (So easy, so good), released one year before the release of "Baião": "The *balanceio* is so easy . . . you don't need to be gifted."

In an interview in 1977 Humberto Teixeira said, "The *baião* slid in on the rug, on the mat, on the trail left by the *balanceio*."[15] The *baião* quickly surpassed the *balanceio*, becoming a dance fad that lasted throughout the decade and into the next, bringing into the Brazilian mainstream northeastern-style dancing and lyrics that often described life in the backlands. In 1947 Gonzaga and Teixeira recorded their third song together. The song, "Asa branca" (literally, "white wing," also known as the picazuro pigeon), described the *saudade* of a northeastern drought refugee who vowed to return to the Northeast once the

Saudade *Asa Branca* "Help Your Brother" *White Wing* *Picazuro pigeon*

rain returned. The song is nothing short of a classic, sometimes described as the "anthem of the Northeast." Gonzaga had effectively transformed himself into the voice of the Northeast. His songs about the Northeast, performed in northeastern rhythms, were protests that lamented migration, demanded recognition, and insisted on the beauty and worth of the backlands. Around the time of the release of "Asa branca," he began performing in a stereotypical costume of a northeastern bandit, in the same vein as the northeastern costumes of Grupo do Caxangá from the 1910s and the Turunas da Mauricéia in the 1920s, and he established an ensemble—a trio of accordion, triangle, and bass drum—that came to characterize *baião*. He also standardized a set of "typical" northeastern musical elements, including a number of dance rhythms and the use of Mixolydian, Dorian, and northeastern (dominant Lydian) modes.

Lauro Maia died prematurely (he was only thirty-seven years old) of tuberculosis in 1950. By 1951, the year of a significant drought, Luiz Gonzaga had come to be known as the "King of Baião," and Humberto Teixeira was the "Doctor of Baião." Gonzaga outshone and outlasted his peers, but his approach to creating a new northeastern genre that achieved national recognition was not unlike that of Lauro Maia in his all-too-short career. Both composers made deliberate efforts to identify and popularize a new dance beat that they could attribute to the backlands, and they wrote lyrics about the region and its customs and landscapes that could add an explicit layer of meaning to their new dance rhythms. In a time in which Rio's samba had become a national dance genre through the radio, the music industry was segmenting its markets, and the concerns and images of the Northeast were engrained in the Brazilian consciousness, the association of a new northeastern dance with pastoral, nostalgic lyrics was a surefire route to stardom.

Luiz Gonzaga's Supplication

By the early 1950s Gonzaga had a long string of hits, most of which he co-wrote with Teixeira and another songwriting partner named Zé Dantas. His songs that referred to drought in the backlands included "Súplica Cearense" (Cearense supplication), "Último pau de arara" (Last flatbed truck; literally, "last parrot's perch"), "Assum preto" (Smooth-billed ani), "Légua tirana" (Tyrannical league), "A volta da asa branca" (The return of the white wing), "Sabiá" (Rufous-bellied thrush), "Baião na garoa" (Baião in the drizzling rain), "Acauã" (Laughing falcon), and "O xote das meninas" (The girls' schottische), among many others. The majority of Gonzaga's songs, whether or not they mentioned drought or rain, described images of life in the backlands, the journey of the drought refugee (the *retirante*), and the challenges of assimilation into city life, and he continued writing and singing about the Northeast and the northeastern experience throughout his career.

The uses of Gonzaga's *baião* were multiple: nation building for President Getúlio Vargas (McCann 2004; Albuquerque Júnior 1999; Dreyfus 1996); reaching new markets for a growing music industry (Silva 2003; Ferretti 2012; Sant'anna 1978; McCann 2004); reaching new markets for the consumption of household goods (McCann 2004; Dreyfus 1996); providing employment and creating community for migrants who worked in the informal sector related to dance music and nightlife (Fernandes 2005); and, relatedly and most significantly, helping northeastern migrants adapt to city life and cope with the experience of diaspora (Vieira 2000; Fernandes 2005; Draper 2010; Loveless 2012). A key debate in the scholarship involves this question: In what ways did *forró* enable or resist assimilation? For one scholar, the rural nostalgia of the genre's midcentury lyrics expressed a conscious resistance to modernization and urbanization among migrants (Draper 2010). Scholars also theorize *forró*'s many effects: it helped construct the notion of a Northeast region (Albuquerque Júnior 1999; Murphy 2006); it was entangled in the construction of Brazilian racial categories (Crook 2009; Albuquerque Júnior 1999); and it located the Northeast in the past in the minds of the Brazilian population (Albuquerque Júnior 1999).

Although many scholars consider the music inherently nostalgic, they often also understand it as apolitical. Paulo Cesar de Araújo (2002), for example, writes that Gonzaga avoided political engagement in his work perhaps because he produced much of his work under the conditions of a dictatorship. Dominique Dreyfus notes that "only some ten" of Gonzaga's songs were explicitly political (1996, 190). Although Luiz Gonzaga's protest avoided engagement with partisan politics, his music was nevertheless a plea for environmental justice, especially via its chronicles of the Northeast. Gonzaga was a one-issue activist, and his issue was drought in the Northeast.

For José Farias dos Santos, Gonzaga's lyrics relate to the sociopolitical consequences of drought (which he calls the "northeastern tragedy"). He identifies four predominant themes in Gonzaga's songs: "the cruelty of drought and migration," "divine protection," "the relationship between man and nature," and "the desire for return and the contrast between the Northeast and the Southeast" (2002, 103). Via these four themes, *forró* made the "northeastern tragedy" vivid for the nation.

Gonzaga intended his music to introduce Brazilian audiences to the lifeways and landscapes of the Northeast as a way of calling attention to the horrors of drought and the people and places it affected. In a newspaper article from 1971, Humberto Teixeira explained how Gonzaga understood their music to be protest music about drought: "The other day, Luiz Gonzaga said that our music was the first protest music, except that we made a kind of lyrical argument, we used the drought refugee, the drought, the famine of the Northeast to grab the attention of our brothers in the South, who were much more privileged, to help them see the tenderness out in that abandoned land."[16]

Even Gonzaga's songs that omitted drought but described northeastern romance, labor, and celebrations were drought protests in that they humanized northeasterners and provided context for the debilitating droughts. His music demonstrated that the problems of the Northeast were about more than its climate. They were problems affecting real people—with loves and desires, a unique cuisine, and so on. His music sought to undermine prejudice against northeasterners by trying to create goodwill for the northeastern population. Letícia Vianna writes, "His engagement had very little to do with confronting those who governed or the status quo, and more to do with feelings of solidarity and obligation to his compatriots from the *sertão*" (2001, 76). She continues: "Luiz Gonzaga's political posture throughout his career was somewhat contradictory. On the one hand, accustomed to discipline and unconditionally respectful of hierarchy, he campaigned for politicians out of sympathy and trust, oblivious to ideology. . . . He was engaged in activism against drought, but did not confront the *coronéis* [wealthy landowners] nor the government, nor did he question the agrarian structure" (79–80).

Dominique Dreyfus also writes about Gonzaga's ambivalent identity as a protest singer, particularly following his recording of "Vozes da seca": "The concept of protest music [*música engajada*] did not yet exist in the era [the early 1950s], but the complaint contained in this song ["Voices of Drought"] profoundly affected Gonzaga, who, then taking on a posture of 'protest singer,' sought to translate, through the songs that he sang, the problems of the Northeast. . . . In truth, the creations of Gonzaga and his songwriting partners constituted, above all else, chronicles of the Northeast, its culture, its society, its behaviors, its way of speaking" (1996, 190).

Gonzaga himself has said he preferred singing about the experience of northeasterners to making direct critiques of the government:

> So I went along singing about the sad things of my people, who departed from the Northeast to the South and the Central-South in search of better days, of work. Because there it rains in an exact period, there you know what the seasons are. In the Northeast, the periods of bad weather are all wrong. When

it should rain, it doesn't, so the people go looking for work in the South, and the Northeast becomes increasingly depopulated. . . . So my music represents the fight, the suffering, the sacrifice of my people. I complain, I criticize the governments, but cautiously, so I do not get involved with those who like to encourage violence. (Luiz Gonzaga, no date, quoted in Dreyfus 1996, 190)

Although Gonzaga was disinclined to address the roots of drought as a social problem—corruption and inequality—he did perform several protest songs directed at the government or the Brazilian populace at large, especially beginning in the 1950s, after he had already become famous. The 1953 song "Vozes da seca" (Voices of drought), by Gonzaga and Zé Dantas, sung in the Mixolydian mode to the accompaniment of a *baião* rhythm, is an overt protest song that makes specific requests and addresses both the social and climatological aspects of drought. Gonzaga makes the following plea to his compatriots in the South on behalf of those "forgotten by the networks of power," the "half of Brazil [that] has gone without eating": fill our reservoirs with water, sell us food at a reasonable price, build more dams, free us from having to beg on the streets, and we will repay you with interest after the drought's end.

In a performance in 1981 to introduce "Vozes da seca," Gonzaga said to the audience: "In the years '53 and '54 there was a bothersome drought in the northeastern *sertão*. Brazil was filled with lures: Help your brother out! Some charity for the northeastern drought victims! Anything will do: money, old clothes, old shoes, old shirts, anything will do. I and Zé Dantas protested, we shouted loudly, 'Dear sirs, the northeasterners,'" and he then began the song. After the first verse, he said, thanking President Juscelino Kubitschek: "One of the people's congressmen cried out, 'Mr. President, this *baião* of Gonzaga and Zé Dantas is worth more than a hundred speeches, as I have said.' So now I praise, loudly, the name of the man who created Sudene [the Superintendency for the Development of the Northeast]: Thank you, Juscelino!"

Gonzaga's 1957 recording of "Sertão sofredor" (Backlands sufferer), by Joaquim Augusto and Nelson Barbalho, begins with Gonzaga speaking as if in the style of a talking blues about the suffering caused by droughts and floods. Referring to the Paulo Afonso Hydroelectric Complex, the Northeast's first hydroelectric power plant, built along the São Francisco River in Bahia in the late 1940s and early 1950s, he says: "Even Paulo Afonso, which was to be the redemption of the Northeast, turned into a thing of luxury. It's just being used to illuminate big cities. Where are the factories? Where's the industry? Where are the good things announced for the Northeast? And what happens if another nasty drought comes?" In the song's last verse, he sings about the goodness, honesty, and orderliness of the northeasterner: "What we lack though / is some actual help / from the big boss / in the federal government." On the liner notes for *O Reino do Baião* (The Kingdom of *Baião*), the album on which Gonzaga released "Sertão sofredor," Nelson Barbalho, the song's lyricist, wrote, "*The Kingdom of Baião* is like a great year of good rain in the *sertão*—it brings some damn happiness to the northeasterner, makes us forget the crisis, bad weather, lent money, the promises of politicians." The same dance music that could bring joy and relief to the northeasterner also aimed a pointed critique at a federal government that promised a hydroelectric power plant that would create drought-proof jobs for *sertanejos* but instead only exacerbated inequality.

Gonzaga's nostalgic chronicles and political demands did achieve at least one known political and practical outcome. In the mid-1950s, following the success of his song "Algodão" (Cotton, cowritten with Zé Dantas in 1953), he was summoned by the minister of agriculture, João Cleofas de Oliveira, who asked what he could do to help. Gonzaga explained, "I said to him that the northeastern people were in great need, and that if he wanted to do something for Exu, I would be very grateful" (quoted in Dreyfus 1996, 191). Oliveira offered to build an agricultural school in Exu, Gonzaga's hometown, and he promptly constructed and outfitted the school and hired faculty. (The school's failure shortly thereafter due to Oliveira's lack of research into whether Exu actually needed an agricultural school when there already was one in nearby Crato underscores the kind of fiscal mismanagement and corruption that characterized twentieth-century Brazilian drought policy.)

Gonzaga also did his own good works in defense of drought victims. He frequently gave charity performances in which he raised money and collected food for northeasterners. In 1979 he founded an organization for needy children called Fundação Vovô Januário (Grandpa Januario Foundation). And he established (and underwrote until 1984) an organization called Ação Contra a Seca (Operation against Drought).

Through the 1950s other musicians joined in the fad and sang about the landscapes and lifeways of the northeastern backlands to the rhythms popularized by Gonzaga and others in order to call attention to the horrors of drought and the lives of northeasterners. Carmélia Alves, anointed the "Queen of Baião" by her friend Gonzaga, recorded Humberto Teixeira's "Ajuda teu irmão" (Help your brother) in 1953. The single was one of the era's most straightforward drought protest songs. The B side was a recording of Alves and her husband, Jimmy Lester, singing "Adeus, Maria Fulô" (written by Sivuca [Severino Dias de Oliveira] and Humberto Teixeira), about a man who leaves his lover at the start of a drought.[17] Marinês, a singer originally from Pernambuco, demonstrated a sense of gallows humor in her song "Urubu tá com raiva do boi" (The vulture's angry with the bull), which tells the story of a bull that refuses to die, thus upsetting a hungry vulture, who cries every day in desperation. In the title track of her 1957 album *Aquarela nordestina* (Northeastern watercolor) (written by Rosil Cavalcanti and Maria Das Neves Coura Cavalcante), Marinês's voice painted a vivid portrait of the images and sounds of drought in the backlands:

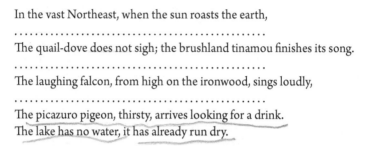

In the vast Northeast, when the sun roasts the earth,
. . . .
The quail-dove does not sigh; the brushland tinamou finishes its song.
. . . .
The laughing falcon, from high on the ironwood, sings loudly,
. . . .
The picazuro pigeon, thirsty, arrives looking for a drink.
The lake has no water, it has already run dry.

In João Mello's lesser-known *toada* "Orós precisa de nós" (Orós needs us) (1960), Mello described the devastating floods in Orós caused by the failure of a dam, which left "families homeless, children asking for bread." He (echoed by his backup singers) sings, "Helping those people is our obligation, my brother." This musical plea to help Orós borrowed its title from a campaign led by archbishop and liberation theologian Dom Hélder Câmara. In 1959 Dom Hélder held a twenty-four-hour telethon, which aired on TV Rio, called *Orós precisa de nós* to raise money for those displaced by the floods.

Throughout the *forró* era, northeasterners turned to religion for solutions to the problem of drought. Fortaleza-born Ary Lobo recorded Gordurinha's "Pedido a Padre Cícero" (Request to Father Cicero) during the 1958–59 drought, bemoaning the current drought to the legendary late priest, who was widely believed to have performed a miracle. Zito Borborema's "Padre Cícero," also released in 1959, was a prayer of sorts, describing a miracle in which Padre Cícero ended the drought. Luiz Gonzaga's 1960 recording of "Meu padrim" (My priest) asks another priest, Frei Damião, to seek God's protection for the northeasterners and insists upon the goodness of the people, who manage to fill many bellies with the scant "emergency money" offered them.

Samba and MPB as Northeastern Protest

While Maia, Gonzaga, Alves, Marinês, and others were singing on behalf of the Northeast in an audibly northeastern voice, with regional rhythms, northeastern instrumentations, and typical modes, other musicians in the 1940s and

1950s continued to perform sambas and other urban genres about drought in the Northeast, highlighting the national interest in the region and the plight of the rural northeasterner. In 1943 Sílvio Caldas recorded the melodically charming, characteristically upbeat samba "Promessa," by Custódio Mesquita and Evaldo Rui, in which Caldas sings about the protagonist's many attempts to ask his god to make it rain: prayer, pilgrimages, offerings, and so on. "Look, my cattle are dying, / my people crying, / my field burning. / The Lord has forgotten me." In 1949 Quatro Ases & Um Coringa recorded "Tive que me mudar" (I had to move), a samba about drought by the great composer Assis Valente. In 1950 Vocalistas Tropicais, originally from Fortaleza, recorded "Tomara que chova" (I hope it rains), a *marchinha* (Carnival march) that became a hit of Rio's Carnival in 1951:

> I hope it rains
> three days without stopping.
> My greatest grievance
> is having no water at home.
> I need to wash myself.

A Carnival *marchinha* from 1954 called "Chuva vá" (Rain go away), by Américo de Campos and Moacir Braga, recorded by Lúcia Martins and Alcides Gerardi, compared the constant rain in Rio to its lack in Ceará. "Rain ruins our Carnival," the song complains.

But the lasting sound of the Northeast resided in the songs of the twentieth century's great *forró* musicians: João do Vale, who recorded only two albums but wrote several of the genre's most enduring songs; Jackson do Pandeiro, who played sambas alongside *forrós* and *cocos* and whose legacy is sometimes compared to that of Gonzaga; Sivuca, an accordionist, songwriter, and arranger who brought jazz to *forró* and vice versa; Dominguinhos, widely considered the heir to Gonzaga's throne; and other musicians. Northeastern music offered migrants a feeling of space, time, and movement in their state of exile as it aimed to raise awareness about the conditions of drought, increase sympathies for northeasterners and northeastern migrants, make specific demands on the government and the southeastern population, and criticize inaction and corruption. It transformed the experiences of drought into sound, reverberating back to effect change.

The early 1960s heralded the end of the first *forró* era, but the pairing of northeastern dance rhythms with tragic yet nostalgic pastoral lyrics had become so prevalent in mass-mediated northeastern music that the sounds came to symbolize the imagery. Already in the mid-1960s Tropicalistas like Maria

Bethânia and Caetano Veloso used *forró* to subtly protest conditions under the military dictatorship that had begun in 1964. Maria Bethânia launched her career in 1965 with a televised performance of João do Vale and José Cândido's "Carcará," a haunting song about hunger in the backlands told through the image of a bird of prey (a caracara) looking for something to "catch, kill, and eat." Before singing the last refrain, Bethânia turned around, her back stiff and shoulders squared, while the band sang the word "carcará" in a crescendoing and ascending sequence, and she said with intensity, "In 1950 more than two million northeasterners lived outside the states in which they were born: 10 percent of the population of Ceará emigrated, 13 percent from Piauí, 15 percent from Bahia, 17 percent from Alagoas."[18] She reprised her performance in 2015 with the same recitation (albeit with a transposition of two of the statistics) in the opening moments of the Twenty-Sixth Brazilian Music Awards, which commemorated the fiftieth year of her career. Bethânia's critique was one of inequality and inaction. Her brother Caetano Veloso's 1971 recording of "Asa branca" implied a comparison of his exile in London to that of the drought migrant (see, e.g., Dunn 2001; Draper 2010; Loveless 2012).

Forró and the sounds of mass-mediated northeastern music became a kind of musical shorthand for protest, exile, drought, and the Northeast itself. Many musicians in Ceará have borrowed *forró*'s melodies, timbres, modes, rhythms, instruments, and lyrics in distinct and sometimes subtle ways to signify the Northeast, its people, and its conditions, from the Pessoal do Ceará in the 1970s, to Massafeira Livre in 1979 and the resulting album *Massafeira* in 1980, to the early electronic *forró* of the 1990s, to the Movimento Cabaçal of the 2000s, and to the burgeoning indie *música autoral* (original music) scene of the 2010s.

Not all listeners have heard the same meaning in *forró* and *baião*. Until the genre was deemed "traditional" following the attention brought to it by artists such as Caetano Veloso and the other Tropicalistas, music critics and members of the Brazilian elite looked down upon it, considering it a product of the culture industry, a cynical tool for nation building under a dictatorship, "music for maids and taxi drivers," and an embarrassing legacy of Brazilian provincialism (see Araújo 2002; Castro 2001; Vianna 2001). It has been called kitsch, tacky (*cafona*), "exotic . . . music from the North" (Castro 2012, 26), and a "kind of filth" (Araújo 2002, 355). One scholar wrote that Luiz Gonzaga was like a rural Carmen Miranda, the legendary camp songstress who, for the benefit of American audiences, danced among birds and giant banana xylophones while wearing fruit in her headdresses, caricaturing *baianas*, Afro-Brazilian women of Bahia (Austregésilo 2012). From such a perspective, Gonzaga, his birds (the picazuro pigeon and others), and his leather bandit costume were little more than broad caricatures of northeastern life made for the southeastern public.

In contrast, the songs of intellectuals such as Caetano Veloso, Maria Bethâ-nia, Gilberto Gil, and Chico Buarque, who is from one of Brazil's most respected intellectual families, among many other Brazilian popular music (*música popular brasileira*, or MPB) singers from the 1960s and 1970s, are routinely understood by scholars to be forms of protest despite their hidden meanings and messages. These coded protests were often relayed via musical allusions to the Northeast and to *forró*. And scholars recognize many other Brazilian genres, including ones that are not protest music per se and some that are primarily dance genres, to be forms of resistance: hip hop, reggae, samba reggae, the music and movements of *capoeira*, *música sertaneja*, Brazilian rock, and many others. Were we to believe the scholarship, much music in Brazil would appear to be protest music.

Why can't the music of Gonzaga, a dark-skinned northeasterner who spoke in a *matuto* (hillbilly) accent to a poor northeastern audience, be considered a form of resistance, *even though he described it as such*? The causes and consequences of drought in the Northeast were a key social concern not just for Gonzaga but for many northeastern musicians of the twentieth century.

CHAPTER 3

The Secret of the *Sertanejo*

Listening to *Forró*, Hearing Drought

A *catingueira* tree blooms: it will rain.
A swallow has flown: there will be a good rainy season.
If the hawk sings, there will be drought.
. . . .
These are the secrets the *sertanejo* knows
And in which he took no pleasure learning to read.

AN ACCORDION, in its high and quavering musette register, opens the song on a lowered seventh scale degree, repeating the note three more times with only the gentlest rubato. It then walks stepwise down to the 5, leaps up to the 1, descends those same three notes again, and then skips down to the minor third. The Dorian mode, the basis of many of *forró*'s and *baião*'s most sorrowful melodies, emerges gradually and ominously, confirmed by the arpeggio that follows. The phrase concludes with a legible and meaningful plagal "amen." The accordionist quietly plays the minor triad, shaking his right hand to produce a soft tremolo, while the vocalist, her voice tense, enters, again on the lowered seventh, to repeat the verse's melody. At the end of the first phrase, a *viola caipira* appears.

This is *forró*, instantly recognizable to many Brazilian listeners as northeastern music—*música nordestina*. The song conjures memories of the *baião* recordings of Luiz Gonzaga and the timbre of his voice and then leads the listener deeper into the *sertão* to the modal *cantoria* improvised duels of the cities in the interior. From there, it travels deeper into the *campo* (field) and the *roça* (farm) via melodic and timbral allusions to *aboios* (herding calls), such as when the vocalist, in a straight tone, sings a microtonal ornament before she steps down from the tonic to the subtonic.

The song I describe here is the 1981 recording of João do Vale's "Uricuri (segredo do sertanejo)" (Arikury [secret of the *sertanejo*], cowritten with José Cândido).[1] Vale's eponymous album featured duets, mostly rerecordings of songs from his first album (1965), with some of Brazil's most famous voices, including Antônio Carlos Jobim, Nara Leão, Chico Buarque, and Gonzaguinha (Luiz Gonzaga's MPB-musician son), as well as northeasterners Zé Ramalho, Alceu Valença, Raimundo Fagner, and Amelinha, the latter two from Ceará. "Uricuri" was sung by legendary Brazilian popular music (MPB) singer Clara Nunes. As Nunes intones the sounds of the backlands, sounds made by men clad in leather and on horseback, she explains the knowledge—the "secrets"—that people in the backlands possess. The arikury palm grows in the Northeast. (Its wax, like that of the carnauba, is a valuable commodity.) The song's lyrics explain that the tree's blossoming is a sign that bees have made honey. *Sertanejos* might not be literate, she sings, but they know how to read the book of nature.

Nunes, primarily famous for singing sambas, recorded this track for a national audience for whom the *sertanejo* was a tragic figure of the past. In *forró's* rendering, the cowboy sang his *aboio* (herding call) not for a human audience but for cattle in order to elicit a practical and physical response. And the *sertanejo* listened to the sound of the hawk not for its aesthetic qualities but to determine whether there would be drought. Yet the *sertanejo* is more than a stock character in the mediated Brazilian imagination. In today's backlands, people find meaning in the sounds of birds, as well as in the sounds of *forró*. And for some, these sounds and the related ways of listening are entwined.

Forró has perpetuated certain symbols and practices of the Northeast—not just images, celebrations, and sounds but also ways of perceiving and knowing. Among these are acoustemologies: acoustic epistemologies, sonic ways of knowing, or understandings of the world made through sound and perceived through sound. Steven Feld (1996), who coined the term, argues that the knowledge of place is bound up in practices of listening and sound making. *Forró* lyrics that explain the meaning of birdsong describe not only a northeastern way of listening but also a particular understanding of the Northeast and how it works—climatologically, ecologically, culturally, spatially, and temporally.

Mass-mediated *baião* has coded certain ways of listening as northeastern. Every January, thirty or so people who identify as rain prophets meet in the city of Quixadá, which is in a microregion of Ceará known as the Central Sertão. The rain prophets, mostly men, share their predictions for the coming season with an audience of hundreds of farmers, college students, local onlookers, academics, politicians, businesspeople, and journalists. To my surprise, many rain prophets, in public pronouncements and private interviews, associate the practice of rain prophecy with the music of Luiz Gonzaga. I heard rain prophets cite the lyrics of Gonzaga's songs when discussing their predictions and the practice more generally. What does it mean that these individuals refer to the lyrics of his commercial popular music, some of which is from nearly seventy years ago, when talking about weather forecasting? When rain prophets listen to (and otherwise observe) nature in ways that radio-era music marked as emblematic of the *sertão*, the act of perceiving and the public sharing of perceptions can be performances of regional identity and celebrations of local knowledge.

Gonzaga's music is meaningful for rain prophets and for rain prophecy not solely because it is considered traditional music, with deep roots in the *sertão*, but because it is popular music crafted and disseminated by a national music industry. Gonzaga's songs are able to give the ecological knowledge in his lyrics an aura of authority and local relevance because of specific characteristics of popular music: mass dissemination, audio recording, fame, and associations between popular music and place and between popular music and identity. Because Gonzaga's recordings were mass disseminated and commercially successful, his nostalgic visions of the Northeast—its landscapes, soundscapes, and knowledge—reached the ears and imaginations of those who lived in the region. Because his music was recorded, his voice and his words have persisted through time. Because of his fame, his voice continues to possess an aura of authenticity and authority. The lyrics of many of his songs, only some of which he wrote or cowrote, mentioned and/or reproduced the Northeast's acoustic ecology and local ecological knowledge as metaphors that were intelligible to his audience. Yet because he and his songs are so profoundly associated with the region and northeastern regional identity, some northeasterners see his music not only as a semiotically rich part of the northeastern musical repertoire but also as a meaningful source of ecological knowledge about the region, a transmission of the *sertão* acoustemology.

This Gonzaguian way of listening (i.e., rain prophecy) is, as Karen Pennesi (2007) has argued, an act of resistance against institutional knowledge generated and shared by the government, which seems to have repeatedly failed *sertanejos*. Moreover, rain prophets understand the communication of knowledge about rain and drought as a meaningful local tradition that has much in common with regional musics and poetry. Traditional rural music, *forró*, and rain prophecy are entangled in a shared *sertanejo* system of local knowledge and cultural production.

I now take a deeper look at the reception of Luiz Gonzaga in Ceará from the mid-twentieth century to the present day to show how Gonzaga's voice has become a vehicle for the transmission of northeastern practices of listening for rain and drought and other related forms of rain prophecy. This chapter is organized in two major sections. In the first section, I explore Gonzaga's musical transmission of the northeastern imaginary, his depiction of northeastern ecological knowledge about rain and drought, his enduring fame, and the ways he has come to be associated with the northeastern region and northeastern identity. In the second section, I turn to rain prophecy to examine its history of mediation, and I assess the rain prophets' citation of the lyrics of Gonzaga's songs, asking how and why these lyrics remain relevant to them.

The Radio and Gonzaga's Enduring Fame in Ceará

As discussed in the previous chapter, through the mid-twentieth century, Luiz Gonzaga's vision of the Northeast traveled across the nation in large part due to the medium of the radio. Brazil's golden age of radio occurred between the mid-1930s and the mid-1950s (by one estimate, 95 percent of households in Rio de Janeiro and São Paulo owned radios by 1950 [see McCann 2004, 23]), and radios were a principal tool for the assimilation of northeastern migrants in the southeastern cities of Rio de Janeiro and São Paulo. It allowed them to establish a connection with national and urban life while still having access to sounds that reminded them of home via shows that specialized in rural musical traditions, including live and improvisatory *cantoria* duels.

Gonzaga, who first left his rural home in the northeastern state of Pernambuco in 1930 to join the army, moved to Rio de Janeiro in 1939 to pursue a career as a musician. In 1940 he started appearing on amateur hour radio programs in which he performed popular music of the time, including waltzes, fox-trots, tangos, and *choros*. Although he initially achieved little success competing against better-skilled musicians who played similar styles, he ultimately realized he could take advantage of the growing potential market for northeastern music (see chapter 1). By the late 1940s his fame had spread nationally, and his voice had become irrevocably associated with the northeastern backlands. He no longer made efforts to speak with the accent from Rio de Janeiro, and he fully adopted his northeastern stage persona.

Despite living in Rio and singing for a national audience, Gonzaga, who sold more records between 1946 and 1955 than any other Brazilian artist (Santos 2002, 54), frequently made radio and concert appearances in the Northeast and took junkets to the region's small towns. In November 1951, for example, he performed a series of live radio shows in Fortaleza, making a stop in the town of Canindé to leave a votive offering for St. Francis, the local patron saint, before returning home to Rio de Janeiro.[2] In April 1953 he performed in a festival in the Cearense city of Iguatú, hometown of his songwriting partner, Humberto Teixeira, around the same time local officials met to plan the construction of the local radio.[3] In May of that year he starred in a "radiophonic show" promoted by Fortaleza's Rádio Iracema and then appeared again in June 1956 in Fortaleza in a radio special called the *Festa do radialista*.[4]

Gonzaga's national popularity began to decline in the mid-1950s, precipitated by changes in the nation's political and cultural climates (Santos 2002, 62). In January 1956 Juscelino Kubitchek assumed the presidency, and with him came plans to modernize and improve the Brazilian economy, which included the expansion of the consumer economy. Sales of televisions eclipsed those of radios, which were responsible for *baião*'s and *forró*'s success, and Elvis and rock and roll, followed by samba and bossa nova, dominated the mediated soundscape (62–63). The front page of Fortaleza's *Jornal o Povo* on December 29, 1956, featured an article that began, "Record stores—where Bach mixes with Luiz Gonzaga—proliferate, national music loses ground, and a tide of luck pushes the ship of adaptors of foreign music." Northeastern regional music had lost its national appeal to music from abroad.

Through the end of the decade, Gonzaga's career shifted primarily to the Northeast, where he maintained only some of his fame. By 1960, when he returned to Fortaleza to perform in a daylong celebration of the fifth anniversary of Rádio Iracema, he was relegated to performing at 9:30 in the morning, finishing his thirty-minute set three hours before João Gilberto "and his 'bossa nova'" took the stage and seven hours before the performance of the headlining act, Carlos Nobre, a popular romantic balladeer of the time.[5]

That same year, Gonzaga recorded a series of campaign jingles for center-right presidential candidate Jânio Quadros, whose conservative platform blamed inflation on outgoing President Kubitchek. Through the sixties Gonzaga toured the cities of the Northeast for Eveready Batteries, performing from the back of a truck while shilling for the company.[6] He also appeared in Eveready print advertisements, which ran a photo of him with his characteristic hat and accordion and which reproduced the lyrics to two jingles, also naming the northeastern rhythm for each song.[7] One of the songs (in a *xaxado* rhythm), called "A pilha pulo do gato" (The Holy Grail battery), says, "He who uses Eveready knows / what he has in his hand. / It's the hottest battery / from North-Central-South to the *sertão*." In an unverified and undated recording he can be heard imploring an audience to join in as he sings an Eveready jingle with a slow *xote* dance rhythm.[8]

Gonzaga recorded jingles for a wide range of products, including Wilkinson razor blades, Fram oil filters, bicycles, cornmeal, flip-flops, coffee, *cachaça* sugarcane liquor, and salt licks for cows.[9] What unites these products, other than the sound of Gonzaga's voice and accordion, is an association with the daily life in the rural Northeast (battery power, cornmeal, coffee, flip-flops, and bicycles), masculinity (razor blades, oil filters, and booze), and agriculture (salt licks).

Despite the decline in his popularity throughout the 1960s, Gonzaga had become an icon of the Northeast by the 1970s. In 1975 he was made an honorary citizen of the Cearense town of Barbalha in the Cariri region, and less than two months later he was made an honorary citizen of the state of Ceará. One newspaper article that year said, "The large amount that Luiz Gonzaga has done for Ceará and for the Northeast deserves to be seen and highlighted, since he was always a defender of our music, of our tradition and customs, publicizing Ceará and Cariri in all of his shows performed in Brazil."[10] Another article called him "a true ambassador of Ceará."[11]

Gonzaga died in 1989 at the age of seventy-six, but his memory became even more associated with northeasternness. In September 2005 President Luiz Inácio Lula da Silva, known as Lula, declared a National Day of *Forró*. The decree, Law No. 11.176, issued by President Lula and the Brazilian National Congress reads in part, "The thirteenth of December is hereby instituted as the 'National Day of *Forró*,' in homage of the birthdate of musician Luiz Gonzaga do Nascimento, the 'King of Baião.'" In Fortaleza in December 2009 the city held a week of free concerts to celebrate the holiday. An article from *Jornal o Povo* claimed that the holiday was necessary to preserve *forró*, which it called a "perfect amalgamation of the ethnic influences that compose the formation of our people."[12] It described the genre as a representation of the northeastern people themselves. Gonzaga's songs were front and center in the concert series.

As with any star, not all people adore Gonzaga. Yet his voice, his songs, and his image are pervasive across Ceará, especially during the St. John's Day season and in other spaces and moments in which northeasternness is emphasized. In the half dozen orchestral concerts I have attended in Ceará since I began traveling to the state, every performance has included a medley of classic tunes by Luiz Gonzaga. Fortaleza's early music ensemble, Grupo Syntagma, plays complex contrapuntal arrangements of Gonzaga's songs alongside pieces by John Dowland and Giuseppe Sammartini. Several rock bands play blues-

FIGURE 5. Supermarket advertisement featuring Gonzaga.

influenced covers of his music. Even Ceará's klezmer band, Banda LeChaim, performs its own version of Gonzaga's best-known song, "Asa branca," as did an Andean pan-flute ensemble I saw on multiple street corners around Fortaleza. Most significantly, traditional *forró* musicians play his music as a substantial basis of their repertoire. Every June for St. John's Day, competitive quadrille performances, which are held in squares and parks throughout Ceará, are accompanied by his music.

Gonzaga's lyrics also appear in nonmusical contexts to signify northeastern-ness. Print advertisements during the St. John's Day season, for example, quote lyrics from his songs and feature his image (see figure 5). Newspaper advertisements for cars, shoe stores, the lottery, health insurance, and countless other products and services depict the holiday's multicolored bunting, drawings of straw (carnauba) hats, and cartoon hillbillies with blacked-out teeth, leather sandals, and plaid shirts. A St. John's Day advertisement for grocery chain Planeta Supermercado from 2008 features a drawing of a smiling accordionist wearing a carnauba hat, his bellows pulled open to reveal the words "Vem pra cá!" (Come here!). Across the top of the ad appear the words, "Êta São João danado de bão!" (Whoa, damn good St. John's Day!), recalling the title to one of Gonzaga's songs, "Danado de bom" (Damn good). His music is ubiquitous in Ceará because it is seen as traditional, as representative of the place, and as representative of the northeastern people.

Traditional Ecological Knowledge, Northeastern Acoustemes, and Birds in Gonzaga's Music

The traditions Gonzaga established (with other musicians of his era) went beyond the musical elements of *baião*. John Bishop (2000) has suggested that post–World War II mass-mediated representations of the northeastern back-lands were responsible for many of the characteristics of St. John's Day attractions in Caruaru, Pernambuco, that catered to the expectations of tourists. As I argue here, Gonzaga's music also codified forms of listening and perception as northeastern traditions, conveying traditional ecological knowledge within a broad range of images and stereotypes of the region.

His lyrics, many of which were written by his primary collaborators, Humberto Teixeira and Zé Dantas, described the region's men as strong, hardworking, and tenacious. The songs spoke of their labor: herding cattle, picking cotton, and planting beans. They depicted the hardships of migration and of assimilation to city life in the Southeast. They pleaded for rain. They explored the pains and pleasures of courtship and romance. They explained the dance moves and the celebrations associated with St. John's Day, the biggest holiday in the Northeast. And many of his songs evoked the soundscapes of the countryside. Birdsong, in particular, appeared frequently in his songs, as did references to birds in other metaphorical contexts, with descriptions of their migratory flights, their cages, and so on.[13] A bird can be seen on the covers of his 1957 album *O Reino do Baião* (The Kingdom of *Baião*) and his 1962 album *Ô véio macho* (Oh old guy), with a blue-fronted Amazon parrot perched on his hat and on the bellows of his accordion, respectively. Some of his best-known and most beloved songs are named after birds, among them "Assum preto" (Smooth-billed ani), "Sabiá" (Rufous-bellied thrush), and "Asa branca" (Picazuro pigeon), which is often referred to as the "anthem of the Northeast."

Embedded into the lyrical depictions of labor, love, parties, and birds are bits of northeastern traditional ecological knowledge, sometimes included merely as passing allusions, and sometimes explained in detail. Gonzaga's song "Marimbondo" (Wasp), cowritten with José Marcolino (1964), suggests that a wasp will try to enter one's house when the rain has arrived, ensuring a good rainy season—and cotton harvest—to come. "São João do Carneirinho" (St. John of the lamb, 1958), by Gonzaga and Guio de Moraes, and Gonzaga's famous "A triste partida" (The sad departure, 1964), a setting of a poem by Patativa do Assaré, allude to a northeastern belief that if there is no rain by St. Joseph's Day on March 19, a drought will follow.

A number of his songs that reference birdsong do so by describing the meaning of the bird's call in relation to the arrival of rain or drought. The lyrics of "Baião na garoa" (*Baião* in the drizzling rain) (1952), written by Gonzaga and Herve Cordovil, say the rufous-bellied thrush will not sing "in the land of drought / when the harvest is no good," while it did sing that "one time it rained in the dry land." The song "Pássaro carão" (Limpkin) (1962), by Gonzaga and José Marcolino, describes the calls of the limpkin and the smooth-billed ani as signs that "rain will fall":

> The limpkin sang.
> The smooth-billed ani sang too.
> The rain will fall
> In my backlands. Someday

Gonzaga was known for his stage banter, and in a filmed segment intended for television in the 1970s he introduces his performance of "Acauã" (Laughing falcon) by talking about the significance of the bird's call in comparison to that of the purple-throated euphonia. The call of the laughing falcon "augurs" drought, while the purple-throated euphonia's call heralds rain.

> There are also many songs about birds, like the story of *assum preto, asa branca, bem-te-vi,* the *juriti.* And there's the story of the *acauã.* The *acauã* has a different story. It's an auguring bird, a bird that nobody wants to hear sing because it calls the drought. It always brings bad news, which isn't what happens with the *vem-vem* [the purple-throated euphonia, literally "come-

come"]. When the *vem-vem* starts to sing, the people say there is good news there, *vem-vem*, in the road and the street, *vem-vem, vem-vem*. Everyone hopes to hear something good, good news. . . . But the *acauã*, when it sings near a poor rural farmer's house, he does everything to send her away, to remove her . . . because she's going to sing an inferno near his house, because she's bringing, she's auguring something bad.[14]

Gonzaga's monologue also mentions the emotional response elicited by the sounds of these birds. The purple-throated euphonia brings happiness, whereas the laughing falcon brings fear and sadness. Through text painting and emotive singing, he carries these sentiments into his performance of "Acauã" in the clip. Following his explanation of the bird's call, he sings a slow and mournful rendition of Zé Dantas's song, accompanied only by his accordion. The first few phrases of the refrain, which starts with the word "acauã," begin on an accented, cried ♭7 of the Mixolydian mode. The piercing timbre of his voice and the tension of the lowered leading tone imply the bird's ominous news.

The song's lyrics clearly explain the meaning of the laughing falcon's cry as it is understood by those who live in the northeastern backlands.[15] As he says in the clip, the lyrics tell that the bird's call "augurs" and "invites" drought:

The laughing falcon sings endlessly through summer
Amid afternoon silence, auguring, inviting drought to the backlands
. . . .
In the joy of the rainy season sing the river frog, the tree frog, the toad,
But in the sorrow of drought you hear only the laughing falcon.

In the song's coda, Gonzaga mimics the bird's call, demonstrating for his audience the very sound that arouses fear and sorrow and that warns of a coming drought. He sings the word "acauã" repeatedly and quickly in a syncopated rhythm for nearly twenty seconds, transitioning from pitched singing to cawing the word in a scratchy falsetto to mimic the raptor's loud cry. The sound of the word "acauã" itself is imitative of the sound of the bird's most typical call, and the rhythm of the word "acauã" also aligns with the rhythm of the call. The laughing falcon sings one pitch and then repeats that pitch and slurs down a whole step, singing "a-cau-ã," long short-short, a distinct quarter note followed by two slurred eighth notes. The bird repeats the call over and over, increasing in tempo and syncopating its rhythm (see Hilty 2003; Barkley et al. 2012). Gonzaga mimics these vocalizations, sounding nearly identical to the bird as he voices its name while imitating its cry, although his melodic contour is unlike that of the bird. "A-cau-ã, 'cau-ã, 'cau-ã, a-cau-ã," he sings, alternating between the syncopated cries and the bird's rapid-fire laughs, between his unpitched, scratchy falsetto and his singing voice.

In this recording of "Acauã," Gonzaga captures the sound of the bird's call, the emotion it provokes in people from the northeastern backlands, and its meaning in relation to traditional ecological knowledge about rain and drought. His music would have provided his audience of northeastern migrants with a nostalgic recollection of the sounds, feelings, and knowledge of the region they left behind. But because of its national exposure, his interpretation of northeastern knowledge reached the ears of audiences that remained in the Northeast who could hear his music in distinct, locally meaningful ways.

Rain Prophecy and the Performance of Traditional Ecological Knowledge

On a Saturday morning in early January 2009 I found myself driving down the pothole-studded asphalt roads of Quixadá, a city in the interior of Ceará, past a big-box hardware store, a lingerie shop, a couple of plazas and churches, some pharmacies, and the like at the suggestion of Lea Carvalho Rodrigues, an anthropologist at the Federal University of Ceará in Fortaleza who thought I might be interested in an event called the Meeting of the Rain Prophets. I turned onto a cobblestone street that led me out of the city center and past the campus of a local technical college until I finally arrived at the banks of a reservoir to attend the annual event, held each year on the second Saturday of January. That year, it took place at the impressive embankment of the Cedro Reservoir, built at the turn of the twentieth century—begun under Emperor Dom Pedro II in 1890 and completed in 1906—as an early and notable effort to mitigate the impact of drought. As I arrived, I saw workers setting up tables with cake and juice—among them was Patrícia Soares Holanda, the daughter of one of the event's organizers, who met with me the previous night, introduced me to rain prophets, fed me dinner, and then took me to a concert of *cantoria* singing, part of the meeting's activities. Camera crews and reporters from national and local TV stations jockeyed for space near a table that marked the stage, pushing me to the side. Volunteers arranged hundreds of white folding chairs, their backs to the embankment. A musician in dark sunglasses tuned a *viola caipira* and warmed up. Rain prophets and guests—an audience of nearly two hundred farmers, students, journalists, researchers, and businesspeople— soon arrived en masse, each making an entrance as he or she walked down a series of stone steps. I ran into a friend, a Brazilian social psychologist, who was joined by one of his students. I took my place behind my video recorder as the prophets, all wearing matching T-shirts, sat down in the front row. Local politicians and event organizers sat on the dais, facing the crowd. To introduce the occasion, a performer sang, followed by short speeches from the politicians and organizers. From late morning to early afternoon, prophets took turns at the microphone presenting their predictions, each including an explanation of his or her methodology and a piece of material evidence, when appropriate, like a map or a bird's nest. One man recited a humorous poem, and another recited a poem in honor of his mother, both in the style of *cordel* chapbook poetry.[16]

For many rain prophets, knowledge of weather and knowledge of sound are entwined. Birdsong, for example, is among the most common indicators of rain or drought. In addition to birdsong, prophets observe the sounds of frogs, the direction in which birds construct their nests, the behavior of ants, the time of year when flowers bloom, the arrangement of stars, and other natural patterns. Rain prophet José Erismá listens to birdsong as one of his primary forecasting methods: "On the first day of the year, at the passing of the thirty-first of December to the first of January, the birds sing differently, like in a party, so they gather and make their show among themselves, since they are happy for the good year that will appear in the rainy season, in the wintry period in Ceará, and also because this is the Northeast. . . . They sing more. They have a different song."[17] When Erismá hears birds singing loudly in large flocks at the start of the year, he understands their calls to be a sign of a good rainy season. Not only is their acoustic volume and the size of their chorus greater than they are throughout the rest of the year, but their song itself, as he hears it, changes.

Like many rain prophets from Ceará, Erismá shares his predictions at the Meeting of the Rain Prophets. Rain prophecy has involved the public performance of knowledge for at least two generations. Until the early twentieth century, predictions were often shared in markets, at religious, athletic, and political meetings, and at other social gatherings (Taddei 2006). Rain prophet Erasmo Barreira grew up watching his father predict to farmers in his home. The gatherings he attended as a child were informal but nevertheless significant for local farmers as a source of information and for establishing a sense of community:

> But I followed my father, my whole life at home. . . . They'd schedule a day in December, on some Sunday or another Saturday in December, to talk about how it was going to be the next year, the perspective for the next year, you know? And here it was as if it were a meeting of any kind of official organization. And one person would argue, and another would say that the rainy season wouldn't be good because there wasn't I-don't-know-what,

the prophecy of whoever and such didn't work. . . . Ninety percent [of the farmers] would go to hear my father's conversation, and I would go along.[18]

"Rain prophet" is a social identity adopted by individuals who have developed reputations for their mastery of traditional ecological knowledge and who perform their predictions publicly, and thus it refers not to those who merely possess the appropriate knowledge but to those who also have an aptitude for oration.[19] Today's "rain prophet" identity resulted from the radio, where prophets could hone their skills in a more formalized setting, making an art of public rain prognostication (Taddei 2006). Since 1997 many prophets have performed their forecasts at the Meeting of the Rain Prophets, attended by farmers, students, university professors, and the television and print news media, which publicize the findings. The event, which was founded and continues to be run by Hélder Cortez, is sponsored by an organization called the Instituto de Pesquisa, Viola e Poesia do Sertão Central (Institute of Research, Viola [Guitar] and Poetry of the Central *Sertão*), which also holds monthly *cantoria* concerts.

At the Meeting of the Rain Prophets, rain prophecy is a performance of northeastern tradition and northeasternness as much as it is an act of communicating practical knowledge about rain and drought. João Soares, who directs the Instituto de Pesquisa, Viola e Poesia do Sertão Central, emphasized to me that he hosts the event not solely to valorize rain prophecy over government weather forecasts but to celebrate the kinds of skills, talents, and values that come from life in the northeastern backlands (also see Pennesi 2007; Pennesi and Souza 2012).[20] In a TV news interview in 2016, Ceará's secretary of culture, Guilherme Sampaio, said, "For the Department of Culture, all of this [rain prophecy] is part of a set of phenomena—experiences—that are associated with intangible cultural heritage."

Soares also likened rain prophecy to *cantoria*, considering them related elements of traditional culture. Singer João de Oliveira, who performed in a concert on the eve of the 2009 Meeting of the Rain Prophets, said, referring to *cantoria* performers, "In some form, we are associated with those who have knowledge of the weather. We certainly have importance for their [those who live in the northeastern backlands] daily lives." That same year, the Meeting of the Rain Prophets opened with a song performed by Guilherme Calixto, who improvised a verse, excerpted below, about the similarities between prophecy and poetry:

This great tradition affects even my spirit.
It seems as if the prophets follow the right path,
Because I wanted to give up my verse to become a prophet.

A prophet is almost a poet in the way he thinks and creates.
The poet thinks about verse and sacred poetry,
And the prophet acquires lessons about our daily lives.

Calixto, Soares, and Oliveira see rain prophecy as "traditional," northeastern, and poetic, even similar to northeastern music. It combines sensory knowledge of nature, including the perception and interpretation of sound, with verbal performance to celebrate local senses of place and identity.

Rain Prophets and the Voice of Gonzaga

On multiple occasions I heard rain prophets cite the lyrics of songs by Gonzaga in their public speeches and private interviews. The citation of Gonzaga's lyrics by rain prophets when discussing rain prophecy can be explained by two similarities between rain prophecy and Gonzaga's music: (1) both are considered reliable sources of knowledge about the Northeast, and (2) both are understood to be expressions of a particular vision of northeasternness.[21]

Because of Gonzaga's national reputation and fame, his voice lends intelligibility and authority to northeastern knowledge. Rain prophet Erasmo Barreira referred to Luiz Gonzaga's voice when he explained to me that the call of the *acauã* is a common indicator of drought. I had asked him if he knew of any examples of rain prophecy that involved sound and birdsong in particular. "The 'cauã," he said, "is one of those occurrences that lots of times, when she enters January singing loudly in the bush, someone once said you call this an 'augur' [*agouro*], you know? Auguring [*agourando*] that the rainy season won't come. This is the 'cauã."[22] That "someone" who had described the laughing falcon's prophetic cry as "auguring," he later clarified, was Luiz Gonzaga in his recording of Zé Dantas's song "Acauã."

By explaining rain prophecy through the voice of Gonzaga, Barreira was able to frame his knowledge in a context that most Brazilians, including those from outside the Northeast (and perhaps even ethnomusicologists from abroad), could comprehend. Brazilian listeners know of Gonzaga and his music; he is a cultural reference that can help people make sense of the Northeast and its practices. In addition, Barreira's reference to Gonzaga's voice added credibility to his knowledge. In our conversation, it was not Barreira who said that when the laughing falcon sings loudly in January it is a sign that the rainy season won't come. It was "someone" else—Gonzaga.

Rain prophecy is more than a rural, hereditary form of weather forecasting. It is a form of local knowledge that has been endorsed by Gonzaga as an index of the region and transmitted—through his voice—in memories and on audio recordings. When I asked radio host and rain prophet Ribamar Lima about the relationship between music and life in the *sertão*, he incorporated the lyrics of one of Gonzaga's best-known songs in his response. For him, Gonzaga and rain prophecy are both examples of traditions that are deeply rooted in the northeastern experience:

> When you see an ant leaving a low place to find higher ground, it's because it's going to protect itself. It knows. It has a god-given gift. When we see, for example, the *mandacaru*—which is a characteristic plant of the Northeast, a cactus—when it blooms during drought, it's a sign that rain has arrived in the backlands, which was said by Luiz Gonzaga. So these are small things that we see, that we start to observe, that make sense, that work. Here we lack water to drink, for home use, and for the animals to drink, which is the worst. Sometimes we have to get water from far, from other states, because we have neither water nor pasture. So we have eternal suffering. And from that comes the northeastern lament.[23]

"When the *mandacaru* cactus blooms during drought, it is a sign the rain has arrived in the backlands," Lima quotes. These words are the opening lyrics of the popular song "Xote das meninas" (Girls' schottische) (1953), written by Luiz Gonzaga and Zé Dantas. The song, about the maturation of an adolescent girl whose only interest is love, is now a standard part of the repertoire of *forró* music. The flowering of the *mandacaru* cactus is, according anthropologist Karen Pennesi (2007), among the most trusted forecasting methods among those she asked in Ceará. To Lima, these lyrics provided evidence for how northeastern music and rain prophecy derive from the needs and "eternal suffering" of the *sertanejo*. For him, Gonzaga's words were "traditional," local, and part of the experience of the region, rather than merely a reflection or representation of it, underscoring the traditional and local nature of rain prophecy. That is, if Gonzaga said it is a locally meaningful tradition, then it must be a locally meaningful tradition.

Rain prophecy is also a public performance with a northeastern rhetorical aesthetic. Certain metrical patterns of speech and internal rhymes, many of which derive from the poetic qualities of *cantoria* and northeastern *cordel* chapbook poetry, are present in both rain prophecy performances and Gonzaga's music. In other words, Gonzaga's music and rain prophecy are rooted in the expressive verbal traditions of the region. Both times I attended the Meeting of the Rain Prophets, the performance of *cantoria* singing and the recitation of *cordel* poetry were integral to the event, and many of the rain prophets recited their forecasts in ways that were themselves poetic and oratorical. At the

Meeting of the Rain Prophets in 2012, rain prophet Antônio Custódio held up a flower from the *mandacaru* cactus and recited lyrics from "Xote das Meninas" before announcing that a good winter would come. His reference to Gonzaga heightened the expressive quality of his prediction in a way that seemed quintessentially northeastern:

> Last year I said the rainy season would begin in December, and that's when it started. It rained for eight months. This year it will already start to rain on the fifteenth of the month. In January and February, however, it will rain only a little. Now, come March and April there will be lots of rain, folks. It's nature that's telling us that. It's the toad. It's the spider. It's the crab. It's the butterfly. It's the birds. It's the bee. And all of nature. . . .
>
> Here's the *mandacaru* flower. [He raised the flower with his right hand.] When Luiz Gonzaga said in the song, "When the *mandacaru* flowers during drought, it's a sign that rain will fall in the backlands. And when the girl gets sick of her doll, it's a sign that love has arrived in her heart." . . . There will be rain. From the 20th of January it will rain. In February it will only rain a little. And in March, April, and May, and June, everything will flood, and it will be a great rainy season. It's certain there will be rain.

When he listed animals that indicate rain or drought, his voice alternated between two pitches, intoning the name of the animal on the higher pitch. His words gradually fell into a cadence, and his voice grew in intensity. As he named each month it would rain, he shook the cactus flower, up and down, accentuating the stressed syllables in his speech, bringing the song's metaphorical lyrics into the present. The metrical and melodic quality of his speech, the physical and visual performance with the flower, and his reference to Gonzaga made the presentation of his prediction not only musical (not to mention local, traditional, illustrative, and authoritative) but also emotional and convincing in a way that his local audience would comprehend.

The Secrets of the *Sertanejo* and Mass-Mediated Acoustemologies

Luiz Gonzaga is not the only Brazilian musician to have sung about the Northeast nor even about the region's birds or its traditional ecological knowledge about rain and drought. But it was lyrics to his songs that I heard uttered by rain prophets, and it was his music that I heard—and continue to hear—in both expected and unexpected settings in Ceará. I have no reason to believe that rain prophets learned their practice directly from Gonzaga's songs, but I do believe that Gonzaga's songs help make rain prophecy meaningful for today's rain prophets. His voice and his words still seem authentically northeastern, symbolizing tradition and local identity because of his role in the discursive construction of the northeastern region; because of the semiotic density of his music, layering musical sound with local knowledge, visual imagery, and linguistic and poetic tropes; and because of his fame and legendary status.

Music that depicted a nostalgic (albeit harsh) vision of the northeastern Brazilian natural environment continues to have an influence on the transmission of northeastern traditional ecological knowledge. The knowledge of place through sound can travel via mass mediation away from the places in which sounds convey local knowledge and then back again. In this case, the commercial nature of Gonzaga's music was central to its ability to reach northeastern audiences and affect individuals in the century long after the music was initially written and recorded.

Practices tied to the comprehension of nature or that are deeply rooted in local cultures can be supported by—even created by—mass mediation and the culture industries. Not only do rain prophets listen to the radio, but the radio helped make today's rain prophets both in the sense that "rain prophet" became a reified identity in part due to performing predictions on the radio and in the sense that the radio helped transmit rain prophecy through Gonzaga's music. Without overstating the role of Gonzaga's songs, I find the citation of his lyrics indicative of a relationship between local acoustemologies, traditional ecological knowledge, and mainstream popular music, demonstrating a process through which the transmission of knowledge about nature and sound came to be mediated through popular music in ways that gave them an enduring aura of authenticity and embeddedness.

The secrets of the *sertanejo* are not so much secrets as they are performances of northeasternness. At the Meeting of the Rain Prophets, the recitation of this knowledge and the knowledge itself, although they are indeed practices of natural observation associated with traditional agriculture, primarily serve as symbols of local belonging that contest structures of governance. And the knowledge itself became locally meaningful in part due to northeastern popular music, its popularity, its persistence through time, and its association with tradition, the Northeast, and northeastern regional identity. Furthermore, the sounds and lyrics of *forró* underscore the notion that northeastern drought-related acoustemologies are a potent element of drought adaptation and self-reliance. If you cannot trust the government, at least you can trust Luiz Gonzaga. And if you cannot listen to the promises and predictions of FUNCEME (the Cearense Foundation of Meteorology and Water Resources), at least you can listen to the laughing falcon.

CHAPTER 4

Sounding the Real Backlands

Raimundo Fagner and the Soundscape of Orós

IN APRIL 2008 residents of the small interior city of Orós measured the water level of the local reservoir every day to predict when it would finally overflow. The bleeding of water over the dam into the Jaguaribe River confirms a good rainy season and transforms a dry cement spillway into a massive roaring waterfall. April 2008 was the first time the reservoir overflowed in four years.[1] According to one newspaper, over ten thousand tourists visited the body of water that month.[2] I first learned about these measurements on a DVD my sister-in-law's brother Neto played at a farewell party one afternoon that June. My (then-future) sister-in-law was moving to the United States to live with my brother, and her siblings had come to a sister's house in Fortaleza to say good-bye.

We gathered on the sofa and around the television near a framed, enlarged photo of the gushing spillway to watch an amateur documentary celebrating the day in April when the reservoir exceeded its capacity. The video began with footage of fireworks exploding over the shimmering reservoir and of revelers dancing *forró* into the night. The mayor gave a speech from a small stage behind a statue of former president Juscelino Kubitschek, responsible for the reservoir, on an overlook at the edge of the dam. Then a local brass band played an arrangement of "Asa branca." The remainder of the movie displayed footage of water. Water flowing over the dam. Water running downstream. Water crashing against boulders. And over the images of water, with the original sounds of splashing and babbling and cascading still audible, the video's editor dubbed a soundtrack of music by Raimundo Fagner.

The family sat rapt. Neto, who beamed proudly as his native city's two claims to fame appeared on the screen before us, pointed at the images of water and explained the importance of that day, the excitement for the city, and the impact on local tourism and agriculture. And then he began to sing. With the sounds of water, the voices of children playing, and the poppy ballads of Fagner streaming from the speakers at the side of the television set, Neto joined in, singing along by heart and gesticulating as if the living room were a bar. My sister-in-law then turned and said, "Water: the happiness of a northeasterner."

Hearing the *Sertão* in the *Sertão*

How is a musical representation of a place heard in that place? How does it affect that place? And who gets to decide how that process works? Just as Luiz Gonzaga's representation of the Northeast affected the region (see the previous chapter), the Orós described and depicted by Fagner articulates with the Orós where Fagner vacations. In his music the city functions as a metonym for the region as a whole and carries the connotations of drought and rurality that the Northeast implies. Yet Orós, like everywhere, is a place with its own particularities and shifting values and tastes. Fagner's presence in Orós as an occasional visitor highlights the distance between his own rockstar subjectivity and that of the people of this small northeastern city, where *forró* and American pop music can be heard alongside Fagner's best-loved ballads.

In his musical Orós, cosmopolitan sounds, images, and values combine with those of the *sertão* to create aural spaces of imagined northeastern Brazilianness.[3] This northeastern imaginary, however, exists beyond the imagination. It also fills the local soundscape, emanating from loudspeakers, televisions, and mobile sound systems. This chiastic interaction (the Northeast in the music and the music in the Northeast) comes into being not only through sound and sound technologies but through relationships of power.

Through sound—the ways we make it, hear it, classify it, and regulate it—we construct modern society, including social hierarchies (Ochoa Gautier 2006, 2014), the workings of structure and agency (Bronfman and Wood 2012), and the boundaries of public and private spheres (Born 2013). In an oft-cited Marxian critique of popular music, Jacques Attali writes that music, which he considers structured noise, is constitutive of society and the political economy: "[Any] theory of power today must include a theory of the localization of noise and its endowment with form" ([1985] 1992, 6). Soundscapes are never benign sites of acoustic production. In its earliest definition by composer R. Murray Schafer in 1969, soundscapes were threatened by the noise of industrialization, and many scholars have since shown them to be sites of contestation (some notable examples include Daughtry 2015; Hirschkind 2006; Thompson 2002).

In Orós music and sound are more than instruments of power; they are carriers and creators of representations of the self propagated through mass mediation and audio technologies, embraced through quotidian necessity and the alluring aura of fame, and brought into relief through conflict as a result of power and resistance. The local soundscape is a site in which an imagined and a lived Orós commingle. It is a space that resonates with the aesthetics and chronotope of "the real *sertão*" yet still celebrates cosmopolitan Fagner for being "an Orós native from the heart." It is a medium through which community is made and where its boundaries are articulated.

This chapter is organized in three sections. I first introduce Orós and its soundscape. I then turn to Raimundo Fagner and analyze his portrayal of the city onstage and in recordings. Last, I examine his effect on Orós and its soundscape through a discussion of his charitable works for Orós, his reception there, and specific ways he has tried (and failed) to manipulate its sound.

The Orós Soundscape

Orós, which sits deep in the interior of Ceará, is a five-to-eight-hour drive from Fortaleza, depending on the condition of the roads and who drives. It is best known for its landscape and its music, but with over twenty thousand inhabitants, it is not an untouched rural idyll. Like many towns and cities in the developing interior of the Northeast, it sustains a striking combination of rural and urban characteristics, traditional and popular music, and old and new audio technologies. In June and July 2009 a foothills *forró* trio played twice a week in a hardware store, while electronic *forró* played from a boom box in a small hair salon. Most homes, including some made of mud and sticks, sport satellite dishes on their roofs (see figure 6).

The city's landmark is a large dam constructed on the Jaguaribe River between 1958 and 1961 as part of President Kubitschek's public works program under the National Department of Works against Drought (see figure 7). Government officials neglected to assist inhabitants of the region flooded by the dam's construction, leaving them to fend for themselves after their homes and farms were submerged (Silva 2006). Until 2003 it was the largest reservoir in Ceará (the largest in the country by some accounts), and despite its tragic origins it remains a primary source of pride for the present-day residents of Orós. It provides water for the city and for agricultural irrigation throughout the region, sending water as far as Fortaleza through the "Worker's Canal" in

FIGURE 6. Home with satellite dish in Orós.

FIGURE 7. Orós reservoir and spillway in June 2009.

times of extreme drought. In periods when the dam overflows, the thundering of water down the spillway overwhelms the Orós soundscape. A local PE teacher told me the sound requires her to shout so students can hear her directions. A banker compared it to the roar of a jet engine.

The reservoir is also a tourist destination for people from other parts of the interior of the state. It is an impressive man-made structure, but most visitors come to see it because it is an oasis in the middle of the *sertão*. Tour buses bring sightseers to a lookout point perched near the edge of the dam, where they gather under a towering statue of President Kubitschek to pose for photos with mountains, the city, and the river running from the reservoir in the background. On the shore of the reservoir, colorful fishing boats rest in the sand, and a floating bar serves beer and fried fish. Local residents use the surrounding bars, the reservoir's beach, and the overlook as meeting places, especially on weekends, when teens sunbathe, children splash in the water, and adults sing together around a guitar and shared liters of beer.

On a Saturday afternoon in 2009 I sat in Orós's central plaza, minutes by car from the reservoir, to interview a local musician. Behind us, a car with an open trunk, equipped with subwoofers, played electronic *forró* hits so loudly I had to lean forward to hear him. The square is home to a pharmacy, a law firm, two bars, a pizzeria, an internet café (where teenagers download music, play video games, and chat online), and a small market. Around the corner is the main street of the city, with several grocers, a few clothing boutiques and shops, another internet café, and the agency, which is run by my sister-in-law's father, where you can buy bus tickets and popsicles and place a bet on the "animal game" (the *jogo do bicho*), a kind of informal Brazilian lottery.

In the plaza, just after dawn on a Monday morning in January 2012, the distant sound of crowing roosters gave way to singing birds and the sounds of passing motorcycles and fruit trucks over cobblestone streets. The metal grates of storefronts rattled as they slid open, and radios and cellphones bleated the hum of electronic *forró*. At 6:00 a.m. a ballad played over a set of loudspeakers on a hill, waking the city as early shoppers began to haggle over prices and cars puttered and rumbled. Throughout the morning and late afternoon, the sometimes-bustling sounds of commerce, radios, and announcements from speakers attached to the backs of moving motorcycles filled the air. Lunchtime was quiet in the square. After dark, bars, restaurants, and parked cars with open doors blared a cacophony of competing electronic *forró*, the out-of-sync *zabumba* rhythms and *forró* timbres creating a sonic wall of triangle, accordion, and pop vocals. *Forró*, which once conveyed an image of the interior of the

Northeast to the rest of Brazil, is now embedded into the soundscape of the Northeast, alongside the sounds of roosters and motorcycles.

Dantas: The Voice of Liberty

In Orós the *radiadora*, a set of six loudspeakers mounted to the roof of the home of José Ribeiro Dantas, its host, constructs and expresses local senses of place, defines town boundaries, conveys alarms and messages, and sanctifies space and time, qualities that other scholars have also observed in European village bells (Corbin 1998; Feld and Brenneis 2004).[4] The *radiadora* is also what R. Murray Schafer would call a "soundmark," "a community sound which is unique or possesses qualities which make it specially regarded or noticed by the people in that community" ([1977] 1994, 274). It has both functional and symbolic significance for Orós (see figure 8).

Nearly every morning since 1972, the people of Orós have been awakened at 6:00 a.m. by the sound of the *radiadora*. On weekdays, children "wake with Dantas" and his "musical alarm clock" to get ready for school. The sound of his morning song enters homes through paneless windows and gaps between tile roofs and concrete walls. His broadcasts reverberate off houses and hillsides, as if dozens of loudspeakers were scattered throughout the streets.

Following six chimes, Dantas plays a recording of an announcer who wishes the people of the city a good morning and thanks God for the sun. He then plays ballads like the 1938 recording of crooner Carlos Galhardo singing "Linda borboleta" (Beautiful butterfly). "One morning," the song begins, "one of those mornings full of light / among the roses of the garden / I saw passing / a gentle butterfly."

After his "good morning" song, Dantas makes the first announcements of the day: a cellphone was left in the square overnight and can be retrieved at the home of the good Samaritan who found it; the hardware store is having a sale; a boy was bitten by a dog, and his family seeks information on the animal; the church is looking for donations of food for a congregant who recently fell on hard times. Local shops, community groups, and individuals can purchase advertisements on the *radiadora*, more commonly referred to simply as "Dantas." The two-real (about one U.S. dollar) fee helps Dantas, who also works as a speaker repairman, maintain his service. He never charges for announcements related to the church, the schools, the hospital, funerals, or causes that he sees as essential for the community.[5] In the afternoon at 5:30, Dantas makes his second and last broadcast of the day. Until not long ago, he ended around 6:00 with a recording of "Ave Maria," which he calls the "prayer of the angel."[6]

FIGURE 8. *Radiadora* in Orós.

Following each series of ads, Dantas plays a song—generally recordings of singers from the early twentieth century, including Luiz Gonzaga[7]—from one of two boom box–style CD players he keeps on a desk. He holds his microphone up to one of the speakers to broadcast the sound. But Dantas is more a source of information, a projection of local values, a citywide alarm clock, and a creator of an acoustic community than a source of entertainment.

In most years during the rainy season, when the people of Orós routinely measure the water level of the reservoir, a representative from the National Department of Works against Drought calls Dantas with readings of the measurement. Dantas then announces the reading on his morning's program. Each year that the reservoir overflows, Dantas informs the city.

Dantas and his *radiadora* played a crucial role in the funeral of my sister-in-law's mother in Orós.[8] When my sister-in-law's mother died, my sister-in-law and my brother flew from Los Angeles to attend the funeral. That morning, Dantas announced that the funeral would begin once the daughter of the deceased arrived from the United States. Once they landed in the nearby Juazeiro do Norte airport, word was sent to Dantas, who announced that the visitors had landed in Brazil and would be in Orós soon thereafter. Life-cycle events, religion, and the daily affairs of Orós are the basis of Dantas's broadcasted soundscape, thus establishing and reinforcing religious and community values among those who live within listening range.

On the blog *Portal Orós*, journalist Josemberg Vieira wrote about a power outage in December 2010 that left Dantas unable to broadcast one morning:

This morning something different happened in our city: the children arrived late for school, workers were late for work, and many people did not wake at the right time, all because the VOICE OF LIBERTY that for almost forty years has woken the city of Orós did not work; but this only happened because on the block where the Voice of Liberty resides, your friend Dantas is without energy since 1:30 in the morning. This good person and a friend of our people deserves our respect and admiration, Mr. Dantas who provides a service of indispensable public utility to our dear Orós, waking and informing our people every day for almost forty years.[9]

Dantas, now in his late eighties, installed his loudspeaker service, as *radiadoras* are more formally called, after noticing that children were arriving late to school and missing class. He had previously worked in Fortaleza as an audio technician and loudspeaker service announcer before moving to Orós, so he had the knowledge and skills to start his own service. He approached the mayor and asked for permission and was granted formal authorization. Building his own loudspeaker tower and setting up his own studio gave him a newfound sense of freedom and autonomy. He named his *radiadora* "The Voice of Liberty."[10] He now describes himself as "number one for the workers in the city," saying his *radiadora* provides an essential public service. In 2002 he received the title of Cidadão Oroense (Citizen of Orós) from the Municipal Chamber of Orós.

Raimundo Fagner's Orós Imaginary

After the reservoir, nationally known popular musician Raimundo Fagner (b. 1949) is the second major source of pride for people in Orós. Orós's residents claim him as a native, and sources often cite the city as his birthplace.[11] That he was actually born in Fortaleza (although he spent much of his childhood in Orós) is of little importance to the city's attachment to the singer. He continues to call himself an "Orós native from the heart." While his music is infrequently regionalist in its sound, he still often evokes the *sertão* and the Orós reservoir by referring to the city onstage, in interviews, and in his music. Orós offers him an air of northeastern authenticity by linking him to rural traditions, the natural environment, and the struggles of the people of the northeastern interior.

In 1971 Fagner began to develop a national audience after success in a competition in Brasília, where he studied architecture at a federal university. His performance of "Mucuripe," which he wrote with Cearense musician Belchior, won first place.[12] The song, about a beach in Fortaleza, became a national success through the voice of Elis Regina, whose iconic status has been compared to that of Janis Joplin and Billie Holiday by NPR.[13] Brazilian journalist Ana Maria Bahiana calls Fagner "the most romantic of the northeasterners [who play] post-Tropicalista fusion" (2006, 290). Fagner was part of the Pessoal do Ceará (Folks from Ceará), an unofficial group of musicians from Ceará who achieved a level of national fame in the 1970s (see Rogério 2008). In an era in which the Tropicalistas from Bahia were dominating the national popular music scene (see Dunn 2001; Favaretto 2000; Béhague 1980), the Pessoal do Ceará joined together to break into the music industry in Rio de Janeiro. They were marketed as a collective and as a kind of alternative to the better-known group of northeastern musicians that included Caetano Veloso, Maria Bethânia, Gilberto Gil, and Gal Costa, as well as to the Clube da Esquina from Minas Gerais.[14] The individual musicians of the Pessoal do Ceará were distinct, and they had no unified musical aesthetic or artistic philosophy. In an interview with sociologist Mary Pimentel, Fagner said, "The Pessoal do Ceará were basically a new thing, a new breath, but we were never constituted as a group, as dependent; we were people from a generation that tried to be professional, but each one with his own work. We arrived really strengthened in the south of the country" (1995, 120). Despite the group's efforts to deny regionalist motivations, the end of the 1970s came to be known as the "boom *nordestino*" by some in the Brazilian music industry. Rita Morelli writes, "These artists . . . never stopped being seen as songwriters and singers who were above all else northeastern" (2009, 83).

Some scholars have written that Fagner was part of a wave of northeastern musicians who, since the 1980s, have combined *forró* with MPB (e.g., Crook 2009; Bishop 2001). Although Fagner did release a *forró* album with Luiz Gonzaga in 1984 and participated in other *forró* recordings, his own music has always been more rock, more fusion, and more MPB than it was *forró*. "Manera fru-fru manera" (1973), composed with Ricardo Bezerra, subtly combined *baião* and a *forró* triangle with tabla drums and a *viola caipira*, a Brazilian steel guitar, played to sound like a sitar. But other recordings were more straightforwardly like the ballads of Roberto Carlos, the Grammy-winning Brazilian rocker/crooner. Although some of Fagner's songs incorporate rhythms associated with *forró* and some of his arrangements include northeastern instruments, he maintains that his music has never been deliberately or ideologically regionalist:

> I never do it on purpose. It may be true that I write songs more connected with the Northeast, . . . but I make international music, with the elements

that it uses: aggressive guitars, the normal instruments that are played in any place, that you record in any place. Just as I recorded in the United States, I also recorded in London. I recorded in Spain, where I drew a little more on northeastern regionalism mixed with Spanish music, but I record the musical foundations here as if I were recording anywhere. I'd be able to use any international musician. . . . I may make a disc of northeastern music . . . [but] I'm not going to carry an accordion. I make my music. Maybe it has a very northeastern feeling, but I make music listening to the Beatles, the same foundation that they have, the *jovem guarda*, a little traditional Brazilian music when it works. Really mixed music. Not even I know what I do.[15]

Fagner was raised in a musical family. His father, a Lebanese immigrant who sold women's clothing and later cattle in Orós, would sing songs from Lebanon at home (see Rogério 2008). But when he was young, Fagner's favorite singer was Luiz Gonzaga. "In the *sertão*," he said, "there used to be lots of *baião*, lots of Luiz Gonzaga. . . . That's what we heard. He was very much the voice of the northeastern people."[16] Fagner is often associated with Gonzaga. Fagner has described him as a close friend ("since Exu is so close to Orós") and a father figure.[17] The two men performed together once in Orós, and Fagner has recorded many of Gonzaga's songs. Fagner said, "I think I still carry a little of [Gonzaga's influence in my music], despite not playing the accordion. . . . But people always relate me to him, they connect me a lot with him."[18]

Despite his efforts to avoid being pigeonholed as a regional musician, Fagner has consistently made references to Orós, the *sertão*, and water throughout his work.[19] In 1968, then only eighteen years old, he competed in a music festival in Fortaleza's Theatro José de Alencar (see Castro [2016] on Ceará's song festivals in the 1960s). He came in first place, beginning his career as a musician (Castro 2008). His winning song, "Nada sou" (I am nothing), which he cowrote with Marcus Francisco and never recorded, began, "I am nothing / I'm a scuffle hoe in the clay of the ground / I'm the *sertão*." In 1977 Fagner released an album called *Orós*, its cover showing him bathing in the reservoir, his long, wet hair obscuring his face. The album features jazzy avant-garde arrangements by Brazilian composer Hermeto Pascoal, and the title track includes the sound of gurgling and howling, rich harmonies, and a *forró* triangle. The third song from the album's A side, "Esquecimento" (Oblivion), cowritten by Brandão, opens with violins playing an undulating pattern, imitating the sounds of flowing water, underscoring a simpler accordion line. Fagner then sings:

Love never fit me
but it always overflowed.

The river of memories that one day drowned me.
And in this current
I stayed to navigate.

The references to water in the violin arrangement, the lyrics, and the cover art are not trivial; water is meaningful and noteworthy in a land characterized by drought.
In the 1982 song "Orós II," composed by João do Vale and Oséas Lopes, Fagner sings:

Don't just speak of drought.
There's not only drought in the *sertão*.
My world almost ended
When Orós flooded.
If it [the dam] snaps, it kills
Everything that we planted.

In his song "Cariribe," from the 1991 album *Bateu saudade*, his lyrics directly recall the hunger, the drought, and the machismo of the *sertão*, referencing his roots in Orós:

I'm from the Cariri *sertão*
I'm from the *sertão* of Orós

. . . .

I'm the cicada and the ant
The drought and the flood.

When Fagner sings the names of familiar places (e.g., Orós, Mucuripe, the *sertão*), he evokes emotions and memories associated with those places. For a national audience, a reference to Orós could conjure images of drought, migration, hunger, perseverance, and perhaps its reservoir. The city serves as a symbol of the Northeast itself. Fagner was promoted with these associations in mind. The concert program notes for a show at the Teatro Tereza Rachel, a now-defunct theater in Rio de Janeiro, at the time of the 1977 release of the album *Orós*, compared Fagner, his music, and the geography of Orós:

Now we are in Orós. Not the disc, but the town of Orós. And the sun already rises, stinging the skin. Those who awoke at dawn saw the big, wild rats called possums entering the yard and eating the growth.
For the Indians who lived in Ceará before white colonization, Orós meant "rare stone." Today, Orós signifies stinging, vast sun, and the continuous work of the men who have already grown accustomed to living between suffering

and music, between the ground that has a surface cracked by the sun and a soft landscape with a reservoir that alleviates the drought but that one day broke its barriers and flowed out, killing and destroying everything in its path. Orós also signifies the pain of the possums. Not the pain of the rats, but the pain of the human possums, who were thus nicknamed because of the subhuman level of life to which they are submitted on the occasion of drought. It was the possums who constructed the dam of Orós. When the dam broke, it was the possums who died. . . .

Orós also signifies this rare stone exposed on the stage of Teatro Tereza Rachel. Orós is the new music of Raimundo Fagner.[20]

The program notes romantically depict Orós as a drought-ridden backwater characterized by hardworking men and a reservoir that is both an oasis and a source of suffering. The description may be specific to Orós, but in many ways it is typical of Brazilian portrayals of the *sertão*, including those of Luiz Gonzaga.

Fagner's allusions to the Northeast are, above all else, nostalgic. "I bring the past into the present," Fagner said. "People are without a present. . . . People are without identity. Everyone is really connected with the same thing of consumerism, of whatever, and I think that this is my passion for music, for poetry, for artistic results."[21] From the popularization of the fox-trot in the 1920s and 1930s through the development in the 1960s of the *jovem guarda* (young guard), which translated American and British pop songs and styles into lyrics and sounds tailored for an adolescent Brazilian audience, intellectuals and artists in Brazil have criticized global commercial musics and their local derivations as threats to music, even to hybrid genres more firmly grounded in national identity. Contemporary genres like electronic *forró*, with sounds and market strategies drawn from other Latin American and North American trends, sustain their bottom lines with planned obsolescence rather than enduring, classic compositions. Kathleen Stewart writes that nostalgia "shatters the surface of an atemporal order and a prefab cultural landscape" (1988, 227). Fagner's desire is that his hybrid nostalgic music, which at times resurrects a particular vision of the Northeast, breaks through the veneer of fungible pop music that he believes to be rooted in neither place nor history.[22]

Fagner's Impact on the Orós Soundscape

Fagner's Social Responsibility to Orós and the *Sertão*

Fagner has long been committed to the social needs of the Northeast. In 1985, the same year as Live Aid and the release of USA for Africa's "We Are the World" and the year following the release of "Do They Know It's Christmas?,"

155 Brazilian musicians came together to record *Nordeste já* (Northeast now), a vinyl EP intended to raise money for victims of drought in the Northeast. Many of Brazil's biggest stars of the second half of the twentieth century, including Gilberto Gil, Caetano Veloso, Maria Bethânia, Tom Jobim, Chico Buarque, Roberto Carlos, and Luiz Gonzaga, gathered in a studio in Rio de Janeiro over three days to support the region that had suffered during the previous five years from alternating droughts and floods. Fagner was involved with the project from the beginning, and he held some of the rehearsals at his home. The single, which was expected to sell a million copies, was mailed to radio stations around Brazil. The cast also filmed music videos for both songs. The clips were similar in style to the video for "We Are the World," with singers soloing emotionally into a studio microphone and swaying together as a chorus during the refrain.

The EP's A side was a song called "Chega de mágoa" (No more grief), composed by Gilberto Gil, with additional lyrics by musicians involved in the album. Fagner sings the last line, "chega de mágoa / chega de tanto penar" (no more grief / no more suffering), before the chorus of celebrities joins in, echoing Fagner. Fagner requested the lyrics for the B-side track from Patativa do Assaré, Ceará's most respected folk poet: "At the time in which we made that song for *Nordeste já*, "Chega de mágoa" [no more grief], which in Ceará they jokingly called "Chega de água" [no more water], and I called Patativa and I said, 'Patativa, I want your lyrics speaking about this moment for our people, about the drought, about the floods, and all of that sort of thing.' And the next day he called me, and I was impressed, because he passed the song over the phone to me, and I copied it down" (2003, 43).

Several musicians involved in *Nordeste já* collaborated to set Patativa do Assaré's lyrics to a *forró* rhythm, resulting in the song "Seca d'água." In Fagner's brief duet in the song with Elba Ramalho, the two perform the chorus in two-part harmony, singing, "Drought without rain is bad, / but an endless rainy season is worse."[23] The song ends with a coda: the descending, alternating melodic accordion motif from "Asa branca."

On his website Fagner explains that he was disappointed with the results of the project.[24] Few radio stations played "Chega de mágoa," which was intended to be a national radio hit, and the musicians never achieved their goal of selling a million copies. On the site Fagner laid the blame on radio broadcasters. In my interview with him, he remembered the project differently, saying it achieved its goal: to raise awareness about drought and suffering in the Northeast. He also contended that the similarities to "We Are the World" were merely coincidental.

In 1984 Fagner and Luiz Gonzaga performed a benefit concert in Natal, the capital of Rio Grande do Norte, for victims of drought in the Northeast. The two sang "Súplica cearense" (Cearense supplicant), a song in which a rural worker begs God for forgiveness, shouldering responsibility for floods in Ceará because he prayed for rain excessively.[25] In an interview Fagner said: "We had one of the most incredible moments of all my life on an occasion in which we were singing for drought—to end the drought—for those afflicted by drought, in Rio Grande do Norte, in Natal, in a football stadium. It had been three years since it last rained, and at the moment we began to sing 'Súplica cearense,' it started to rain, with the multitude of approximately fifty thousand people crying" (2003, 57).

In 2000 Fagner inaugurated the Raimundo Fagner Foundation (Fundação Raimundo Fagner) in Orós.[26] The foundation is a nonprofit organization that teaches music, theater, visual arts, and sports and offers after-school tutoring to at-risk youth. The organization, now headquartered in Fortaleza, has won awards from groups associated with UNESCO and UNICEF and from several Brazilian and Cearense organizations.

The Reception of Fagner in Orós

For those who live in Orós, Fagner's efforts to advertise his personal connection to the city and the *sertão* on the national stage are an affirmation of the city's significance. People in Orós hear the nationally targeted music of the "northeastern boom" in particularly local ways. "Unlike other musicians from the interior," said Janett Lima Silvers (my sister-in-law and Orós native), "Fagner always publicly announced his love for his hometown on national television and radio." On prime-time variety shows and late-night talk shows, Fagner often mentioned his friends in Orós by name and talked about the city, the reservoir, and the *sertão*. In an appearance on a national TV comedy program from the early 1990s, a famous comedian named Chico Anysio, also born in Ceará, asked Fagner where he was from in Ceará. "I'm from Maranguape," Fagner said, referring to Anysio's hometown, a city in the Fortaleza metropolitan area. The comedian responded, joking, "You're from Maranguape. I'm from Orós." The audience erupted in laughter, and the comedian continued, "I was born in Orós because there wasn't a worse place to be born."[27] Fagner's fame brought Orós to a national stage. His reception in Orós and personal involvement with the city, on the other hand, has made his national sound locally meaningful. What is heard as a musical representation of nostalgic rurality to a southeastern urban audience is a representation of the self to those from the city.

Today, Fagner lives predominantly between apartments in Rio de Janeiro and Fortaleza, but he also owns a home on an island in the middle of the Orós reservoir and another on the top of a hill in the city, along with, I believe, one or two other homes elsewhere.[28] He is a source of local mythology. Rumors of sightings with other Brazilian celebrities, such as television icon Xuxa, are commonplace. In the past, Fagner would walk around Orós barefoot and shirtless, drinking beer with friends at local bars and chatting with people in the streets. His extended family in Orós is large, and he still has friends in the city. When he visits, he often plays soccer. On some occasions, he closes the local community center and invites friends on an exclusive guest list to party with him. Once, he paid for a new pool table at Chico Pinto's bar, where he has brought some of his celebrity friends to drink.[29] Many people in Orós consider him a friend and say, "We drink beer with him" when he visits, and they downplay his difference by saying, "He's just another person from Orós."

In January 2012 Fagner returned to Orós for a tennis tournament he organized at his foundation. With nearly 150 people from town, I pressed my face against the net surrounding his clay court to watch him play the final doubles match. His partner, a young, fit athlete, helped lead him to victory over two heavy-set, gray-haired opponents. Everyone listened intently as the ball thwacked off the red earth and against rackets, the sound accompanied by whispers and the amplified voice of the referee who called out the score. The match was faintly backgrounded by Catholic hymns from a nearby church. At one point, a harsh grinding noise—I was told it was a water pump—interrupted the game. With one hand Fagner held his racket, and with another he angrily and swiftly pointed toward the source of the sound. Someone scurried up the hill and into the street, and the grinding abruptly ceased. After the game, people ran to pose for photos with the star. While he showered, they snapped images of themselves with the racket he left on a table near the bathroom. "For Orós," Janett said, "he is a god. Orós doesn't exist without Fagner. And Fagner wouldn't exist without Orós."

"We live under his influence," said Janett. "Everyone has posters in their houses. You hear his music at parties, in stores." A tire repair shop displays a large poster of Fagner next to a poster of a girl in a bikini on a motorcycle. A barbecue restaurant in the square has two posters on its wall, one of the reservoir's spillway and one of Fagner. A local woman has hung photos of herself as a child posing with Fagner on her wall among family portraits; in permanent marker, his signature and a personal note decorate an adjacent wall.

Fagner's music is integral to the sound of Orós both because it imagines the city and because it is played there. One evening, a series of Fagner concert DVDs played on a loop on a small television in a restaurant facing the reservoir. A bar in the town's hills played a video of one of the concerts late into the night, the sound of the music spilling into the street. A restaurant on the main street played his music in the morning as the owner swept the floor. A local man has a reputation for performing impersonations of Fagner, and he is said to sing and play with an uncanny resemblance to the star.

In the past, Fagner has exerted political influence in Orós, specifically in terms of his support for the Batista family, one of the city's major political families. Fagner grew up as a close personal friend of theirs. His father's first wife was a Batista, and Fagner once had plans to marry someone from the family. The night before Election Day in a year in which Eliseu Batista ran for mayor, Fagner gave a free concert in Orós. Regarding Fagner's involvement in state politics, Wellington Batista said, "The paving of the road that provides access to the reservoir . . . was done quickly thanks to his request [to the Ceará state government]."[30] Eliseu Batista said, "When things get tough, we call him: 'Raimundo, let's go to the governor.' And then everything works out."[31]

Today, Fagner avoids visiting the city center. Too many people asked for money, help, or an impromptu concert, and he grew weary of the responsibility. When he was out at night, locals used to offer to sing his own songs to him. Now he prohibits the live performance of his music in his vicinity. Bar owner Chico Pinto said, "If someone takes out a guitar, he doesn't like to hear his own songs. I think he's gotten sick of it."[32] Lately, Fagner has been reluctant to spend long periods of time in Orós. According to local gossip—no news sources seem to have reported on this, but Fagner alluded to it in our interview—he was the victim of a major theft perpetrated by someone in Orós, possibly a family member. Fagner had to start touring again. The situation highlights Fagner's insider/outsider status in Orós, where he is simultaneously seen as an abstract icon, a financial provider, and kin.

Orós FM: The Sound of the Waters

Although Fagner loves and is beloved in Orós, his taste and power, which are consequences of his artistry, wealth, cosmopolitanism, legend, and political leverage, have clashed on occasion with the local soundscape. His musical preferences are those of an experienced, successful, and cosmopolitan musician. His aural preferences are those of the wealthy and urban. And his sway in Orós is considerable. As a result, Fagner's seemingly insignificant musical hobbies and auditory concerns have had the potential to transform the sound of Orós in meaningful, lasting ways.

In March 1992, following the suggestion of a friend in Brasília, Fagner converted a small room off the foyer of his hilltop home in Orós into a radio station he called Orós FM, "O som das águas," the "sound of the waters." The radio,

now self-sustaining through advertising, was initially created by Fagner as a hobby. He told me:

> The radio is something that I have, but I don't participate in it. I made it more for pleasure.... It was something that happened without me having committed much.... So since I don't live there, at first I was still interfering, I was doing the programming, because at the time I got the radio I had more than fifteen thousand CDs, I produced a lot of CDs, and I was inside the labels, and I received the recordings from all the labels, so I had lots of discs. And one of the things that made me have the radio was the possibility of using those discs. So at the start of the radio, I was really in love. I kept doing the programming in my own way, for my own taste. And it wasn't, that is, a region where there's another kind of audience, an audience from the real *sertão*, so I no longer participate. I don't see what the programming is, programming directed at that kind of listener from the interior of the *sertão*.[33]

Fagner opened his radio station, which people in Orós often call "Fagner's radio," as a mere diversion and as a use for his growing CD collection. He realized, however, that people in Orós were actually listening, that his radio station had an impact and an audience, and that his own aesthetic preferences were unlike theirs. He handed the radio's programming over to its staff—in 2012 it employed two workers and two interns—who could better program music for "an audience from the real *sertão*." Despite Fagner's claims to the Brazilian public that he is an "Orós native from the heart," his experience of the world and his tastes share little in common with those of his fans and his radio listenership in Orós. Today, the radio station's programming is a mix of electronic *forró* (including *forró* covers of older American and British successes: its rotation in 2012 included a *forró* version of Foreigner's 1984 "I Want to Know What Love Is," which had recently been repopularized by Mariah Carey), *brega, música sertaneja,* and mainstream Brazilian and international radio hits, including Ivete Sangalo, Justin Bieber, and Rihanna.[34] Part of each day's programming on Orós FM also comes directly from a major radio station in Fortaleza.

Around the time Fagner opened his radio station, he is rumored to have taken a public stand against Dantas's *radiadora*.[35] The noise, it is said, bothered him, and he made his displeasure known. The majority of Orós sits on two facing hills, and the principal street runs through the valley between. Fagner's home sits at the apex of one hill, and the broadcast tower above Dantas's home sits high on the other (see illustration 1). Fagner complained that the sound traveled directly into his second-story bedroom window. He felt so inconve-

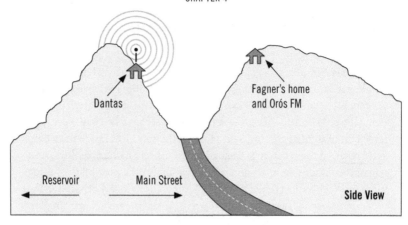

ILLUSTRATION 1. Dantas broadcasting to Fagner in Orós, side illustration. Not to scale.

nienced by having his sleep disrupted early each morning that on three occasions he sent a police officer to order Dantas to stop his morning broadcasts. Fagner's actions temporarily silenced the local announcer.

To Fagner, the sound of the *radiadora* is noise—unwanted sound. To the people of Orós, it is a useful and meaningful soundmark. Fagner, whose habitus includes the proclivities and behaviors of the Brazilian "class A," its wealthiest social class (especially in terms of how he conceives privacy and hears sound), was at odds with a city that values and appreciates its "musical alarm clock," which many people in Orós describe as a "public service" and understand as both practically and symbolically important.

The residents of Orós—a church group, members of the Orós Social Center, and others—came together in protest and signed a letter requesting that Dantas be allowed to resume his 6:00 a.m. announcements. Regina Dantas, who periodically substitutes for her father, estimates that they collected one thousand signatures in her father's support. They brought the letter to a local judge, who granted permission for Dantas to resume his broadcasts. Fagner has now constructed walls and windows that block out the sound, and Regina claims that residents today "believe in the *radiadora* more than the radio." When Dantas begins his announcements, people turn off their radios to hear what he has to say.

Regarding those who oppose his *radiadora*, Dantas said, "There are many ignorant imbeciles who ignore my work for reasons having to do with the sound bothering them, that this and that and thus and such, but in any case, I think the following: When these people have this criticism against me, this is what I say: God already gave you twice what I have ever expected in life."[36]

The Real *Sertão* from the Heart

Fagner's music envisioned an Orós that articulated with an ongoing national dialogue about drought and the northeastern region. In an era in which fusion and regional identification were mainstream in Brazilian popular music, Fagner's allusions to the small city, water, and northeastern music gave him, like the other Pessoal do Ceará, a unique voice in a national milieu. He also understood his music and his nostalgic Orós as antidotes to widespread consumerism in Brazilian music that valorized sameness over artistic quality and difference.

Fagner, though, has long related to Orós and the Northeast as more than expedient symbols of authenticity and nostalgia. He participated in projects that raised awareness about drought in critical moments, such as *Nordeste já* and his performance with Luiz Gonzaga in Rio Grande do Norte. He created a successful nonprofit organization for underprivileged northeastern youth. And he has remained involved with local politics in Orós, helping elected officials with various projects. His affection for his friends and family in Orós, like the townspeople's affection for him, is sincere, while their adoration of him, by gathering to watch him play tennis, hanging posters and paintings of him on walls, and playing his music as a soundtrack to ordinary afternoons, holds him aloft.

Despite his involvement, Fagner—the man, not the legend—is in some ways distanced from the aesthetic and aural subjectivities of Orós, and his disproportionate authority can turn fleeting hobbies and minor annoyances into powerful restructurings of local sound and senses of time and place. His desire for quiet as a vacationer was at odds with the meaningful sounds of Dantas's *radiadora*, which marks time each morning and afternoon, sanctifies the place and certain times with "Ave Maria," and articulates notions of work and community. And he relinquished the programming of his radio station, which was initially little more than a fun way to make use of giveaway CDs from record labels, because people "from the real *sertão*" were listening.

The "real *sertão*" and Fagner's imagined one align on a large scale through the images and consequences of drought, the needs of *sertanejos* as a general population, and a pride in the northeastern backlands as a subordinate place in the Brazilian cultural imaginary. On a small scale, however, the "real *sertão*," itself an imaginary, is a place in which the goods and desires of global capitalism (including American pop music and commercial *forró*) come into contact with the exigencies of a small city in which everyone knows practically everyone else; where a reservoir is a driver of economic activity through pisciculture, regional tourism, and irrigation for agriculture; and where Catholicism is dominant, despite a recent surge in Evangelicalism. Local audio technologies, like the *radiadora* and mobile sound systems, fill the city's soundscape with the meanings inherent to its economic and cultural context. The intersection of these quotidian sounds and values with Fagner's mediated northeastern imaginary permits him, with his multiple homes around Brazil, extensive world travel, and substantial fame, to be an "Orós native from the heart" without ever being "from the real *sertão.*"

CHAPTER 5

Real or Plastic *Forró*

Soundscapes of a Changing Economy

AS TOURISTS EXITED the baggage claim at Fortaleza's Pinto Martins International Airport in June 2008, they encountered a *forró* trio and a pair of professional dancers. The performers were there as part of the Ceará Secretariat of Tourism's efforts to promote seasonal tourism. Dressed in stylized St. John's Day costumes, with large patches shaped like palm trees, radiant suns, and *jangada* sailing rafts rather than the standard plaid patches that mock rurality, the dancers welcomed visitors to a paradoxical Fortaleza, a coastal paradise characterized by the dances and sounds of the northeastern backlands. The trio, each musician wearing jeans and a carnauba straw hat, played Luiz Gonzaga's "Olha pro céu" (Look to the sky), a classic song of the June festivals that describes a romantic encounter and the beauty of the colorful paper hot air balloons that light up the St. John's Day night sky in the backlands. Someone nearby handed out hats (the same ones worn by the musicians) that had stickers on them that read "Ceará: Terra da luz" (Ceará: Land of light).

Between 2000 and 2013 tourism to Fortaleza more than doubled—from about 1.5 million visitors per year to over 3.14 million.[1] Brazilians account for a majority of these tourists, averaging a little above 90 percent of the visitors to the coastal metropolis over this thirteen-year span.[2] Brazilians travel to Fortaleza primarily to enjoy Ceará's famous beaches and to encounter typical northeastern culture. In roughly that same period—the years surrounding the turn of the twenty-first century—the Brazilian federal government, along with the Ceará state government, expanded cultural policy and the public support of traditional culture. New programs emerged to pay salaries to "masters of culture" (*mestres de cultura*) who continue to practice *reisado*, sing *cantoria*, craft *rabeca* fiddles, and possess knowledge about folk medicine. Other programs offered grants to help musicians produce albums, put on shows, and host workshops, paid for primarily through the federal Rouanet Law and Ceará's Jereissati Law, both of which gave tax incentives (mostly to businesses, but also to individuals in the case of the Rouanet Law) for supporting expressive culture. Community centers were built, the creative economy was stimulated, and locally and nationally significant practices were recognized and funded.

This same period was also marked by a notable decrease in extreme poverty and an expanding middle class with increased access to consumer credit and interest-free payment plans. Between 2003 and 2013 some twenty-six million Brazilians were lifted out of poverty, leaving only 7.4 percent of the nation below the poverty line in 2014.[3] In Ceará between 2002 and 2012 the poverty rate (the percentage of the population with an income below R$140 per capita per month, approximately US$75 in January 2012) dropped from 48 percent to 21.3 percent, a 55.6 percent decrease (IPECE 2014). The rate of extreme poverty, defined here as an income of R$70 or less per month (approximately US$38 in January 2012), dropped in Ceará from 19.8 percent of the population to 8.5 percent. Between 2006 and 2014 cellphone subscriptions jumped from approximately one subscription for every two people to nearly 1.4 cellphone plans per capita, an indication of expanding consumption and access to modern communications technology.[4] In Ceará these structural changes, aided by state-paid pensions for aging drought victims and conditional cash transfers to the poor that required children to attend school and get vaccinated via President Lula's Bolsa Familia program, assuaged the consequences of drought and left fewer people vulnerable.

The everyday music of Ceará changed as the realities of its population changed. In the years following redemocratization in the 1980s and 1990s, new, highly profitable electronic and electrified regional dance genres arose around Brazil (see De Marchi [2015] on the rise of independent record companies for niche Brazilian markets in the 1990s). Bahia saw the explosion of *axé* music. Pará, a northern state at the mouth of the Amazon River, became home to *tecnobrega*. Rio de Janeiro saw the emergence of *funk carioca*. And Ceará introduced its people to *oxente* music, a term that was quickly forgotten in favor of the more general *forró*, which some refer to as electronic *forró* and others call stylized *forró*, but most everyone else calls just *forró*. As Ceará's middle class grew, so too did its taste for this dance music. Through the first decade of the twenty-first century, electronic *forró*'s popularity and presence never waned. On the contrary, it replaced foothills *forró*'s position as the prime local genre.

I argue that the same leftist government that brought people out of poverty also increased access and recognition to traditional music and cultural expression more generally. Yet members of the new middle class were less interested in government-aided cultural expression than in the trappings of the consumer class. Did their desires undermine the efforts of the cultural policy of the same period? How do you protect traditional music not just from indifference or irrelevance but also from the profound dominance of commercial music in a moment of an expanding consumer class?

Most scholars no longer promote the kind of preservationist heritage management that was once prevalent in academic and applied settings, in which musical culture was regarded as a set of objects (songs, instruments, dances, techniques, and the like) to be maintained. Under the rubric of musical (or cultural) sustainability, several ethnomusicologists have argued that music exists in a multilayered musical and cultural ecosystem that has many properties in common with—and in fact may be part of—biological ecosystems (e.g., Titon 2009; Schippers 2010; Grant 2016; Lühning 2013). This idea resonates with emergent discussions from posthumanism and object-oriented ontologies and more straightforwardly refashions a functionalist understanding of music's place in society. The applied method that follows from this theory is that music cultures, especially those that are significant to history, senses of identity, and communities, can be sustained following models of ecological sustainability (to varying degrees) (Grant 2016; Schippers 2010; Titon 2009).

Foothills *forró*, which is significant to Ceará's history, identity, and community, is perceived by many musicians and cultural activists as endangered. A key threat, they argue, is electronic *forró*, a genre that is inherently commercial and mainstream. During the era discussed in this chapter, some elements of Brazilian cultural policy—based on my observations—exemplified the ecological premise of cultural sustainability.[5] The Brazilian government created a network of programs that funded and promoted music and art as dynamic and interrelated elements of the economy and Brazilian society more generally. Programs supported practitioners of rural traditional culture alongside urban popular musicians, and they encouraged music and expressive culture as practices rather than artifacts.

In this chapter, the case of *forró* in Ceará illustrates that cultural policy nevertheless came up against the economic and political realities in which the policy was crafted and in which it operated. Daniel Sharp (2014), who conducted an ethnographic study of a traditional northeastern music ensemble in the interior of Pernambuco and a cosmopolitan urban band whose members were originally from the same small city and remained (musically, professionally, and semiotically) connected to the traditional ensemble, arrived at the same conclusion. Sharp argues that cultural *resgate* (rescue) in northeastern Brazil in the early twenty-first century is not a free-floating ideal but a fraught endeavor tied to changing and unequal definitions of citizenship developed through the process of redemocratization in the postauthoritarian era and wedded to the demands of cultural tourism, which has been inspired by mass-mediated music that romanticizes the interior of the Northeast.

Foothills and electronic *forró* are both elements of the same local musical ecology, and discourses and practices surrounding the sustaining of traditional *forró* have frequently involved electronic *forró*. This music ecology has a range of elements and variables, some abstract, some concrete: images of the backlands as memory, identity, and home; an understanding of the government as a key source of support for the arts; a legacy of political corruption; a history of drought; expanding consumer capitalism; the practices, values, and products of cosmopolitanism; tourism and the tourist economy; the political and social outcomes of the Workers' Party administration under Presidents Lula and Rousseff; and northeastern timbral aesthetics (the accordion, the *forró* triangle) and dance rhythms (xote, *forró*), among other things.

Electronic *forró* towers over foothills *forró*, which remains a neotraditional genre meaningful as a symbol of the Northeast and local identity. The drought protests of Luiz Gonzaga and the *forró* era are no longer relevant in the same ways they once were. With its nostalgic representation of the backlands and the rhythms of bygone rural lifeways (by 2013, 73 percent of Ceará's population lived in urban areas),[6] foothills *forró* stood poised as the sound par excellence of Cearense cultural heritage, ideal for festivals that celebrate the northeastern backlands, such as St. John's Day, and for cultural tourism, which benefits from locally iconic sounds.

At the same time, foothills *forró* found itself in need of support from the local tourist economy and from cultural policy intended to prop up fading practices associated with local heritage. The Jereissati Law, introduced into Cearense law in 1995 (and repealed in 2006, but still partially in effect through some of its corollary programs), was intended "for the encouragement and financing of cultural activities traditionally not absorbed by the formal market." Although foothills *forró* was originally a commercial genre, its transformation into folklore has made it dependent—if not entirely, then at least partially— upon such public sources. Yet as the neotraditional subgenre found access to state support via contracts to perform at St. John's Day festivals, among other public contexts and means, so too did electronic *forró*, which policymakers and cultural event producers came to understand as a surefire way to draw big (and satisfied) crowds.

Traditionalists, cultural activists, and foothills *forró* musicians alike recoil at this reality. For many, the concern is not only about representation and authenticity but also about morality. Ethnomusicologist Felipe Trotta (2009) draws such a distinction between the two subgenres, describing foothills *forró* as primarily about the *sertão* and electronic *forró* as about partying and sex, suggesting that one is wholesome, while the other is "malicious" because it debases northeastern values. He cites a blogger who, referring to electronic *forró*, writes, "I want my *sertão* back" (Trotta 2009, 12). Others have noted a correlation between *forró* and international sex tourism (e.g., Lamen 2014). The characterization of certain musical genres, often those correlated with lower-class audiences, as immoral is one of the perennial narratives of popular music.

In Ceará I have heard many middle- and upper-class individuals speak of electronic *forró* in a similar moralizing fashion, echoing critiques made by the Brazilian elite against working-class genres in the twentieth century (see P. Araújo 2002; S. Araújo 1988). They understand electronic *forró* as a direct threat to foothills *forró* in terms of radio airplay, presence at local celebrations, and commercial success. I should note, however, that the association between these subgenres and types of people is hardly straightforward. There are professional musicians who play both electronic and foothills *forró*, there are musicians who play one but appreciate the other, and there is occasional overlap between the two in terms of repertoire and performance venues and contexts. Both genres, as I have said, typify the St. John's Day seasonal soundscape in Ceará. Foothills *forró* is often associated with the middle-aged and elderly, and electronic *forró* is generally associated with youth. Electronic *forró* fans tend to be of the lower middle and lower classes. Yet there are fans of electronic *forró* who also enjoy foothills *forró*. Foothills *forró* is popular among young intellectuals in Fortaleza, and there are many middle- and upper-class individuals in Fortaleza—some of whom are in their thirties and forties—who listen and dance to electronic *forró*.

In this chapter, I first discuss the history and context of the electronic *forró* industry in Ceará. Then, I explore the foothills *forró* scene in Fortaleza and examine the concerns of foothills *forró* musicians in relation to electronic *forró*. Last, I discuss cultural policy as it relates to sound and *forró* in Fortaleza.

The Emergence of Electronic *Forró*

Since the era of Luiz Gonzaga, *forró* has changed substantially with the incorporation of electronic instruments and drum sets, *lambada*-influenced dances, and quicker tempos. The history of the incorporation of electronic instrumentation and rock and pop hybridity into *forró*, however, is nuanced.

Luiz Gonzaga himself performed electrified, amplified *forró* in 1972—released on CD in 2001—in the Teatro Tereza Rachel in Rio de Janeiro, with an electric guitar and an electric bass in his band. As previously discussed, Gonzaga and his oeuvre were experiencing a national resurgence in popularity at that time due to the incorporation of *baião* into Tropicália. And although Gonzaga's national reputation had waned in the 1960s, his northeastern fans continued to celebrate him as their aging, symbolic "King of Baião" throughout the remainder of his life. That he included electronic instruments in his later performances seemed of little importance to his fans, and other *forró* and *baião* musicians, including João do Vale and Marinês, incorporated electronic instruments as well.

Other musicians throughout the 1960s, 1970s, and 1980s—including the pop rock *jovem guarda* (young guard), the Pessoal do Ceará (Folks from Ceará), and the Tropicalistas—updated the *forró* sound with rock instrumentation, contemporary lyrics, and blues- and MPB-influenced vocal techniques. *Jovem guarda* pop singer Sylvinha recorded a cover of Luiz Gonzaga's "Paraíba" in 1971, with guttural, wailed vocals and distorted rock and roll electric guitar, leading one music journalist to call her the Brazilian Janis Joplin.[7] Her husband, *jovem guarda* pop singer Eduardo Araújo, recorded Gonzaga's canonical "Juazeiro" that same year in a similar style, singing "Juazeiro, yeah, yeah, yeah!" each refrain. Other musicians, such as Elba Ramalho (who is sometimes known as the "Queen of *Forró*"), Alceu Valença, Geraldo Azevedo, and Fagner, made *forró* rock popular for new audiences through recordings, televised song festivals, touring, and the radio throughout the 1970s and 1980s.

Northeastern audiences that continued to enjoy *forró* as dance music, however, heard *forró*-influenced MPB and rock—sometimes referred to as *forrock*—as something other than *forró* itself. Still, *forró* as dance music increasingly incorporated rock and pop instrumentation and vocal styles. For example, a Cearense singer named Eliane, who, like Elba Ramalho, refers to herself as the "Queen of *Forró*," released her first album, a four-track EP called *Brilho das estrelas* (Starshine), in 1983. (She was fifteen years old at the time.) The title track, a love song, features a Moog synthesizer sustaining notes throughout the recording. Another song, "Amor pra mim" (Love for me), in the *arrasta pé* rhythm, includes both an accordion and a saxophone.

It was in the last decade of the twentieth century that *forró* in Ceará underwent a vast and deliberate transformation. In Fortaleza in 1989 an entrepreneur named Emanuel Gurgel, a soccer referee and owner of a T-shirt manufacturing company, decided to change careers and enter the music business. He began by managing a *forró* band called Black Banda, a task that offered him insight into the music industry in Ceará. He noticed how dancers cleared the floor when musicians took breaks, and he heard party-goers complain that shows ended too early in the night.

He left his position with Black Banda and created his own *forró* band following his marketing insights. Gurgel auditioned musicians to craft his ideal, marketable ensembles, similar to the boy bands of the 1990s in the United States. His first dance band, Aquarius, played 50 percent *forró* and 50 percent other kinds of popular dance music. His second group, Mastruz com Leite, formed in 1991, was his first group to achieve real success. The name, which means Epazote (an herb) with Milk, refers to a common home remedy in the Northeast. Gurgel based the design of the band on his observations from working with the other bands: more *forró*, longer parties, and marketable sounds and lyrics. Mastruz com Leite, with three singers and eleven musicians by 1992, could play nonstop sets for five hours from 11:00 p.m. to 4:00 a.m. It had three drummers, two electric guitarists, two bass players, a saxophonist, and three accordionists, so individual musicians could take breaks while the band continued to play.[8] They played only *forró*, and within their first two years they had acquired a repertoire of approximately 350 songs, including the classic *forró* standards of the Gonzaga era, the contemporary hits of Eliane and others, and original songs. Gurgel established a recording studio, called SomZoom, and his business, including his bands, employed nearly two hundred workers by 1992. Gurgel's early empire comprised sound equipment, a sound system car, four tour buses, an audio engineer, and a small factory that produced T-shirts, signs, and posters. Each show employed approximately fifty individuals, including security guards, ticket salespeople, drivers, stage crew, sound and lighting crew, and musicians.[9]

By 1994 Gurgel had created seven bands, each with a distinct but not substantially different "personality."[10] By 1996 he had twenty-nine artists under SomZoom's management.[11] Today's *forró* bands trade some of their musicians and singers as if they were athletes on professional sports teams. A 1993 newspaper article from Fortaleza's *Jornal o Povo* describes the similarity between the groups: "The difference between the bands is small, almost imperceptible, only remaining in the principal voices and in the vocal part that shouts the names of the bands in the middle of the tracks."[12] To distinguish between the groups, Gurgel had his bands call out their names in the middle of songs during shows, allowing radio broadcasters to play the live recordings without needing to pause between songs to announce the band's name.

A copyright scandal in 2010 called the WikiLeaks of *Forró* revealed striking similarities between the sound, songs, and format of Cearense *forró* band Aviões do Forró (Airplanes of *forró*), which was the number one *forró* band at the time, and copycat competitors, also from Ceará, Garota Safada (Nasty Girl).[13] The two groups allegedly recorded the same song within twenty-four hours, initially failing to acknowledge the existing copyright of a musician from Pernambuco who was also accused of plagiarizing the song's refrain from a 2006 children's song. The scandal was revealed on an anonymous blog—hence the allusion to WikiLeaks—and the story was eventually picked up by the mainstream press, including Fortaleza's *Diário do Nordeste* and the nationally distributed *Revista Globo*. When asked about the scandal by *Revista Globo*, Neto Leite, vocalist for Mastruz com Leite, responded, "Everyone has the same voice, the same drive. Put it on to listen to, without seeing the images, bands a, b, c, d . . . you can't identify who's playing. They lack identity."[14] The WikiLeaks of *Forró* scandal illustrates the continued prevalence of Gurgel's format from the 1990s, now evident in bands managed by production companies Luan Produções and A3 Entretenimentos, which is currently the biggest *forró* management company.

Ethnomusicologist Nonato Cordeiro (2009) identifies six strategies underlying SomZoom's early business model: (1) the studio owned the copyright to its own compositions, and multiple bands recorded and performed the same songs, (2) all musicians earned fixed salaries, (3) the studio's arrangers wrote the arrangements for all groups, (4) it mass produced recordings, (5) its advertising was centralized, and (6) it distributed music nationally via the radio and television.

Although electronic *forró* is frequently described as having no musical resemblance to its traditional form, there are a number of evident musical transformations from traditional to electronic *forró*: electric guitars, which at times play rock solos, and the drum set accommodate the part of the triangle and *zabumba*; saxophones and synthesizers, along with accordions, play the traditional accordion lines; whereas foothills *forró* was sung in unison or in thirds, electronic *forró* involves backup singers who sing homophonic harmonies, creating a dense vocal texture; and traditional melodies, with short note values, short pauses between phrases, and meandering, modal melodic lines, gave way to longer note values, longer pauses between phrases, and a smaller melodic ambitus. Cordeiro (2009) also notes that while cover songs were uncommon in foothills *forró*—with the exception of musicians rerecording their own songs or other well-known *forró* hits—in electronic *forró* cover recordings of non-*forró* popular music are very common. Electronic *forró* also includes dance moves associated with *lambada*, which was popular in Brazil (and internationally) in the 1980s. Today's electronic *forró* includes horn sections, professional dancers who share the stage with musicians, and elaborate stage lighting and effects. Its studio recording aesthetic, as Felipe Trotta and Márcio Monteiro (2008) note, includes the use of reverb, compressors, and filters.

Gurgel's approach was not solely about updating *forró* music for a youth demographic that liked to dance until four in the morning but also about creating a music-based empire with business tie-ins and both vertical and horizontal integration. In the mid-1990s he controlled the majority of the *forró* industry in Ceará and around Brazil. Early on, Gurgel rented the venues in which his bands performed, so he earned revenue not only from ticket sales but from drinks, merchandise, and record sales. SomZoom's bands performed simultaneously in different venues, so the best options for his target demographic on any given night were all SomZoom-controlled bands and venues. Individual bands also performed in multiple venues in a single night. In 1993 Gurgel signed a ten-year lease for a radio station—FM Casablanca—to play SomZoom's recordings.[15]

Ultimately, Gurgel acquired his own venues, established a music publishing house, created his own speaker and amplifier factory, founded a production company that produced events and rodeos, and opened his own CD shops, including one in Fortaleza and one in São Paulo (Lima 2007).[16] In 1995 Gurgel, who in 1993 became president of Ceará Sporting Club, the organization behind the professional Ceará soccer team, sought corporate tie-ins linking soccer, Mastruz com Leite, and milk (to take advantage of the band's name), including the milk brands Leite Betânia and Parmalat. A 1995 sports editorial from *Jornal o Povo* quips, "Gurgel intends to utilize the brand of the group together with that of a sponsor. We can soon have on our black-and-white jerseys [the colors of the Ceará team] Mastruz com Leite Betânia, or even Mastruz com Parmalat."[17] Gurgel earned US$6 million in 1995 for SomZoom, in part due to promoting his bands and records on FM Casablanca in Fortaleza and on two radio stations he owned in the interior Cearense city of Sobral and another in beachside Canoa Quebrada.[18]

Gurgel also took a number of steps to market rurality as part of the SomZoom *forró* brand, even while rurality was not an explicit attribute of the lyrics or the music itself. In 1996, frustrated with payola—called *jabá*—he opened a satellite radio station, which he called SomZoom Sat. On the satellite radio, which is streamed and broadcast on local radio stations around Brazil and also accessible over the Internet, his announcers present in northeastern accents and promote SomZoom concerts throughout the nation. Musicians who are not affiliated with SomZoom but who wish to have their music played on the station are charged payola, either in cash or in unpaid performances. In 2001 SomZoom Sat broadcast twenty-four hours per day on ninety-eight stations in ninety-five cities in fifteen Brazilian states. Gurgel also founded the Mastruz com Leite Rodeo Circuit and created *Revista Conexão Vaquejada* (Rodeo connection magazine), which advertised the rodeo circuit, the SomZoom bands, the satellite radio station, and the rural lifestyle promoted through his company (Pedroza 2001). Throughout the year, electronic *forró* bands continue to play at crowded parties in the interior of Ceará, at times overtaking town squares or filling large outdoor *forró* venues that are generally little more than fields surrounded by cement walls with a stage in the back.

The electronic *forró* model has changed only slightly since the mid-1990s. Because of the prevalence of CD piracy in northeastern Brazil (see Bishop 2004; Dent 2012) and online file sharing, contemporary electronic *forró* bands now distribute CDs for free to those who attend shows, parties, and rodeos. In turn, fans play the recordings loudly on their car stereos as they drive through city streets, or they play them from parked cars and trucks on sound systems called *paredões de som* (singular, *paredão de som,* meaning "big wall of sound") built into trunks or truck beds or sometimes towed behind vehicles. The electronic *forró* practice in which musicians shout their band's name has expanded to include the shouted names of businesses and products. These "shout-outs" are called *alôs* (hellos), and companies will pay between R$500 and R$1,000 (approximately US$280 to US$565 in 2012) to have a band announce its name in the middle of a song during a live performance. Posters with the companies' names are placed on the floor of the stage or held by someone in front of the stage as reminders to the vocalists, who shout, "Alô," followed by the name; businesses can assume the performance will be recorded, distributed on CD or online for free, and then played loudly over sound systems at bars or parties or in neighborhood streets.

Hermano Vianna (2011) has observed that in the northern city of Manaus in the state of Amazonas, the poor buy pirated *forró* concert DVDs from street vendors. He suggests that they buy DVDs because televisions with embedded speakers and DVD players that can also play CDs are less expensive for lower-class consumers or bar owners than a "reasonably good sound system" (Vianna 2011, 245). However, I would suggest that this is interesting not just because it highlights the inexpensive cost of televisions versus sound systems but because it indicates the considerable growth of consumer spending among the middle and lower classes in Brazil, which are widely known as classes C, D, and E, categories established by the Brazilian Institute of Geography and Statistics (IGBE). In the latter years of Lula's presidency (which lasted from 2003 to 2011), many of these people were able to buy sound systems for their vehicles and flat-screen televisions, DVD players, and other electronics for their homes with consumer credit and increased disposable income. In 2010 class C (defined as those with a monthly household income between R$1,530 and R$5,100—approximately US$870 and US$2,900) spent R$864 billion (around US$490 billion) on consumer goods, nearly matching the consumer spending of the wealthy classes A and B combined.[19] Consumption among classes D and E grew 4.2 times between 2002 and 2010. The consumption of televisions, video players, and home sound systems by class C, called the "new middle class," accounted for 44 percent of domestic spending in Brazil in 2011.[20] With members of the new middle class, I have listened to, danced to, and sung along with recordings of electronic *forró*, either blaring from the back of a car or from a television, at pool parties, at bars and restaurants, in living rooms and on front porches, at a religious pilgrimage site, on street corners and in town squares, in markets, and in various other places where members of class C gather.

Contesting Electronic *Forró*

The electronic *forró* industry lies outside the mainstream Brazilian and multinational music industries and functions with its own set of rules and parameters, all guided by late capitalism and a contemporary northeastern subjectivity. Because of the prevalence—and acoustic volume—of mobile sound systems, the distribution of free CDs, and the dominance of local radio broadcasting, as well as the pervasiveness of payola, many musicians in Ceará see electronic *forró* as a threat to their livelihoods. Musician Orlângelo Leal, the lead singer of a regional rock band called Dona Zefinha, expressed to me his concern that his band was unable to afford distributing CDs for free at their shows, something that audiences had come to expect from electronic *forró*.

Much music in Fortaleza is seen in opposition to electronic *forró*; there is *forró*, and there is everything else. A T-shirt I found in the Galeria do Rock—a cluster of tattoo parlors, heavy metal–themed clothing stores, oral surgery clinics, and CD shops in the dark and hidden top three stories of a dilapidated shopping center in downtown Fortaleza—characterizes this dichotomy simply. It reads "*Forró* bad. Metal good" (see figure 9).

In my conversations with foothills *forró* musicians, electronic *forró* was a common topic. One foothills *forró* musician explained to me that there is not a fight between the two genres. Rather, because of the dominance of electronic *forró* in Fortaleza, foothills *forró* musicians must compete for resources and airwaves so the two can coexist. Foothills *forró* has a smaller audience and less control of the market than electronic *forró*, so musicians depend on cultural policy, seeking support from the government or other organizations by way

FIGURE 9. "*Forró* bad. Metal good."

of legislation, grants, and inclusion in civic festivals. Many locally produced recordings, for example, are paid for with competitive grants from a local, state, or federal source or from corporations that support the arts to receive tax benefits guaranteed by the Rouanet Law, which, according to the Brazilian Ministry of Culture, paid out over R$1 billion in 2015 (approximately US$250 million in 2015).

In early 2010 many of Fortaleza's more prominent foothills *forró* musicians came together to form the Cearense Association of *Forró* (ACF). By 2012 the organization included nearly four hundred musicians—accordionists, triangle players, *zabumba* players, and others—and between fifteen and forty musicians attended the group's weekly meetings, held at Kukukaya, a foothills *forró* venue decorated in the style of a mud-and-stick home from the *sertão*. The owner of Kukukaya, Walter Medeiros, was also the president of ACF at the time and presided over meetings. The organization existed to promote foothills *forró*; to identify and create new venues, spaces, and opportunities for the performance of foothills *forró*; to apply for grants; and to lobby for cultural policy that privileges traditional culture over commercial culture. The members of the association were careful to refrain from speaking out publicly against electronic *forró*.

Nevertheless, discussions at meetings often turned to the commercial genre, drawing a distinction between what they perceive as wholesome foothills *forró* and commercial, base electronic *forró*.

There were two lines of reasoning offered by members of ACF as to why foothills *forró* is "true" and "authentic" and why electronic *forró* is unworthy of being called *forró*. The first concerns the music. Accordionist Adelson Viana, who has accompanied Fagner, Dominguinhos, and others onstage in national tours and is one of Fortaleza's most respected foothills *forró* musicians, explained the difference:

> Electronic *forró*'s beat is something with less swing, based on the *vanerão*, a style from the South, by musicians who didn't have much lived experience with foothills *forró*. But it's a culture that's important, and I wish them success. We defend another kind of music, the true *forró*, because we consider that to be *forró*. It needs to have *zabumba*, accordion, and triangle as the basic elements, just like rock has electric guitar, bass, and drums. So we think these three elements can't be hidden, and in electronic *forró* we perceive that what appears most aren't these three elements but the production itself: the dancers, the drums, the horns. So it's a music with . . . more percussive elements. *Forró* isn't. It has the rhythm that's purer, truer, and these three elements are more evident. . . . In truth, I think this all descends from the *lambada*, and I think it shouldn't be called *forró*, because *forró* is something else.[21]

For Vianna, *forró* needs not just the typical rhythms, which are sometimes but not always part of electronic *forró*, but also the typical trio of accordion, triangle, and *zabumba*, which, he suggests, must not only be present but also be emphasized. When Vianna performs *forró* before audiences, he plays his accordion center stage, with a *zabumba* player to one side and a triangle player to the other. A drum set player, a bass player, and an electric guitarist perform behind them, obscured by the trio in front and by dimmer stage lighting.

The second argument against electronic *forró* concerns morality. In its lyrics, foothills *forró* describes the *sertão*, they say, whereas electronic *forró* emphasizes sex and partying. Vianna says, "Foothills *forró* talks about things that are more about the daily lives of our people."[22] Both *forrós* do talk about the conditions of life in the Northeast, but they talk about different conditions. Trotta and Monteiro (2008) believe that electronic *forró* owes its success to its "content," which they call the "trinomial party-love-sex," suggesting that the lyrical content enables and underlies the social context in which individuals hear the music. Indeed, contemporary electronic *forró* addresses sex, partying, and love far more frequently than drought, rurality, and bittersweet suffering, but it also addresses other topics. One popular contemporary band, for example, is called Calcinha Preta (Black Panties), and many of their more popular songs are love songs. A large number of the songs performed by electronic *forró* bands are covers of *música sertaneja* hits from central-southern Brazil or popular songs from the United States or Europe. Still, there are exceptions in which electronic *forró* bands discuss rural themes. Mastruz com Leite, notable for its closer connections to foothills *forró*, performed a song on their 1993 album *Coisa nossa* (Our thing) called "Raizes do Nordeste" (Roots of the Northeast), which describes a romantic *sertão* and mentions the song of the *sabiá* bird—the rufous-bellied thrush—and the strength and virtue of the northeastern worker:

> In my *sertão* there's a bit of everything good that you can imagine.
> It's got the bright sky up where the *sabiá* sings.
>
> There's goodness in the eyes of the working man
> Who wears a straw hat with humility, yes sir.

Many of Mastruz com Leite's songs have rural topics. Although their popularity peaked in the 1990s, they have remained famous as the first popular electronic *forró* band, they still tour, and many current groups still cover their songs.

More to the point, foothills *forró* also had sexual lyrics. Gonzaga's work (and the work of Jackson do Pandeiro, Dominguinhos, Trio Nordestino, and others) depicted sexuality much less explicitly than the *forró* of the turn of the twenty-first century, but the *forró* of the mid-twentieth century was dance music just as electronic *forró* is dance music, and it was also associated with drinking, dancing, and amorous and erotic encounters. Many of Gonzaga's best-known songs, especially those associated with St. John's Day, describe partying and dancing. The name of contemporary *forró* group Cheiro de Menina (Smell of Girl) has been cited to me as an example of the vulgarity of electronic *forró*. Juxtaposed with lyrics from Luiz Gonzaga's 1949 "Vem morena" (Come, dark-skinned girl), which he cowrote with Zé Dantas and is considered a classic, it is no more or less sexual:

> This, your salty sweat, smells nice and has a flavor,
> Since your sweaty body with its smell of flowers
> Has a seasoned taste of the flavor of love.

Cearense musician Messias Holanda (1942–2018), whose biggest *forró* hit was "Pra tirar coco" (To remove a coconut) in 1981, complained in January 2012, "Today they have forgotten the poetry of the music. They're demeaning to women. In my music I talk about *cachaça* [Brazilian rum] and women, but I tell stories without offending."[23] At an ACF meeting on June 8, 2010, one musician called electronic *forró* "vulgar" and claimed that the genre promotes prostitution and *cachaça*. He argued that the city government invites electronic *forró* musicians to perform at local events and on civic holidays because it is what the people want. Another musician agreed and said that the support offered by the government is misguided. If the mayor wants to give people what they really want, he joked, it would be cheaper to supply the population directly with *cachaça* and prostitutes and forget the electronic *forró*.

References to sex may be more explicit in electronic *forró* than in foothills *forró*, but I would argue that this is due to changes in sexual expression that have occurred in Brazil and elsewhere in the last half of the twentieth century and not to a cheapening or debasing of *forró* per se, as many scholars, intellectuals, and musicians contend. Furthermore, and contrary to what Trotta argues, the *sertão* remains equally relevant to both genres of *forró*. The difference lies in the relationship between audiences and the *sertão*. Early fans of foothills *forró* consumed the music because it constructed a *sertão* imaginary that reminded them of distant homes and the values and images they left behind before migrating to urban metropolises. Foothills *forró* concerns the *sertão* imaginary. Contemporary fans of foothills *forró* enjoy it as an expression of northeastern culture. Electronic *forró* fans—at least those in Ceará—live in cities and rural areas in the *sertão* or on the periphery of Fortaleza, and the music fills soundscapes, including kitchens, town squares, rodeos, and rural-themed venues like the Clube do Vaqueiro (Cowboy Club), on the outskirts of Fortaleza. Foothills *forró* depicts a nostalgic backlands landscape. Electronic *forró* fills today's backlands with sound.

Since 2010 a *forró* venue in the interior city of Russas, Ceará, has hosted an annual *forró* party called Tomara que Chova (I Hope It Rains). At the I Hope It Rains party in April 2011, partygoers were promised a free glass of wine if it rained the night of the event. The implication, of course, is that rain was unlikely. Drought, the *sertão*, and the importance of rain remain materially—if not semiotically—relevant to electronic *forró* and the dance and party culture associated with it.

The most significant distinction between the two *forrós* is the underlying financial structure of each. At ACF meetings in 2010, musicians expressed a sense of resentment about the government supporting electronic *forró* and musicians from outside the state. At the meeting on June 8, 2010, association members fretted about the image of St. John's Day propagated by the media and the city. The newspaper *Jornal o Povo* had run a series of articles celebrating the longevity of electronic *forró* in Ceará and the career of Emanuel Gurgel, and ACF musicians found the articles troubling: it was the St. John's Day holiday season, and electronic *forró* groups were performing at the major parties and stealing headlines in the paper. Messias Holanda mentioned that he was asked in an interview with *Jornal o Povo* about his feelings regarding electronic *forró*, and he told the newspaper that the biggest threat to foothills *forró* was not the large electronic *forró* bands but the small ones, because they tended to undercut foothills *forró* musicians. "Because they charge so little," he said, "they play lots of parties, which means that we have to go running after space.... Our money's been used up." At a meeting on June 25, 2010, the day after St. John's Day, a musician complained that a *música sertaneja* duo, Victor & Leo, originally from the southeastern state of Minas Gerais and based in São Paulo, was going to play a St. John's Day party the following night at the high-end Marina Park Hotel. "We should be supporting northeastern music," she said, "not music from the South during this festival, which is symbolic of the Northeast." A *sertaneja* duo, as opposed to a *forró* trio, represents the wrong Brazilian rurality for her, and St. John's Day is the most iconic rural northeastern holiday. Another musician lamented that a compilation *forró* CD produced in the northeastern state of Piauí selected a track from an electronic *forró* band, rather than a foothills *forró* band, to represent Ceará. Adelson Viana expressed his concerns to me:

> The municipality supports *forró* principally during this season [St. John's Day], but they could support it more. But there exist financial interests behind this: electronic *forró* aggregates, gathers, generates much more cash than foothills *forró*. This is because there are businesspeople behind it, behind all of the politics that make it happen, and this is important.... What is in the media the most is electronic *forró*, but that doesn't mean that there aren't groups and musicians who are preserving and sharing roots music. It's an issue of the scene.... If it were a little more balanced, divided, if there were space for both, it would be ideal.[24]

In the northeastern state of Paraíba, musician and state minister of culture Chico César found a solution for the imbalance of power between the two *forrós*. In April 2011 he announced that the state of Paraíba would only contract foothills *forró* performers and not electronic *forró* bands, which he referred to as "plastic *forró*," during the St. John's Day season: "As secretary of culture, I say that the state will neither contract nor pay musical groups and artists whose styles have nothing to do with the heritage of the northeastern musical tradition, which has its apex in the period of the 'June festivals.' It will not. I will not pay *forró* bands that aren't characterized as traditional northeastern culture.

But we would never intend to prohibit or suggest the prohibition of any such tendencies."[25] Secretary César's announcement became a widely publicized controversy, and many northeastern musicians took sides and issued statements. He was ultimately forced to clarify his position and his use of the term "plastic *forró*," which many saw as inappropriate. He said, "The two [*forrós*] are legitimate, and I'm part of the market myself, but these bands don't need the support of the state [of Paraíba] to survive, as is the case with the historical bands of *forró*. Our job is to give visibility to those who have no market."[26] In an interview with *Jornal o Povo*, ACF president Walter Medeiros expressed a similar belief: "It is not the role of the state to finance the dismantling of popular culture. And the largest sponsor of these plastic bands is the governor of the state of Ceará."[27] At a meeting of the ACF before St. John's Day, Medeiros asked, "What *forró* is this? What St. John's Day is this?" He continued, "We must have this conversation with the people who have the task of preserving culture."[28]

Some state politicians see ACF as a valuable constituency and are willing to partake in the dialogue desired by Medeiros. In 2010, an election year, two candidates for state deputy, the equivalent of a state representative in the United States, visited ACF meetings to campaign. On July 6, 2010, candidate Tony Nunes gave a speech in which he argued that electing him would benefit the foothills *forró* community. Nunes, formerly a singer, is the presenter of a television show called *Forrobodó* on TV Diário, an affiliate of Rede Globo. The show features *forró* bands performing in the TV studio, and Nunes described it as the only show in Ceará dedicated exclusively to *forró*. In his speech, he appealed to the morality associated with foothills *forró*. He claimed that *forró* is stereotyped as a musical culture associated with crime, prostitution, and alcohol but that, despite the negative stereotype, no single *forró* musician in Ceará had committed a crime in the past twenty years. "Musicians are good," he said, "but this is ignored because of the attitude perpetuated by electronic *forró*." His solution was to change the role of traditional music in Fortaleza, requiring that 50 to 60 percent of all musicians paid with municipal or state funds be from Ceará. "This will even save the city money," he argued. "This culture is ours, this culture of *forró*," he said and emphasized that if he were elected, he would "moralize" *forró* and find new venues for traditional musicians. By characterizing electronic *forró* as immoral and foothills *forró* as moral, Nunes was also characterizing the morality of different populations.

On August 3, 2010, Luiza Lins, another candidate for state deputy, attended the meeting. Lins, a member of the Workers' Party, the same party as Presidents Lula and Rousseff, is also the mother of Luizianne Lins, the mayor of Fortaleza between 2005 and 2012. Lins came dressed in a red shirt and wearing a star necklace and star earrings, the iconography of the party. In her speech, she spoke about health care for musicians, and she took credit for organizing free foothills *forró* concerts on Sunday evenings at the newly renovated Pinhões Market, where the majority of ACF members have performed. A musician told Lins that while he appreciated the Pinhões Market gigs, the city took too long to pay musicians. Lins blamed local bureaucracy and reminded them that she only allows local *forró* musicians to play there. Chico Pessoa, a *forró* musician born in the neighboring state of Paraíba who moved in 1982 to Fortaleza, where he began an illustrious career, came with Lins to speak on her behalf. Pessoa was perhaps a questionable choice for Lins: at the July 6 meeting when Tony Nunes spoke, ACF members complained that Chico Pessoa was hired by the mayor to play at an event organized by ACF, but he was not a member of the association. One person said, "Chico Pessoa isn't a part of the association, so he doesn't deserve to perform under its name. People who come to meetings should be rewarded."

In 2010 the ACF was successful with many of its initiatives. A plan for the creation of the first Cearense "sanfonic" orchestra (*sanfona* is the term used in the Northeast for the accordion, as opposed to *acordeão*, which is used elsewhere) came to fruition, and the group, comprising thirteen ACF-affiliated accordionists, performed several times in Fortaleza at citywide festivals. The celebrations for the Municipal Day of *Forró* in honor of Luiz Gonzaga were organized by ACF and funded by the Secretariat of Culture of Fortaleza (SE-CULTFOR). The Secretariat of Tourism of Fortaleza (SETFOR) sponsored Sunday evening *forró* concerts, organized by ACF, on the city's boardwalk in July and August 2010, the tail end of the St. John's Day season in Fortaleza. On its website, SETFOR explains: "With the objective of strengthening the festive and hospitable characteristic of the city, Holidays in Fortaleza unites attractions like Chico Pessoa, Neopineo, Diassis Martins, Adelson Viana, and Os Januários to demonstrate the best of *forró* to our visitors who will pass these holidays in the capital. And, for more interaction and fun with the public during these five weekends, four couples of dancers will occupy the plaza and will teach the tourists to dance the rhythm of *forró*."[29]

Ceará's tourism industry underwent many changes as Fortaleza prepared for the 2014 World Cup. The city of Fortaleza, which was promoted as a beach paradise during the so-called Government of Changes, which ended in 2002, is now promoted for both the sea and the *sertão*.[30] The Secretariat of Tourism of the state of Ceará began constructing a large aquarium on Iracema Beach, the city made progress on its light rail, and it proposed a tram that would run the length of the boardwalk, from Iracema Beach to Mucuripe Beach. Music and arts from the *sertão* are promoted as if they were Fortaleza's traditional culture, and the government runs a chain of handicraft shops—many of the items come from the interior—and also heavily promotes its St. John's Day concerts and quadrilles. Interior cities like Quixadá, where a national chain constructed a luxury hotel and conference center in 2011, began to acquire large-scale tourism infrastructure and were marketed for their natural landscapes and picturesque traditional cultural practices and handicrafts. These works, projects, and initiatives for tourism and culture were funded by local, state, and national entities in part due to the preparation for the World Cup and the broader vision of then mayor Luizianne Lins.[31]

In October 2009 the Fortaleza municipal government created the Municipal Council of Cultural Policy through its Secretariat of Culture. The council was intended to oversee, create, and evaluate cultural policy and projects. At ACF meetings in July 2010, members encouraged one another to vote for representation on the municipal council. Any citizen who registered with the Secretariat of Culture could vote for one of the council's twenty-one representatives (each creative sector has one representative, with the exception of "traditional and popular culture," which has two), and ACF members debated the idea of registering themselves as from both "traditional and popular culture" and "music" categories so the association could elect two representatives to the council. The council includes representatives from municipal agencies, including the Secretariat of Tourism, the Secretariat of Culture, the Secretariat of Economic Development, and the Secretariat of the Environment and Urban Control, among others. Elected representatives from the creative and cultural community include Walter Medeiros from the ACF, the president of the Association of Quadrilles of Ceará, and the president of the Cearense Folklore Commission.

At ACF meetings, members proposed a number of strategies—in addition to organizing local events and seeking political representation—for increasing the visibility and viability of foothills *forró* while limiting the expansion and ubiquity of electronic *forró*. One plan involved forming a coalition with the Association of Radio Listeners, which similarly felt that electronic *forró* had disproportionate control of the radio. Another strategy involved an alliance with the local Catholic community, which considered electronic *forró* sinful and believed it to be promoting prostitution and alcoholism. But the most successful regulation of electronic *forró*, it seems, came not from foothills *forró* musicians who heard the genre as immoral or as undeserving of being called *forró* but from people who heard it as noise.

Quieting Electronic *Forró*

When I asked his opinion of electronic *forró* in 2009, composer and land-scape architect Ricardo Bezerra explained that what bothered him about the genre was not the quality of the lyrics or music nor the monopoly-like en-terprises behind it but the volume at which it is played. Electronic *forró*, said Bezerra, is "noise pollution." He explained how he was bothered by the sound systems—the *paredões de som*—that loudly play electronic *forró* at all hours of the day regardless of the neighborhood or the day of the week. Many individu-als in Ceará, especially (but in no way exclusively) in upper-income neighbor-hoods, consider the *forró* from the sound systems invasive.

These sound systems are common means of broadcasting and listening to electronic *forró* and are central to the business model that includes publicly playing recordings of bands that shout out their own names and the names of local businesses in the middle of songs. *Paredão* sound systems are status symbols among *forró* fans and convey both taste and purchasing power. They also allow individuals—often members of the new middle class—to occupy public spaces with sound. These individuals may experience this as a form of staking claim to public areas to which they, until recently, have been otherwise denied access. And the music they broadcast perpetuates the market control of the electronic *forró* industry and the business interests of the companies mentioned in "Alô" shout-outs.

As Fortaleza's middle class expanded and the city prepared to welcome an onslaught of foreign and national tourists, a distaste for noise grew.[32] (Other ethnomusicologists have noted a similar correlation between class and listening in Latin America, e.g., Waxer 2002; Hernández 1995). Paradoxically, although the growing middle class desired quiet, the city became noisier as it expanded. A January 9, 2012, article from the *Diário do Nordeste* begins with a quote from Brazilian author Mário Quintana: "Progress is the insidious substitution of ca-cophony for harmony."[33] In Fortaleza this apparent contradiction—that urban growth leads to both noise and a preference for quiet—has been negotiated legislatively. Signed into law by the mayor of Fortaleza on March 4, 2011, Mu-nicipal Law 9756/11 posed a threat to electronic *forró* culture and its presence in the local soundscape. The *Paredão* Law, as it is commonly known, is a noise abatement ordinance that prohibits the use of mobile sound systems in public spaces or in private spaces to which the public has access, such as gas stations and parking lots. It also limits the volume of mobile sound systems in com-mercial locations to a maximum of seventy decibels between 6:00 a.m. and 10:00 p.m. and a maximum of sixty decibels at all other hours. For most infractions, authorities confiscate the sound systems and charge the perpetrators a fine between R$849 (US$472 in 2012) and R$8,490 (US$4,720). Individuals playing music louder than eighty-five decibels run the risk of imprisonment. The *Paredão* Law is enforced by the Municipal Secretariat of the Environment and Urban Control (SEMAM), which in 2011 received more noise complaints (60.8 percent) than any other kind of environmental complaint.[34]

For Leonardo Cardoso, Brazilian efforts to legislate noise (in São Paulo, the case he studies) entail understandings of citizenship and are matters of nothing less than "universal equality and individual freedom, welfare principles and economic gain at the micro (i.e., municipal) level" (2016, 4). By passing noise control laws, municipal governments determine who can or cannot be heard and whose sounds are acceptable and whose are disruptive or distasteful.

Until the passage of the law, *paredão* sound systems characterized the general soundscape of Fortaleza's Carnival celebrations, as well as the street parties each weekend between New Year's Eve and Carnival known as Pre-Carnival. During the 2012 Pre-Carnival and Carnival season, SEMAM promoted the law heavily through the television, radio, and the newspaper and advertised the phone number and website for registering complaints. Fortaleza's secretary of culture, Fátima Mesquita, issued the following statement in January 2012: "In addition to being illegal, *paredões de som* disturb the public order and disrespect the common good, as well as harm the good progress that was organized by us so that Carnival revelers could enjoy themselves the best way possible. We will work with the police and, principally, with the population in the sense of monitoring and inhibiting this type of practice through public complaints."[35]

The topic of the complaint hotline was widely publicized during the Carnival and Pre-Carnival season in Fortaleza, and middle- and upper-class individuals reminded one another of the law and the disturbance caused by *paredões de som* on Facebook and Twitter. A widely circulated image on Facebook showed a pickup truck with a large *paredão de som* in its bed with text that read, "Does this bother you? Then call SEMAM 3452-6923." In one weekend during 2012's Pre-Carnival, SEMAM confiscated five sound systems. An article in the *Diário do Nordeste* about the law featured a photo of a police officer holding a decibel reader near a *paredão de som*.[36]

People associated with electronic *forró* voiced opposition to the law. A Fortaleza-based electronic *forró* band called Forró Estourado released a song in 2011 in protest against the law. The song, called "Não proíba o paredão (Lei do paredão)" (Don't prohibit the sound systems [*Paredão* Law]), argues that those who like electronic *forró* are "good," "peaceful," and just seeking to enjoy themselves:

Hello mayor, city councilman

. . . .

Our parties cause no turmoil.

. . . .

There's no crime, there's just enjoyment.

. . . .

No! No! Don't prohibit the *paredão*!
No! No! We just want to have fun.

Despite the *Paredão* Law, sound systems remained prevalent, perhaps less so than in previous years, at Fortaleza's 2012 Carnival and Pre-Carnival celebrations, but they had virtually disappeared by 2016. Yet they remain dominant in Carnival parties in towns and cities outside the state capital where mobile sound systems continue to be legal in public spaces. *Paredões de som* and sound trucks are also important tools in political campaigns, as they drive through the streets of Fortaleza and other northeastern cities playing *forró* campaign jingles. Mayor Luizianne Lins's 2008 campaign jingle, "Eu quero mais" (I want more), sung by a choir with an underlying *xote* rhythm and an accordion emphasized in the mix, became a soundmark of the city and the election season while she campaigned for reelection. The long-term consequences of the law on the electronic *forró* industry remain to be seen, but many have speculated about its potential impact on future political campaigns—some have suggested that politicians will make an exception for themselves.

Forró Symbolism and the State

Both subgenres of *forró* were, during their prime, working-class dance genres derided by the elite, who considered them musically and morally repulsive. Both *forrós* also articulate relationships between the city and the *sertão*. One depicts the *sertão* in its lyrics and its sound—first because of migration, nationalism, and nostalgia, and now because of cultural tourism, the valorization of local music, and an ideology concerning traditional culture. The other involves rodeos, rural performance venues, and a direct connection to the material conditions of *sertão* life in Ceará, where urban migration continues to increase, where urban media is easily accessed in the *sertão*, where rodeos and *forró* parties remain popular, and where many individuals were able to rise out of poverty and into the new middle class at the end of the first decade of the twenty-first century.

In the present-day context, the significant distinction between the two *forró* cultures is that one treats music as a commodity, while the other now, despite its commercial origins, treats music as a social good, necessary for maintaining a unique local identity and encouraging traditional values and now dependent upon legislation and taxpayer funding. Those with a vested interest in foothills *forró* voiced little animosity toward electronic *forró* itself aside from their musical and moral criticisms. Their primary concern with electronic *forró* was, specifically, that it limited access to audiences and acoustic space by way of unfair business practices. Quasi-monopolistic control of venues and radios, payola, disregard for copyright law, and an endless pursuit of profit left foothills *forró* musicians struggling to survive in the local soundscape. With the creation of the Cearense Association of *Forró*, traditional musicians gained a voice in local cultural politics and strengthened their position in the soundscape. Meanwhile, increased prosperity and sensitivity to noise led to legislation that limited the sound of electronic *forró* in public spaces.

The greatest achievement of the Workers' Party under Presidents Lula and Rousseff was the eradication of extreme poverty, especially in the rural Northeast, through programs like Fome Zero (Zero Hunger), introduced by Lula in 2003, and Brasil sem Miséria (Brazil without Misery), introduced by Rousseff in 2011. It seems ironic that welfare programs that allowed many northeasterners to overcome the issues described by foothills *forró* would help make that same genre—and the musicians who play it—dependent upon state sponsorship, which has been exploited by electronic *forró* as well. Can public funding and soundscape legislation maintain foothills *forró*'s symbolism as environmental conditions and socioeconomic contexts change and as electronic *forró* remains popular?

Forró, or Bread and Circuses

Carnival in Times of Drought

EACH YEAR, ONE SONG emerges as the hit of Carnival. It becomes the holiday's refrain. You hear it repeatedly in cabs and shops, on the radio, at private parties, on beaches, and in the streets, where it blares from *paredão* sound systems as revelers sing and dance. Musicians also transform it into *forró* and *pagode* covers, melding the song to local musical aesthetics for crowds at live shows held in town squares during Carnival. In Ceará in 2012 that song was "Eu quero tchu, eu quero tchá (tchu tchá tchá)" (I want tchu, I want tchá). The song, a *sertanejo universitário* recording by duo João Lucas and Marcelo, reverberated across the nation. The recording combined regional rhythms and timbres into the sound of a regional Brazilian nowhere, blending the timbre of *forró* accordion with a hint of the southern Brazilian *vanerão* rhythm and the vocal style of and generic attribution to *sertanejo universitário*, a hybrid genre from the south-central region and originally associated with college-age audiences. Its lyrics introduced the "sensual" dance that accompanied the song's new rhythm and bragged about its popularity.

To one Brazilian cultural critic, the Carnival hit symbolized the bread and circuses politics of a Brazilian government that spent large sums of public money on parties and events in times of economic and environmental turmoil. In a mural in São Paulo, graffiti artist Mundano depicted a protester saying he wants water instead of "tchu" or "tchá," a shorthand not just for Carnival but for misplaced priorities (see figure 10). Mundano is known for his environmentalist artistic interventions, including graffiti and site-specific installations, and many of his projects concern drought.[1] His 2015 mural in São Paulo shows protesters

FIGURE 10. "São Paulo tá fervendo" (São Paulo's boiling). São Paulo, Mundano, 2015.

standing on cracked earth. The Brazilian Southeast experienced severe droughts in 2014 and 2015 that led to a water shortage in São Paulo, a megacity with a population of over twenty million, prompting the city to ration water for its residents. People protested about having their water shut off for several hours each day and took to the streets, blaming a corrupt and spineless government. In Mundano's mural, picket signs read: "It's not the rain's fault!" "Water for whom?" "Don't sell water, defend it," "Will trade 1995 Escort for cistern," "Water is a universal right," and "Water isn't a commodity." In the middle of the mural, a man wearing a T-shirt with a picture of a car, its trunk open to reveal a sound system, holds a sign that shows a multiple-choice question with three possible responses. One of them is selected: "I want: ( ) Tchu; ( ) Tchá; (X) Water."

This critique, that the people want water, not parties, is especially meaningful when unrecoverable expenditures from Brazil's 2014 World Cup and 2016

Olympics stand in stark contrast to a national recession that pundits consider the deepest and most prolonged since the 1930s, a recession that put an end to the previous moment of economic optimism. These monumental sporting events also took place in a period marked by significant and costly environmental disasters, including far-reaching droughts and the breach of an iron ore mine tailings dam near Mariana, Minas Gerais, that killed seventeen people, left another six hundred or so homeless, buried a town, and transformed the Doce River into a toxic mudflow that traveled through two states and into the Atlantic Ocean, killing wildlife and destroying fishing and tourist economies along the way. The Mariana dam breach is widely understood to be one of the worst environmental disasters in the nation's history, and its environmental impact could be felt for another century.

Environmental crises of historic magnitude reached across Brazil. A drought that began in Ceará in 2012 and lasted into 2016 is considered the worst drought since the one in 1915—the drought that inspired Eduardo das Neves's song "Ajuda teu irmão" (Help your brother), the one that became the topic of Raquel de Queiroz's most famous novel, and the one that expelled songwriter Humberto Teixeira's family from the *sertão* when he was young. The 2012–16 drought was so severe that it instigated new waves of migration and disrupted the social progress that had been achieved in the backlands in the previous decade. At the time of Carnival in 2015, 176 of Ceará's 184 municipalities had declared a state of emergency.

Although the first decade of the twenty-first century left fewer people vulnerable to drought, bringing many out of extreme poverty or even into the middle class (examined in the previous chapter), the costs of emergency drought relief, coupled with a national recession, prompted politicians to reconsider allocations for music and popular cultural events. In 2014, 2015, and 2016 the Public Ministry of Ceará called on the state's municipalities to cancel any public Carnival celebrations so public funds could be saved for drought relief and other needs. Cancel Carnival in Brazil? Things must be bad.

But many municipalities in Ceará spend large sums of money on free parties throughout the year. Costs include bands—most of them electronic *forró*—and event planners, as well as infrastructure and marketing, including stages, sound equipment, lighting, portable toilets, security, electricity, signage, and advertising. Payments to bands to perform during the holiday typically range from more than R$10,000 to nearly R$500,000, depending on the number of bands and their individual fees.[2] In 2004 the city of Acarau spent R$250,000 on its Carnival. Caponga paid much less, a total of R$77,000, for six bands to play in its town square and on its beach during Carnival in 2004. A big city like Sobral or Fortaleza can spend well over R$1 million on its Carnival.

Many people, including politicians, consider these expenses to be wasteful in precarious times. Are they? Is Carnival not a significant element of cultural heritage and citizenship worthy of public support? And should parties—especially those that use public monies to pay commercial *forró* bands—be funded privately, even when they are considered important for senses of local and national identity and sources of revenue for local economies? More generally, to what extent are musical events, concerts, and festivals environmentally costly? Mark Pedelty (2012) notes that global rock concerts are ecologically taxing, given the carbon footprint of air and bus travel, electricity for stage lighting and sound, and so on. Music festivals also often leave large quantities of trash and human waste in public spaces. Event organizers and musicians are becoming increasingly cognizant of issues surrounding sustainability, sometimes making visible efforts to offset environmental damage (e.g., see Pedelty 2012). In Ceará environmental activists, like my friend biologist Cátia Riehl, now lead workshops for event planners through organizations like Fora do Eixo, which promotes independent music outside the Rio / São Paulo axis, on waste management and sustainability at music and arts festivals.

My argument in this chapter is simple: the cost of drought affected the practice of expressive culture, and it did so for a number of interrelated reasons. The politics of environmental justice were as relevant to the context as the politics of musical taste, the workings of the local music industry, and state and local cultural policy. Key factors included corruption, understandings of government's role in and responsibility to drought relief and to (expressive) culture, visions of local and national identity, and musical aesthetics.

My own ethnographic observations, along with an examination of news coverage and budgets, expenses, and memoranda from municipal payment requests, as well as documents and statements released by government officials, suggest three specific justifications for the cancellation of Carnival in times of extreme drought. First, in an era of austerity, funding these expensive parties is irresponsible; worse, it appears to be related to entrenched corruption, which only aggravates efforts to mitigate drought. Second, Carnival has limited importance to Ceará's sense of identity and history when compared to St. John's Day or New Year's Eve or to a number of locally meaningful religious and agricultural festivals, and it is in the state's interest to prioritize more traditional events. Third, Carnival uses public funds to pay for electronic *forró*, which is known to be lucrative and self-sustaining and which is understood as not representative of local cultural heritage. On the other hand, there are reasons to defend a publicly funded Carnival. First, some people do not trust the politicians with their money. Out of fear of embezzlement, people prefer knowing their taxes are spent on parties they themselves can enjoy, ensuring they reap some tangible benefit from their tax contribution. Second, and more significantly, some people consider Carnival a significant element of Brazilian democracy and a cultural right guaranteed by the Constitution of 1988 and underscored by the cultural policy achievements of the first decade of the twenty-first century. According to this argument, Carnival is not only a right to be protected but a practice to be paid for and organized by the government.

The various arguments for and against withholding Carnival funds suggest that as drought took a toll on public coffers, politicians placed limitations on public funding for music festivals, encouraging the private sponsorship of them instead. Such limitations hinged on notions of cultural heritage and tradition, as well as on the neoliberalization of culture. Although the cancellations themselves are temporary, they point to an increasing privatization of music in a place where musical experience is also understood as a basic right.

In addition, it is important not to overestimate the progress made in the previous decade. I conducted research for this chapter primarily in 2015 and 2016, a moment that marked the decline of the Workers' Party in Brazil. Many began to see the party as corrupt and President Rousseff as inept. The white and monied classes felt ignored as the value of the U.S. dollar increased. And despite significant social improvements, including the reduction of extreme poverty, Brazilian society—especially in the Northeast—remained marked by vast inequality. Extreme overcrowding in hospitals and medicine shortages in public clinics were national concerns and were evident throughout Ceará.

Carnival Cutbacks

State governments across Brazil demanded cutbacks to their Carnival celebrations in 2016. According to one newspaper, at least nine Brazilian states called for the reduction or cancellation of government-sponsored Carnivals.[3] In most cases, the economic crisis and the resulting difficulty paying emergency expenses were the justifications. In the city of São João del-Rei, Minas Gerais, the R$350,000 Carnival budget was instead to be used to fill potholes and for public health.[4] A city in São Paulo state promised its R$150,000 for the purchase of a new ambulance. A city in the northern state of Rondônia planned to use its R$120,000 to build three classrooms. A city in the southern state of Rio Grande do Sul intended to reassign its funds for reforms to a youth shelter.[5]

Even Rio de Janeiro had to reduce its support for the city's legendary Carnival parades. Mangueira, one of Brazil's best-known samba schools, had fewer floats and fewer musicians and dancers as a result. The samba school also felt the effects of the recession on the private sector, as the cost of imported fabric for costumes rose and as corporate sponsorship of the samba school declined.[6]

In Ceará Carnival cutbacks were blamed on drought and the troubled economy in equal measure.[7] As explained above, government agencies, including the Ceará Tribunal of Municipal Accounts and the Public Ministry of the State of Ceará, requested Carnival reductions in three consecutive years, beginning in 2014. In 2015 and 2016 Ceará's governor, Camilo Santana, a member of the leftist Workers' Party, suspended Carnival expenses from all state entities and organizations, excluding only those supported by the State Incentive of Culture System, which funds traditional culture. His action was widely praised in 2015. Representative Heitor Férrer, from the center-left Democratic Labor Party (PDT), said in an interview for a newspaper, "It was very much the right decision, because we cannot consider having festive events in times of drought, when water reserves are at only 1 percent in some municipalities in the state."[8] Lula Morais, of the Communist Party of Brazil (PCdoB), said, "Camilo's decision is correct. We cannot spend on parties while families suffer from a lack of water."[9] As a result of the governor's request, the city of Sobral planned to redirect its R$800,000 Carnival budget in 2015 to drought relief, promising the money for water tanker trucks and digging deep wells. That year, some twenty-four cities withdrew their bids to use municipal funds for Carnival.

Extreme drought is expensive. A simple fifty-two-thousand-liter cistern can cost around R$18,000, and it costs between R$15,000 and R$25,000 to install a new well. One worker estimated that in 2013 and 2014 five times as many wells were dug in Ceará as in 2012. A federal program initiated in 2012 called Operation Tanker Truck (Carro-Pipa) supplied 1,227 tanker trucks of water in 2014 to Ceará (and nearly 8,000 across the Northeast and elsewhere), which were paid for with a combination of state and federal funds. Nearly 80 percent of Ceará's municipalities benefit from such programs. For example, Santa Quitéria, a city with almost forty-three thousand residents, was given twenty-four of those tanker trucks. Additional federal drought emergency programs have provided Santa Quitéria with 1,732 cisterns, more than a thousand small monthly Drought Grants (Bolsa Estiagem), which are paid on top of Bolsa Família payments to qualifying farmers, and payouts to almost ten thousand families from drought insurance called the Crop-Guarantee Program (Garantia-Safra), which pays monthly salaries to low-income farming families in municipalities that have reported a crop loss of at least 50 percent. Farmers in Santa Quitéria have received nearly thirteen hundred emergency lines of credit, totaling almost R$12 million in low-interest drought-related loans.[10] State and federal governments have also subsidized the cost of corn in areas affected by drought, and another program, Planting Time Project (Projeto Hora de Plantar), distributes seeds for beans and drought-resistant corn at strategic moments in the climate cycle. In 2015 federal drought assistance was inadequate to cover the costs of the drought, and municipalities had to purchase water trucks and dig new wells, as well as buy equipment to clean the water.

This is not the first time drought has affected Carnival in Ceará. In 1916 there was debate in the press about whether to cancel lavish Carnival celebrations in the state while the population still recovered from the drought of 1915. The community decided to allow the wealthy to hold private Carnival balls with the assumption that profits from the parties would be used to help drought victims (Rios 2002, 113). Historian Kênia Sousa Rios describes objections to Carnival in 1932, which was a year of drought, as preoccupations of Fortaleza's Catholic bourgeoisie, who considered the holiday "four days of the devil's presence" (108). "These representatives of Joyful Ceará dance and celebrate on the graves of the victims of a horrible tragedy, the climatic crisis from which we have not yet been freed, delivering the madness of Carnival," said a February 10, 1932, article in *O Nordeste* (109). For Catholic protesters, disregarding the needs of drought victims and submitting to the sin and temptation of Carnival were symptoms of a singular "moral crisis" and contributors to the "de-Christianization" of Cearense society (109). In response, wealthy capitalists threw charity balls and advertised their humanitarian deeds while aligning with the Catholics to keep drought victims in refugee camps away from the city.

Carnival as Pandering and as Drought Industry

Cearenses of all classes have complained to me that expensive Carnivals and other parties are wasteful when so much needs to be done for Ceará's population, ranging from health care and education to repairing potholes and addressing drought. Some state politicians have publicly suggested alternate uses for Carnival budgets. On the Facebook page for *O Povo*, the newspaper asked readers if they thought city governments should cancel their Carnivals in 2016 because of drought. Readers overwhelmingly said yes but consistently added that drought was only one of many concerns facing the Cearense population.

Yet many mayors and city governments prefer to maintain the parties for their local populations, despite pressing needs. For example, approximately

three weeks before Carnival in 2016, days before the governor officially prohib-
ited the expenses, the mayor of Orós announced that the city would hold its
Carnival, only one of four cities in the state to submit a bid that year. A news
blogger from Orós shared the mayor's confirmation and then offered a brief
commentary: "My opinion about this Carnival in Orós and throughout Brazil
is this: I know this traditional event generates revenue for the cities, but how
many expenses are left unpaid? If there is sufficient money destined for such
an event, why is there a lack of resources to invest in public health? How can
we make sense of that? If there are ultimately enough resources to contract so
many bands, why do they tell us that there is no money to hire more doctors?
How can we make sense of that?"[11]

In addition to the expenses seeming wasteful, they have also been described
as unnecessary, given that most Carnival parties happen regardless of public
funding. Several cities in Ceará are known as poles for celebrating the holiday.
Rather than canceling the parties, many seek private sponsorship. Espedito Carneiro, the president of the Association of Municipalities of the State of Ceará,
argued that many cities attract enough partygoers to be able to find businesses
to underwrite the events and use them as opportunities for marketing. Carneiro
also said that in 2015 cities began exploring the option of renting their town
squares to beer companies that could fence in the spaces while selling only their
own brand of beer. The beer companies could then sponsor the city's Carnival
and make a profit on beer sales, even while allowing free admission. Many cities succeeded in finding private sponsorship. Orós ultimately paid for its 2016
Carnival, which featured several high-profile electronic *forró* shows and one
axé music show, with private funding from businesses and wealthy friends of
the mayor. Banabuiú, a small interior city near Quixadá, also threw a privately
sponsored *forró* Carnival; the municipality provided only logistical support.
Acaraú charged admission to its *forró* and *axé* Carnival.

Most Carnival celebrations require little sponsorship at all. In Beberibe,
a popular beach city during Carnival, the municipality canceled all live music performances and instead helped organize a "circuit" of privately owned
paredão sound systems. In parties called *blocos* in cities across the state (and
country), brass bands typically lead groups of partiers through streets and
into public parks, where informal-sector beer and *cachaça* vendors supply the
alcohol. Samba schools parade and perform in front of bars where partiers
fill the neighboring streets and sidewalks. In Várzea Alegre, a small city in the
interior of Ceará, a samba school of farmers paraded from the dusty field into
the town to their Carnival theme, "Water: Source of Life." Fortaleza hired only

local musicians, mostly indie rockers, to play at its mainstage Carnival shows in 2016. It also paid for the stages, musicians, sanitation, and grandstands for the *maracatu* and samba parades and a few neighborhood *blocos*.

If spending large amounts on Carnival is wasteful and unnecessary, why do politicians continue to do it? One reason is to buy votes, a common practice in the Northeast. In 2015 a Cearense federal representative (*deputado federal*), Ronaldo Martins, accused mayors throughout Ceará of buying votes with the materials intended for drought-related works: "There are cisterns that have been held up . . . because many mayors are waiting for the elections to arrive. People are going hungry, thirsty, while there are cisterns kept in soccer fields."[12] Politicians can also buy votes by pandering to voters and throwing popular parties. Pandering was a frequent criticism of Fortaleza's mayor Luizianne Lins (from the Workers' Party, 2005–12), who was known for her spectacular New Year's Eve fireworks displays launched over raging beach parties with performances by some of Brazil's most famous musicians. Lins saw these festivals as a way to encourage cultural tourism. Even more suspect is the use of scant municipal budgets for big parties in small interior cities, especially near and in election years.

Arguments to defund Carnival reflect not just a prioritization of drought but also a growing preoccupation with corruption, especially in 2016, a municipal election year. In the second decade of the twenty-first century, as the middle class grew, Brazilians began voicing their exasperation with corruption at all levels of politics, culminating in the Operation Lava Jato (Car Wash) inquiries of the federal government, which began in 2014 and uncovered a major scandal involving Petrobras (the state-run energy company). The mid-2010s also saw demands from members of the Right to impeach President Rousseff, whom they consider corrupt, as well as extreme calls to return to a military dictatorship. In the Facebook discussion hosted by *O Povo*, referenced above, commenters who believed municipalities should maintain their parties despite the drought tended to view their local officials as untrustworthy. If cities paid for Carnival parties, commenters argued, they could be certain their taxes were spent on something they could experience themselves, rather than on enriching politicians and their cronies: "There's no sense in cutting expenses if the money will go into bank accounts in other countries." "It would be very good if they actually invested it where it should be invested, but in my city we haven't had [Carnival] in a long time, it's nothing now, and I have no idea where [the mayor] invests the money." "If the money were really to be used for drought, then yes [cancel Carnival], but since the money is going to end up being diverted, no!"

Even a number of those who supported redirecting Carnival funds to drought relief expressed similar concerns: "I'm in favor of cutting costs for Carnival, but with lots of monitoring, because if not, this money will go into the pockets of the officials of each city." "Yes [cancel Carnival]. And use this money that would be invested in Carnival to combat drought that affects our state, but I'm doubtful. With these cuts, do you think they're really going to invest this money in the Cearense population?" "Election year, dangerous year, keep an eye on the administrators."

In some cases, state-government-issued calls for cancellations were met with resistance by local authorities who had a political stake in upholding the celebrations. In 2014 the mayor of Santa Quitéria refused to cancel the city's four-day Carnival despite the request of the state Public Ministry. The city's mayor, who had taken a public stand against corruption at his mayoral inauguration in 2013, insisted that the municipality had enough money to cover the expenses and that it was not behind on any of its bills. Santa Quitéria, with a population of almost forty-three thousand, had proposed spending more than R$400,000 on its Carnival that year, around half of one percent of the city's annual budget.[13] Santa Quitéria's refusal to cancel its Carnival was taken to a judge, who prohibited the city from using any public funds for the event and threatened to impose a fine of R$100,000 per day if the city disobeyed the judge's order. The city was permitted, however, to maintain its "traditional" Carnival celebrations, including *bloco* street parties and *paredão* sound systems. In 2016 in Paracuru, one of the most popular beach destinations for Carnival in the state, the city reduced expenses from previous years but still held its *forró*-centric holiday. To compensate for the impact of tourism on the local water supply, the mayor had three new wells dug and sought assistance from Petrobras to dig another ten.

Carnival Has Marginal Significance in Ceará

Although some of Brazil's Carnivals are world famous, such as the celebrations in Rio de Janeiro, Salvador, and Olinda, Carnival in Ceará is generally a local affair: a highly anticipated four-day vacation and an opportunity to party, to let go of life's worries and frustrations, and to experience all the meaningful social reversals and chaos that Carnival offers. Although many Cearenses say they look forward to Carnival's arrival, many also say the holiday has little bearing on the state's unique cultural heritage.

Fortaleza does have a unique Carnival celebration that involves *maracatu* parades on a major thoroughfare in the city's downtown, with a unique rhythm, elaborate costumes, and a notable history that dates back at least to the nineteenth century. But *maracatu* has low visibility in Ceará. Few people attend the parades, and the *maracatus* only began to receive city funding and recognition in 2006 due to Lins's efforts to increase cultural tourism and strengthen senses of local cultural identity (see Cruz and Rodrigues 2010). The city's Carnival also involves small Rio de Janeiro–style samba schools, a phenomenon that began in the 1960s, which parade down the same street as the *maracatu* nations and which tend to attract bigger crowds (Cruz and Rodrigues 2010). Street *blocos* with brass bands that play *marchinhas* have also been an element of Ceará's Carnivals since the 1930s, a decade in which Carnival itself became a national practice and a symbol of *brasilidade*. In Fortaleza *blocos* have only been funded by the city since 2007 and were relatively unpopular for many years (Cruz and Rodrigues 2010). Popular opinion and my own observations suggest that the public funding and promotion for the *blocos* and *maracatus* has, in fact, increased not only participation in these local Carnivals but also their significance in the local imagination as a part of the annual cultural calendar. Starting in the 1990s, those who could afford to do so either left the state or, since 2000, traveled to a (publicly and privately funded) jazz and blues festival in Guaramiranga, a charming Cearense mountain town with cooler temperatures. Meanwhile, the vast majority of Cearenses celebrate Carnival to the sound of *paredão* sound systems and electronic *forró* or *axê* music shows performed from stages or *trios-elétricos* (sound trucks with live bands atop them) in beach towns or in cities in the interior.

Other holidays possess greater significance for Cearense cultural identity. St. John's Day, with the surrounding June festivals, is the primary annual holiday, followed by Christmas and New Year's Eve. Other smaller holidays, such as Epiphany, Holy Week, a range of saint's days, and some historical commemorations, have meaning for individual cities and communities. An internet meme echoes a sentiment I hear repeatedly in Ceará: "Carnival is good . . . but I prefer St. John's Day." A Ceará newspaper headline from 2011 captured the same sentiment: "Our Carnival Is St. John's Day." Although St. John's Day festivals were canceled or notably reduced in cities around the Northeast in 2015 due to the economic crisis, the celebrations suffered no significant cancellations in Ceará. Regarding threats to St. John's Day elsewhere in the Northeast, the media termed the holiday the Day of "St. John of the Crisis." Petrobras, embroiled in its high-profile scandal, threatened to withdraw its patronage of many of the region's June festivals, especially in Bahia, leading many affected cities to reconsider their celebrations.[14] Ceará's St. John's Day, however, remained strong.

The famous pilgrimages to Juazeiro do Norte to leave votive offerings for Padre Cícero, which were affected by drought, saw no mandated changes or accommodations. In October 2015 there were fears that the influx of religious pilgrims into the city in early November would worsen conditions for the local population, as many of the city's neighborhoods were without water each morning.[15] Yet little was done, and Ceará's government focused its attention on Carnival rather than these other events, calling for the cancellation of only a few egregiously expensive festivals.

Electronic *Forró* Does Not Deserve Public Funds

A third motive for restricting Carnival funding is musical in nature, primarily aesthetic. A comment I hear often in the context of my research is that such state-sponsored events, like a number of other changes, are leading to the loss of Ceará's unique characteristics, a process called *descaracterização,* or "decharacterization." Some blame municipal and state governments. Others take aim at the local population: "People only value what comes from outside the state," and its corollary objection, "Nobody respects what's from here." Electronic *forró* is included among the musical genres that are said to "decharacterize" Ceará, despite its local origins. Like the bourgeois Catholics of 1932 who believed that Carnival was bringing about the de-Christianization of Ceará, bourgeois traditionalists in 2016 believe Carnival—at least the wrong kind of Carnival—is bringing about the decharacterization of Ceará. Proper Carnival in the state involves *marchinas, blocos, afoxés, maracatu,* and sometimes *frevo,* but never *forró. Forró* is either the music of St. John's Day or commercial pop music that is not and cannot be considered traditional in any context.

In an effort to save its Carnival, one city employed tropes of "tradition" and "cultural revival" to defend its party that featured *axê* music from Bahia and electronic *forró.* The city of Tauá, after being prevented from using municipal or state funds for its Carnival in 2014, swiftly applied to the federal Ministry of Culture to pay its expenses. In its application to the ministry, Tauá's mayor's office offered a justification scattered with keywords associated with federal cultural policy and platitudes about culture appropriated from academia. The application's primary argument hinged on a defense against (unnamed) individuals or entities that "staunchly opposed" the celebrations for involving "mediated" and commercial activities in a time of urgent need. The city, it argued, was requesting a necessary investment in the rescue or revival (*resgate*) of its popular culture, a kind of discourse most often associated with traditional culture. Furthermore, it argued that although the city was undergoing an era of development, it had not lost sight of "keeping traditions alive."

On the day before Carnival began, the Ministry of Culture approved Tauá's request for R$488,634. The city hired four prominent *axé* bands from the state of Bahia; a young Cearense pop singer who garnered attention for being a northeasterner and who sang southern-central *sertanejo universitário* music; three electronic *forró* bands; and Chico Pessoa, a foothills *forró* musician discussed in the previous chapter. One could argue that such an event would help maintain local cultural heritage, as Tauá's mayor did, especially given that the city had purportedly held similar events for twenty consecutive years. But the use of public funds to pay commercial bands—primarily electronic *forró* and music and musicians from outside the state—is the very issue that most concerned foothills *forró* musicians at the meetings of the Cearense Association of *Forró* that I attended (see chapter 5).

When the city of Santa Quitéria refused to cancel its Carnival in 2014, Déric Funck Leite, a state prosecutor who took the issue to a judge, argued against the expenses on musical grounds: "The unbridled spending of public money on *forró* bands, in and of itself, catches the eye in dealing with public affairs, since such a high amount to produce a Carnival event, in the face of the social demands of a poor municipality in the *sertão*, sounds like an affront to and contempt for the suffering of the Cearense *sertanejo*."[16]

In addition to an aesthetic argument against electronic *forró*, Leite and others opposed paying the bands with public monies because *forró* bands tend to be so lucrative. *Forró* was devised to be a highly profitable industry in the 1990s, and it has continued to thrive. Yet many of these bands benefit greatly from public contracts. Since the expansion of the *edital* competitions in the 2000s, a fierce debate has grown around the payment of mainstream recording artists with public money. In 2013 the Ceará state government paid Ivete Sangalo, an *axé* and pop-samba diva—truly a national star—from Bahia R$650,000 to sing at the inauguration of a new hospital in Sobral. The Public Ministry of Ceará protested, asking that money be returned to the health care budget. Amid statewide controversy, the state Tribunal of Municipal Accounts refused to pay Sangalo until the governor (Cid Gomes) was able to justify the cost. One month after the inauguration, the new hospital's poorly constructed façade collapsed, injuring two workers. The situation called attention to the prioritization of appearances—the building's façade and Ivete Sangalo's show—over necessities. In 2016 a federal agency, the Tribunal of Accounts of the Union, determined that events with "lucrative potential" and that "can attract private investment" would be ineligible for receiving funding through Rouanet

Law tax breaks to corporations and individuals (see chapter 5). The agency's study showed that a significant amount of tax revenue had been lost to profitable events like Rock in Rio, an annual music festival that had benefited from Rouanet Law sponsorship.

The State Incentive of Culture System, which was not restricted by the governor in 2015 or 2016, has continued to fund all other forms of Carnival celebration, including *maracatus*, samba schools, *blocos*, *afoxés* (which are associated with Afro-Brazilian Candomblé religious practices), and *cordões* (which are costume parades with percussion). In 2016 the state of Ceará made over R$1 million available for these Carnival celebrations. What distinguishes these various musics and practices from the *forró* and *axê* Carnivals that have been curtailed? Primarily, these celebrations—parades, parties, and so on—are considered traditional for Carnival. The state provides incentives to musics that it understands as concordant with a particular vision of Carnival and a particular vision of Ceará. But by cutting support for these *forró* and *axê* Carnivals, the government is not limiting their prevalence. It is only handing them over to the private sector.

An Argument in Favor of Carnival

It may seem like an obvious decision to eliminate or reduce expenses related to four-day parties characterized by debauchery, especially in times of need, but to at least some Brazilians, the significance of Carnival exceeds this. The holiday is a glue of social cohesion and a nationwide exhalation. It is deserved, anticipated, and savored. It is an expression of the nation and of Brazilian democracy. Vinicius Wu, the secretary of institutional articulation for the federal Ministry of Culture, believes the cancellation of Carnivals around Brazil in 2016 signals a weakening of national cultural policy, which had been so strong in the previous decade. "It does not take much effort to conclude that cultural management is under attack in Brazil," he writes. "The economic crisis, coupled with a poor understanding of the relevance of cultural rights by part of the government and sectors of society, is leading cultural management into an alarming situation. The idea of culture as something superfluous—that should be immediately cut in periods of crisis—can bring about a significant setback to what was accomplished in the last decade."[17] For Wu, strong cultural policy is necessary for a properly functioning democracy. From his perspective, cultural policy in the previous decade had only begun the hard work of creating a wholly inclusive and democratic Brazil and had done so in part by symbolic means. That Carnival became the immediate target of reductions and a hot topic in the press suggests that many Brazilian politicians disagree about the role of cultural policy and events like Carnival. In Brazil artistic and musical cultures are often considered integral to the country's political and economic goals.

In an opinion piece published in *Diário do Nordeste* a week before Carnival began in 2016, Cearense law professor and cultural rights expert Humberto Cunha argues that the Brazilian constitution guarantees culture as a right with the same protections as "public heritage, administrative morality, and the environment." He continues, "There is no doubt that Carnival parties, present in distinct forms across this country of Carnival, are integral to Brazilian cultural heritage." These parties, he claims, are constitutionally recognized as intangible culture and are inherently related to identity and cultural memory. In his opinion, the government is tasked with guaranteeing these cultural rights for all Brazilian citizens, and the recommendations to cancel Carnival reject this obligation by dismissing the celebrations as little more than leisure, which, he says, is also protected by the 1988 constitution. City Carnivals, he recommends, should keep their expenses within their budgets, but the calls to impede the celebrations should be made with special care and attention given to the cultural rights of Brazilians, who, he implies, have already suffered enough.[18]

But city- and state-sponsored parties are not straightforward and benign gifts given out by the government to protect the cultural rights of the people. Referring to the increased municipal control over and financial backing of Carnival that occurred during Luizianne Lins's tenure as Fortaleza's mayor, Danielle Maia Cruz and Lea Carvalho Rodrigues argue that although Brazilian Carnival is widely understood as a period characterized by the inversion of social hierarchies (e.g., see DaMatta 1991), the local government's role in planning and financing the parties alters this logic: "[Carnival] transformed into a time that is now permanently negotiated between the municipal administration and revelers" (2010, 19). By planning and funding Carnival celebrations, city and state governments employ the holiday in ways that not only benefit local economies but also exert a certain amount of social control over citizens, as well as aesthetic control over the music. As Cruz and Rodrigues demonstrate, Carnival sponsorship determines the neighborhoods where Carnival may be celebrated, what music is appropriate for Carnival, and what music is adequately representative of the place and of local and regional identity.

Has the cancellation of these publicly sponsored parties returned Carnival from the state back to the people? No, as I stated earlier, Ceará's Carnival has simply shifted from being controlled by the state to being controlled by industry and the impresarios behind electronic *forró*. Drought, in a sense, has accelerated the privatization of music in a place where musical experience is celebrated as a social good. These changes coincide with the expansion of electronic *forró's* horizons, as *forró* singer Wesley Safadão (his stage name roughly means Really Lascivious Wesley) has become a national phenomenon and one of Brazil's highest-paid performers. Emanuel Gurgel's famous description of *forró* "as a product" has, perhaps, become a convincing justification for the state to diminish its cultural responsibilities.

At the start of her first term as mayor, Luizianne Lins tried to prioritize foothills *forró* and *maracatu* in the events she sponsored with city money. But she quickly learned that these local musics were relatively unpopular, despite their rootedness in senses of regional and local identity. The genres may work well for tourists as musical symbols of local ethnicity, but folklore is *chato*, "no fun," for much of the local population, especially for the (increasingly tenuous) new middle class. This reality left her government with the choice of either sponsoring parties that feature this commercial music, which many people believe will lead to the decharacterization of the state, or encouraging private companies to pay for them, thus privatizing cultural celebrations that some Brazilians believe are constitutionally guaranteed.

Many programs that support the arts and culture through Brazilian federal, state, and municipal cultural policy and related tax incentives—such as those of Itaú Cultural, the Banco do Nordeste and other financial institutions, and non-profit organizations such as local Social Service of Commerce branches—are inclusive and embrace many kinds of traditional and popular practices, ranging from an urban art like hip hop to a rural calendrical dance drama like *reisado*. A consequence of this egalitarianism is that a commercial cultural expression such as *forró* can benefit from the same values and budgets as smaller, less lucrative practices. The approach in Ceará, to limit Carnival expenses to only those that are traditional, thus excluding solely *forró* and *axê*, seems to have had little effect on the success of Carnival. On the contrary, as one person said to me, "The crisis has been good for Carnival!" More people stayed in the city, she argued, and the *blocos* were more popular than ever. But the situation nevertheless highlights the way in which commercial musical culture has come to dominate the local musical soundscape. In 2016 traditional music carried on during Carnival with minimal public funding, and such funding remained a government priority. Commercial *forró* found other ways of making money, generally from businesses, wealthy individuals, and admission-paying concert-goers, rather than state or city government. And cosmopolitan, indie youth genres that are relatively inexpensive acts and have local audiences were able to fill the void left by costly shows from out of state.

Indeed, the deductions also resulted in genuinely local Carnival events. As I mentioned above, Fortaleza's Carnival in 2016 exclusively featured local bands. Electropop vocalist Daniel Peixoto, who performed on Carnival Saturday, wrote on his various social media accounts that a local Carnival helps support the local music scene:

> This year, Fortaleza's Carnival will be special! Special because we are only going to include local attractions on the official calendar! Absolutely nothing against artists from other states, like those we have had in previous years, who bring their shows here and throw a lovely party with us, but it is also extremely important to strengthen and affirm Cearense culture in such a rich and creative moment in our music! By the way, Cearense music is doing very well, thank you, and I think that 2016 will be a very rich year for us, coming from a 2015 with such brilliant albums from Karine Alexandrino, Marcos Lessa, Cidadão Instigado, Johnatta Doll e Os Garotos Solventes, Selvagens a Procura da Lei, Daniel Groove, etc. . . . In 2016 we will have the albums of Veronica Decided Morrer, Laya Lopes, Vitor Colares, and mine and many others that are in the oven, bubbling over and about to explode! So my message is: APPRECIATE LOCAL CULTURE!

This local indie music scene, supported by Fortaleza's 2016 Carnival, was hardly traditional or representative of local cultural heritage. On the contrary, it was more cosmopolitan than Brazilian, more queer than macho, and for listening as much as for dancing. Was this music a more appropriate public expenditure than electronic *forró*? Perhaps so, if only because *forró* has come to represent a crude musical form of capitalist greed—disposable music that seeks the lowest common denominator, irrepressible and capable of surviving in harsh economic and environmental moments. Privatized *forró* parties, with high-priced admission for the rich in luxurious locales like Porto das Dunas Beach just outside Fortaleza and at free privately funded public events in cities in the interior, continued to thrive during the holiday despite the prohibition against using public monies.

The *Sertão* Will Become the Sea, and the Sea Will Become *Sertão*

The privatization of *forró* carnivals in Ceará involves perceptions of *forró* music, realities of the *forró* industry, and changing frameworks of cultural policy, as well as the cost of drought, the failures of drought policy, and fears of corruption and the drought industry, alongside a national recession. The pressures of an environmental crisis ultimately outweighed the government's responsibility to throw Carnival celebrations, forcing politicians and citizens alike to assess the value of Carnival. The demands of drought—starvation, thirst, disease, crop failure, mass migration—and the state sponsorship of expressive culture are entangled in a complex political web, but they are also distinct in kind and distinct in degree. Water, not tchu or tchá.

In 2016 it rained along the coast of Fortaleza on Carnival Sunday—not water, aside from a light overnight shower, but thousands of *forró* CDs and designer sunglasses suspended from little pink parachutes. Wesley Safadão and his associates paid to have them dropped from helicopters above the city to promote his latest release and the brand of glasses for which he serves as a spokesperson. That same day, women's thong underpants rained from a heli-copter onto Porto das Dunas Beach, where Aviões do Forró were to play that night and where Wesley Safadão had performed the previous night. Newspapers ran stories making light of the irony that it rained lingerie and *forró* CDs rather than water. These stunts—called a "rain of panties" and a "rain of glasses" by marketers—epitomize the objectification of women and the cross-promotion of forró with consumer goods that typify the ethos of contemporary neoliberal *forró* culture in Ceará. Less than a month before Carnival, the rain prophets in Quixadá had predicted a good rainy season, despite the dire forecasts of FUNCEME, which warned against a fifth year of drought. And they were right: It rained. It rained *forró*.

Conclusion

ON SOME HOT, hypothetical day in the early twentieth century—maybe in the 1910s—hydrocarbons, alcohols, and acids combined on the surface of a Cearense carnauba frond to form a wax to protect the leaf from the blazing sun and to slow evaporation. With long hooks, workers trimmed the fronds from the tall trees on which they grew. Donkeys carried the leaves to other workers, who then removed the waxy powder from the leaves and melted the dust into a solid. American industrialists imported the wax from Brazil and then sold it to the recording industry, where workers melted it down again and combined it with other ingredients so it could transform into a soft disc. A sound recording engineer took the soft wax master record and placed it on a lathe for musicians, who sang and played as the lathe etched their sound onto the wax. A few steps later, and the engineer produced a shellac 78 rpm record. A music industry entrepreneur living in Rio de Janeiro purchased the record and others like it, imported them to Brazil, and then made more of his own with Brazilian musicians. The Brazilian recording industry expanded throughout the 1920s.

In the 1930s Luiz Gonzaga, following a population of drought refugees, left the land of carnauba trees for Rio de Janeiro, bringing his accordion and his memories into a recording studio where, in the 1940s, a wax master captured his voice and the sound of his accordion. An engineer transferred these etchings onto a phonograph record. The record traveled back to the place from where the accordionist came. A radio deejay placed the record on a turntable and broadcast it over the air. A merchant with a radio set on a counter in the front of her shop played the music into an interior city plaza. In the music Gonzaga poetically described the beauty of a plaza and a merchant not unlike these. He also sang about why business was bad for the merchant and why she had moved to the small city following several years of hardship in the *sertão*, a place he romanticized in a way that eased the merchant's longing for the past. He also demanded that she get some help: loans, reservoirs, at least some respect. She sang along with the record, her voice melding with his. In the 1950s and 1960s she taught the songs to her daughter, who also sang along with her and the *forró* records. Her daughter internalized the songs' sounds and lyrics as a kind of truth about the way things used to be and sound. Some of the songs explained how to listen for drought, a technique the girl also learned from her father. One such technique involved listening for changes in bird vocalizations: some birds make certain calls, or they sing together, or they fail to sing at all before periods of rain or drought. When the daughter grew up, the lessons in the songs reinforced and celebrated the ways of listening that her cousins in the coastal city never needed to know.

Some musicians the same age as the daughter made careers for themselves in Rio in the late 1960s and 1970s, following in the footsteps of the musicians the daughter grew up hearing. It was now the era of vinyl, but many of the topics of songs were the same. One of these musicians, Raimundo Fagner, sang about Orós, the small city he left behind, going so far as to show himself on an album cover bathing in the city's reservoir, a famous symbol of drought and resilience. He even named the album after the city. Through the end of the century, the people of the city celebrated him as their own, and they hung his image on their walls and played his music on their stereos and into public spaces. Into the digital age, his legacy in the city endured. But Fagner began returning home, where he—and local residents—learned he had changed. One member of the community made daily announcements over a loudspeaker to wake the town for work and school and to share local news, sometimes related to the reservoir. The celebrity, who visited primarily to escape the fast life of the big city, had no desire for such public noise. He may have once romanticized the town in his music, which became part of the local soundscape, but he was now trying to alter it with his desire for quiet and an effort to silence the announcer. He failed.

Other changes were taking place in the music industry as the twenty-first century neared. A capitalist instigated the creation of a new genre of dance music that shared a name and only some musical elements with *forró*, the music the merchant's daughter grew up hearing. With the intention of selling music as a product, this man exploited all the elements of a local music industry, from the recording studios and the musicians to the venues and the radio. He and other regional music industry executives also took advantage of funding intended for cultural heritage, which performers of the related neotraditional genre resented. In the early twenty-first century, despite the cries of tradition-alists like the merchant's daughter, audiences for local music, with newfound class distinctions in an era of economic and social change, did come to see this new popular music as heritage, appropriate for seasonal holidays and symbols of regional identity. The merchant's granddaughter, who lived on the coast, where she drove a new car and accessed media on her smartphone, spent her Friday nights dancing to *forró* with her friends. However, a protracted drought, coupled with a political and economic crisis, undermined recent social mo-bility and brought about unwelcome austerity. The crisis prompted questions about government, heritage, and the response to drought. People, including the granddaughter of our hypothetical merchant, were left asking, "Which do we need more, music or water?" Although it may appear to be a false dichotomy, the question emerged when the state government blamed the cancellation of publicly funded Carnivals on the cost of drought.

So goes the narrative I have told in this book. I began by exploring how wax, which formed on carnauba palm trees in Ceará as an adaptation to drought, transformed into 78 rpm records, the medium for early foothills *forró*. The wax became the music—and not just any music, but music that described the very places from which the wax came and that was subsequently audible in those same places. I ended the last chapter with an anecdote about how Wesley Safadão rained thousands of *forró* CDs onto Ceará's coast. The music became the rain—and not just any rain, but rain that carried the meaning of the commercial genre and the neoliberal moment to which it belongs and that showered places in which rain was greatly needed, paradoxically offering scant relief aside from pleasure. The relationship between Ceará's landscape and its music is vibrant and dynamic, and it became especially so through the advent of recorded sound and the development of popular music.

In the book's opening pages, I introduced five concepts that run through the six case studies: vulnerability, materiality, listening, nostalgia, and policy. Rather than review these as discrete concepts here, I would like to explore how they work in tandem to suggest some implications for future research on music and the environment in Brazil or elsewhere. There are three conclusions I hope readers will have drawn from this book. First, ecological change and crisis affect musical culture via the political economy and the workings of social difference and stratification. Second, popular music—that is, commercial music created by a music industry—is connected to an environmental phenomenon such as drought not solely via lyrical treatments of landscapes but in material ways as well. Third, the discursive invention of Brazil's Northeast region has had material effects on the Northeast and on the northeastern experience. More generally, discourses about places affect the material realities of those places.

Ecology, Music, and Society

Many of ecomusicology's key questions can be answered by asking how music and sound constitute society and social relations. The connections between meaning and sound, between sound and natural materials, between natural materials and musical instruments, between musical instruments and instrument makers or musicians, and between musicians and environmentalism have social contexts with histories and hierarchies. Stories of music and nature are, in other words, also stories of social relations.

For example, there are several pertinent questions involving the materials of musical instruments. One concern is whether natural resources are sustainable and whether the changing availability of materials threatens the continuance of traditional musical practices. I have observed the musical adaptation to the changing cost and availability of materials myself in Ceará as musicians have substituted PVC pipe for bamboo in the construction of *pífanos* (fifes) and gourds for wood in the construction of *rabecas* (fiddles). It is also noteworthy that the declining availability of materials, particularly for mass-produced instruments, is also a consequence of global capitalism and systemic inequality. Such is the case in my investigation of a wax used in the fabrication of early sound recording technologies.

Environmental protest songs or other music that scholars might describe as environmentalist in nature are also often rooted in social, rather than ecological, needs. Blues and gospel songs about the Mississippi River Flood of 1927 were more than responses to flooding, as they explored themes of racism and the black experience as much as they described the devastation of the floods as environmental phenomena (Evans 2006). Woody Guthrie's dust bowl ballads chronicled the Great Depression as much as dust storms and drought (Curtis 1976; Gold 1998; Lookingbill 1994). The drought protests of *forró* demanded no changes to the treatment of nonhuman natures or to drought as a climatological phenomenon, pleas for rain notwithstanding. Rather, the protests concerned the experience of exile, the prejudice and scorn directed at northeasterners, and the needs of workers, including drought-proof employment and fair loans.

Even the musical conveyance of ecological knowledge is bounded to meaningful social relations: between musician and listener and among institutions such as governments, industries, and traditions. For some *sertanejos*, local ecological knowledge is especially meaningful because of the singer who sings about it. The knowledge is worthy of continued celebration and dissemination because many consider government-provided knowledge about rain and drought untrustworthy due to a history of corruption and false promises. Perhaps ironically, traditional music and events like the Meeting of the Rain Prophets also rely on government (especially local and state) support.

Soundscapes are also relational. They are produced by the constructive clashing of images, sounds, social formations, and individuals. The soundscape of Orós, a small city in the *sertão*, took its shape through a negotiation of power between townspeople and Raimundo Fagner, a famous musician who spent much of his childhood in the city. Fagner's national fame has made his music, which often describes the city in its lyrics, a common element of the local soundscape. His status also led him to attempt altering the local soundscape to his own preferences by creating a radio station and trying to silence an announcer who broadcasts daily from a homemade loudspeaker system. Local sonic expectations and subjectivities, which link sound to local social and environmental values, ultimately won out over those of the wealthy star.

Ecological models for the sustainability of traditional musical practices must consider economic conditions and political motivations. In Ceará two leftist federal programs achieved contrasting results: social welfare efforts brought vast numbers of people out of poverty and into a growing middle class; cultural policy, meanwhile, came up against the desires of the new consumer class, which broadened demand for commercial popular music, namely, electronic *forró*. The popular music genre competed against traditional music—foothills *forró*—for access to the same resources and opportunities offered by a robust cultural policy that treated expressive culture as elements of the economy and the practice of citizenship and as systemic and thus ecological. That is, an ecological understanding of music cultures recognizes the cultural significance of commercial popular music, even genres that some call vulgar and musically bereft. More to the point, cultural sustainability is oftentimes, but not always, a concern of the intelligentsia, while the consumption of popular dance music can be a prerogative of the working class (or anyone else), and both of these realities warrant recognition.

For the Ceará state government, the ecological cost of drought had to be weighed against the social benefit of expressive culture—specifically Carnival. In an era of continuing drought and a national economic recession, politicians redirected allocations for Carnival to urgent drought-related needs. A range of factors were considered in the less-than-straightforward decision: Exactly how costly is drought? How significant is Carnival to the local population? To what extent does the government have a responsibility to fund mainstream music cultures if they are considered culturally meaningful to some people? And to which people? How economically viable is *forró*, and can a Carnival that is available to all social classes still take place without government resources? Environmental and economic crises, I claim, have quickened the spread of neoliberalism and the privatization of the culture industries.

Popular Music, Meaning, and Material

Popular music is often a vehicle for expressing visions of past, present, and future places and selves. Yet its connection to the natural environment goes beyond meaning and expression. Because popular music is produced through an industry, it is connected to a range of social, economic, and political mechanisms. These various mechanisms interface with attributes of the environment and consequences of environmental change, including natural resources, the cost of drought, soundscapes, and ecological exile.

The music industry is one that peddles sound—it captures it, manufactures it, mass-produces it, markets it, creates demand for it, and lobbies for it. It is an industry that is and has always been inherently global, not because of musical hybridity or transnational music markets, but because the materials of music technologies travel on global commodity markets, even in the era of the mp3. The manufacture of consumer electronics also involves the extraction of natural resources, and its environmental and cultural impact is substantial. Just as the materials of small-scale, locally made instruments are awash in local significance for instrument makers and musicians (Dawe 2016), as they are for *rabequeiros* and *pífeiros* in Ceará with the materials of *rabecas* and *pífanos*, the materials and resources of mass-produced instruments carry local meaning. Like wood and bamboo, commodities such as wax feel one way or another in a laborer's hand, betraying stories of working the land, of social formations, and of ecological knowledge. The manufacture of the equipment of popular music thus involves multiple and interlocking fields of cultural production, some of which directly and indirectly affect nonhuman natures.

Live music is environmentally taxing as well. The energy used in amplification, lighting, and travel has a significant carbon footprint (Pedelty 2012), and concertgoers produce considerable solid waste. When governments finance festivals, taxpayers and politicians might consider music and public celebrations frivolous expenses in the face of increasing environmental costs. In Ceará, as more state resources went to the cost of ecological crisis, fewer went to expressive culture, which, despite a history of many Brazilians considering expressive culture an essential element of citizenship, came to be seen primarily as the responsibility of the market, not the government. Environmental decline feeds into the politics of austerity and aggravates the effects of neoliberalism on expressive culture by transforming music and the arts from practices tied to citizenship, community, and heritage into products, as well as by failing to regulate the industries that sell these artistic products, thus limiting certain kinds of expression.

On the other hand, the material conditions of environmental crisis also create the conditions for certain forms of expression. For example, drought led to ecological exile, which resulted in *forró*. Popular musicians tend to respond to the market, but it also seems a banal truism to say popular musicians in a great many music cultures also sing about everyday experience. In *forró*, efforts for national integration, the nostalgic desires of northeastern migrants, and the experiences and memories of northeastern musicians coalesced in the radio era to create what was in many respects—but not exclusively—a musical response to drought.

Popular music also interfaces with the soundscape in meaningful ways. Music technologies—speakers, amplifiers, radio transmitters and tuners, microphones, and personal computers, to name but a few—allow spaces to fill with sounds made by musicians in the past or elsewhere. This transmission of aural distance, both temporal and spatial, materially reconfigures the soundscape in the here and now. The soundscape also affects popular music, as when singers mimic birds, thus transmitting webs of local meaning and knowledge back into the soundscape.

The mass mediation of popular music also spreads ecological knowledge and environmental imaginaries to large, disparate, and distant populations. Shared notions of ecological knowledge shape ideas about the land and about the people who consider that land home. Such ideas can affect policy, contribute to prejudices, and generate sources of pride by transforming practical knowledge into cultural heritage.

Imaginaries, Landscapes, and Places

In the middle of the Cearense *sertão*, an hour or so from a beach paradise called Jericoacoara and a few hours from Fortaleza, sits Sobral, a city whose residents have gone to great lengths to resist associations with the *sertão* and *sertanejidade*, "*sertão*-ness." Sobral is a vision of idealized cosmopolitanism. The city's main plaza is called (in English) Central Park. Nearby, on Avenida Boulevard, stands the Arco do Triunfo. There is a museum dedicated to Albert

Einstein and the theory of relativity (an observatory in Sobral helped prove the theory in 1919) and a decent sushi restaurant. A former mayor proposed a new city hall in the shape of the Twin Towers as a memorial. Throughout the city, yellow school buses, imported from the United States, circulate, with their common name, in English, "school bus," painted on the backs. Residents claim to prefer playing baseball to soccer. I once gave a talk at a university there, and the students nodded as I explained my ideas about the image of the *sertão* in contemporary regionalist music in Ceará. When I finished, however, they made sure I understood one thing. In Sobral, we don't go out *forró* dancing, they said. (One of them was wearing a baseball cap.) No, here we go to a club to dance to Top 40, mostly from the United States.

Sobral did not emerge like this by chance. Its cosmopolitan image was the brainchild of Cid Gomes (b. 1963), a former governor who was born and raised in the city. It now stands as a foil to other cities that emphasize the regional imaginary. If Sobral borrowed its symbols from mass-mediated visions of cosmopolitanism, many other places in Ceará have taken some cues from mass-mediated visions of the *sertão*. That geographical imaginaries affect places is not a new observation. Scholars have noted that mass-mediated representations of rurality and natural space have affected the expectations of tourists, for example. Consequently, tourist industries and others modify places to meet those expectations (e.g., Sharp 2014; Crouch 2006; Bishop 2000).

My emphasis in this book has been on the nature of these media-influenced modifications and the extent to which they become naturalized. At what point does a mass-mediated vision of the *sertão* actually become the *sertão*? At what point does the mass-mediated experience or expectation of weather patterns affect how weather works—not climatologically but epistemologically and even ontologically? How is the "real *sertão*" made of sounds and images of an idealized *sertão*? And what are the limits of the influence? Popular music can be didactic. It teaches how the world should look. How it came to be. How we should listen. How we should long for home.

The northeastern imaginary I describe here is characterized by several things, including agriculture, poverty, out-migration, Luiz Gonzaga, machismo, the *sertão*, *caboclo* identity, and drought. Each has its own history, although they are related, especially through mass media. None of them is representative of the entirety of the northeastern experience, and some of them came into being expressly through the culture industry. Yet together they form a particular vision of the region I observed in Ceará. They have become part of the narrative within the region itself, affecting local knowledge, trade, and policy as much as music and social life.

Politics, Matter

Climate change and other forms of environmental decline will affect a greater range of human activities than we typically acknowledge. As natural resources become unavailable, new, sustainable materials will need to be used to produce (and reproduce) music. With rising sea levels and worsening droughts come displacements, and with displacements come new forms of human expression, including new kinds of music that may potentially replace older kinds of music. With changing weather patterns come challenges to (or renewed activations of) forms of local ecological knowledge. If populations of birds, whose calls convey vital knowledge to farmers, migrate to more hospitable places or become extinct, local ways of knowing become obsolete. Mounting costs of disaster relief align with shifting values—such as an understanding of music primarily as a product—thereby leaving an even greater number of expressive practices vulnerable to a marketplace that prioritizes novelty over heritage.

By emphasizing the social, rather than the environmental, facets of the concerns outlined in this book, I have sought to underscore the role of neoliberalism in linking current environmental decline to the cultural changes I observe in Brazil. I understand this not as some bogeyman but simply as a current state of affairs in which deregulation and privatization have left more people—farmers and accordionists alike—vulnerable to the vicissitudes of both the climate and the market.[1] Not all people will become ecological refugees, nor will all people find their ways of listening and knowing obviated. We must ask not merely about the songs that might vanish or the instruments that must evolve but also about the people who find themselves choosing between music and water.

Notes

Introduction

1. In a critique of ecomusicology, Ochoa Gautier (2016) has questioned the hegemonic ontology that conceptualizes a nature/culture binary. Some people (such as some Amerindians in lowland South America) have boundaries of human *being*—of humanness—that extend into beings that post-Enlightenment cosmopolitans often take for granted as nonhuman, thus demonstrating the constructedness of what can be considered "nature" and "natural." Anthony Seeger (2015) has similarly cautioned ecomusicologists about terms such as "nature" and "human." I agree with them but nevertheless employ the term "nature," as I insist on its discursive constructedness.

2. See Aragão (2013) for a wonderful short ethnographic study of this practice. Aragão writes that the use of the triangle by street vendors influenced *baião*, not the other way around (also see Dreyfus 1996), although the *baião* may have since affected its use by street vendors.

3. For example, see Grey (2007, 2013) on *saudade* in Portuguese *fado*; and see Feldman-Bianco (1992) on *saudade* in broader social contexts in Portugal, Brazil, and the Lusophone diaspora.

4. See Draper (2010, 44–52) for an extended treatment of *saudade* in *forró*, especially his discussion of what he terms *material saudade* and the musical conjuring of smells and other senses associated with life in the northeastern backlands.

5. Another zone, the *meio-norte*, characterizes parts of the northernmost northeastern states of Maranhão and Piauí and links the *sertão* to the Amazon.

6. In the colonial era, Brazil was divided into semifeudal land grants. The Pernambuco Captaincy included the present-day states of Ceará, Pernambuco, Rio Grande do Norte, Paraíba, Alagoas, and part of Bahia.

7. In 1884 Ceará became the first state in Brazil to abolish slavery, four years before the rest of the nation.

8. There still exists a popular debate about the origin of the word *forró*. Many claim it evolved from the English phrase "for all," which was presumably written on signs outside of parties held by British railroad workers—or American soldiers—living in northeastern Brazil in the early twentieth century. However, the consensus among scholars today is that *forró* is a shortened form of *forrobodó*, a word with Bantu origins meaning "party" (see Silva 2003; Cascudo 2012).

9. This ensemble is known by many names around the Northeast, including *terno de zabumba* and *esquenta-mulher*, along with the other names already listed. The most common name in Ceará is *banda cabaçal*.

Chapter 1. Hills, Dales, and the Jaguaribe Valley

1. Some notable examples include Dawe (2016) on the local significance of materials to instrument makers and Allen (2012) on the cultural significance of trees as related to the sustainable production of violins.

2. See Ryan (2013) on the qualities, meanings, shared agency, and music of gumleaves for Aboriginal Australians and Roda (2014) on the qualities (relational and inherent) of materials associated with tuning a tabla drum.

3. "250 Communicado: Considerações sobre as seccas—indústria, oleo de copaiba, cera de carnauba," *Pedro II*, March 2, 1850, 5.

4. Walter Newbold Walmsley Jr., "The Carnauba Palm and Its Wax," *Bulletin of the Pan-American Union* 73 (1939): 31–42, quote at 31.

5. Brazil sold 293,800 kilograms from two locations in Rio Grande do Norte alone in that period (Moreira 1875).

6. A document released by the United States Bureau of Foreign and Domestic Commerce (July 22, 1921) said regarding exports from Bahia: "The total exportation of carnauba wax during 1920 amounted to 4,384 bags of about 140 pounds each, of which the United States took 2,368, England 1,640, and France 789, the remainder going to Germany, Denmark, and Argentina. During 1919 the exports amounted to only 2,858 bags. *The principal use of this wax in the United States is for the manufacture of phonograph records*" (1921, 409, emphasis added).

7. This idea was inspired by the work of Catherine M. Appert, who writes about musical palimpsests. See, e.g., Appert forthcoming.

Chapter 2. "Help Your Brother"

1. Although drought has never been the sole driver of migration from the Northeast region, it is widely understood to be the primary catalyst (see Hall 1978; Kenny 2002; and Barbieri et al. 2010).

2. See Reily (2002) for a powerful ethnography of the *folias de reis* and society, music making, morality, and religious enchantment in the Brazilian Southeast.

3. The song's title is unknown, as are its original Portuguese lyrics. Denis translates the lyrics directly into French in the original edition: "'Quand s'arrête le mois des fêtes,'—dit une chanson populaire,—'pour l'entrée de janvier,—le peuple se prend à écouter qui entendra le premier gronder l'orage. . . .—Il n'y a plas de vie si satisfaite—que la nôtre dan le sertaon,—quand l'année donne un bon hiver, et que dans le ciel gronde l'orage'" (1910, 272).

4. The composer's full name was Jayme Rojas de Aragón y Ovalle. Arleen Auger, Maria Lúcia Godoy, and Kathleen Battle have all recorded the piece, and Renée Fleming and Felicity Lott performed it in recitals in Brazil in 2012.

5. João Pernambuco was his stage name. His legal name was João Teixeira Guimarães.

6. See also Travassos (2000) and Wisnik (1977) on music and Brazilian nationalist modernism in the 1920s.

7. For example, Jararaca recorded "Tem de tudo" (It's got everything), a 1939 song by Sá Róris about drought in the Northeast.

8. On regionalist literature and drought in the Northeast, see Anderson (2011) and Perrone (2017).

9. Oswald Barroso, personal communication with the author, April 17, 2017.

10. "Maringá—Cidade canção," *Maringá turística*, http://www2.maringa.pr.gov.br /turismo/?cod=nossa-cidade/4, accessed December 10, 2015.

11. Terra da Luz (Land of Light) is a nickname given to Ceará by nineteenth-century writer and abolitionist José do Patrocínio to describe both the state's sunshine and its status as the first Brazilian state to abolish slavery.

12. Nirez and Humberto Teixeira, "Sou apenas Humberto Teixeira," *Jornal o Povo* (Fortaleza), April 7, 2000.

13. "Humberto Teixeira—O parceiro oculto," *Jornal do Brasil*, May 1, 1971.

14. Ibid.

15. Ibid.

16. Ibid.

17. The song was later recorded by Miriam Makeba. (Sivuca arranged many of the songs on the album on which she recorded "Adeus Maria Fulô," including "Pata pata.")

18. Schuyler Whelden (2017) has noted that in her 1965 performance, Bethânia appeared to be imitating the bodily movements of the caracara itself.

Chapter 3. The Secret of the *Sertanejo*

1. The song's title refers to the arikury palm, which, according to the song, signals that bees have made honey when it blooms. The spelling of the song title varies from recording to recording, including "Uricuri," "Ouricuri," and "Oricuri."

2. "Luiz Gonzaga vem novamente ao Ceará!," *Jornal o Povo* (Fortaleza), November 5, 1951.

3. "Iguatú festejará o primeiro de maio," *Jornal o Povo* (Fortaleza), April 27, 1953.

4. "Hoje na festa do radialista estréia de Luiz Gonzaga o rei do baião," *Jornal o Povo* (Fortaleza), June 20, 1956.

5. "Programa Irapuan Lima Rádio Iracema," *Jornal o Povo* (Fortaleza), July 2, 1960.

6. "O precioso," last modified February 1, 2009, accessed November 18, 2011, http://revivendoteixeirinha.wordpress.com/category/novidades/.

7. "Causas dos reis: Pilhas Eveready," accessed February 2, 2012, http://www.luizlua gonzaga.mus.br/index.php?Itemid=32&id=14&option=com_content&task=view.

8. "Jingles: Pilhas Eveready," accessed February 2, 2012, http://www.luizluagonzaga .com.br/jingles/12.htm. The unofficial website, www.luizgonzaga.com.br, contains an online archive of recordings in which Gonzaga can be heard performing political and commercial jingles. I cannot authenticate the recordings on the site, but the voice in the recordings does sound like Gonzaga's.

9. See Dreyfus (1996, 210) for more on Gonzaga's career in advertising.

10. "Luiz Gonzaga vai ser cidadão barbalhense," *Jornal o Povo* (Fortaleza), October 2, 1975.

11. "Luiz Gonzaga é afinal cearense," *Jornal o Povo* (Fortaleza), November 27, 1975.

12. "Sobre o forró," *Jornal o Povo* (Fortaleza), December 12, 2009.

13. Both Sulamita Vieira (2000, 45) and Megwen Loveless (2010, 223) mention the prevalence of birds in Gonzaga's songs. José Farias dos Santos (2002, 122–126) describes the association between birds in his music and the northeastern knowledge of drought, also briefly mentioning birdsong in particular.

14. "Luiz Gonzaga Canta Acauã," accessed October 17, 2010, http://www.luizluagonzaga .mus.br/index.php?option=com_content&task=view&id=648&Itemid=47.

15. Gonzaga is not the only northeastern Brazilian musician to have sung about the laughing falcon. Dominguinhos, often considered Gonzaga's successor, praised the wisdom of the northeastern people and their ability to recognize drought from the laughing falcon's call in his 1976 song, "O canto de acauã" (The laughing falcon's song). Clemilda, a *forró* singer best known for her bawdy lyrics and double entendres, attributes the opposite meaning to the bird's call in her 1977 song, "Canto do acauã" (Song of the laughing falcon), in which she claims that the laughing falcon's song brings happiness and rain to the backlands. Relatedly, in his book *Waiting for Rain*, Nicholas Arons writes that the laughing falcon's call is a "symbol of hope and a harbinger of plentiful rain" in Ceará (2004, 5). In fact, according to anthropologist Karen Pennesi (2007), the laughing falcon's call can have both meanings to present-day rain prophets in the Northeast, depending on whether the bird sings while perched on a green branch or a dry branch. Furthermore, according to ornithologist Steven Hilty (2003), the laughing falcon's vocalizations are most frequent during the rainy season, and not periods of drought.

16. On cordel, see Slater (1982); Curran (2011); and on cordel, northeastern spoken poetry, and drought, see Arons (2004).

17. José Erismá (rain prophet and accountant), interview by the author, September 3, 2011, Quixadá, Ceará.

18. Erasmo Barreira (rain prophet, radio announcer, retiree), interview by the author, September 3, 2011, Quixadá, Ceará.

19. See Rios (2003) on the use of elevated language in rain prophecy.

20. The event was initially conceived to provide useful information for the management of local agribusiness and to send a message to the government that local forecasts should be considered in decisions regarding the distribution of seeds (Taddei 2006, 2012).

21. My experience with the rain prophets was not unique, and I can assume they did not mention Gonzaga in my presence simply because they knew I was researching northeastern music. Anthropologist Karen Pennesi, who has conducted extensive ethnographic research with the rain prophets, writes that rain prophet Chico Leiteiro often sang for her the songs of Gonzaga "inspired by the topic or lesson of the moment" (2007, 49).

22. Erasmo Barreira (rain prophet, radio announcer, retiree), interview by the author, September 3, 2011, Quixadá, Ceará.

23. Ribamar Lima, interview by the author, January 9, 2009, Quixadá, Ceará.

Chapter 4. Sounding the Real Backlands

1. Honório Barbosa, "Orós sangra após quatro anos," *Diário do Nordeste*, April 7, 2008, http://diariodonordeste.verdesmares.com.br/cadernos/cidade/oros-sangra-apos-quatro -anos-1.689183.

2. Honório Barbosa, "Sangria do Orós atrai 10 mil pessoas," *Diario do Nordeste*, April 15, 2008, http://diariodonordeste.globo.com/materia.asp?codigo=529143.

3. Frederick Moehn (2007) has written that race, class, and nation were envisioned, contested, and articulated in Brazilian popular music at the turn of the twenty-first century. Borrowing a term from Josh Kun (2005), who was himself building upon Foucault, Moehn describes this alternative musical imagination of place and citizenship as an "audiotopia," a "'third Brazil' between the two Brazils" (2007, 183). Fagner's northeastern imaginary can be likened to the idealized Brazilian audiotopias described by Moehn.

4. Writing about bells in the French countryside in the nineteenth century, Alain Corbin explains, "Bells shaped the habitus of a community, or, if you will, its culture of the senses" (1998, 97). Bells, he argues, constructed a local sense of place for a migrant proletariat, defined town boundaries, conveyed alarms and messages, made public spaces sacred, and were believed to have the power to scare away demons and storms. Steven Feld calls bells in Europe "part of an acoustic ecology that joins space and time in history." He says bells "make communities audible," and they can express authority and "disruption" (Feld and Brenneis 2004, 469). See Vasconcelos Solon (2006) for a historical study of the loudspeaker service in Teresina, Piauí, in northeastern Brazil, which was removed from the city's downtown in 1952. Through oral histories, Vasconcelos Solon depicts the role of the loudspeaker in commerce and community, as well as its contemporary role in the memory of his interlocutors.

5. Regina Dantas, interview by the author, December 13, 2011.

6. Regina Dantas claims that in the past several years, Dantas, her father, has only played "Ave Maria" for funerals and masses.

7. Dantas claims to own the entire Luiz Gonzaga collection.

8. See Taylor (2002, 432) on radio weddings and funerals of the 1920s in the United States.

9. "Seu Dantas, Voz da Liberdade," http://portaloros.blogspot.com/2010/12/seu-dantas -voz-da-liberdade.html, accessed April 14, 2011.

10. José Ribeiro Dantas, interview by the author, December 13, 2011.

11. Fagner has in fact contradicted himself regarding his place of birth. In his interview with Ana Bahiana (2006), he claims he was born in Orós but raised in Fortaleza. He says exactly the opposite in his performance on the 2001 TV program *Ensaio*, later released as a CD/book, *A música brasileira deste século por seus autores e intérpretes: Fagner* (Fagner 2003). The confusion is due in part to the fact that Fagner claims he falsely registered his birth in Orós when he was young.

12. There are accusations on the internet that I can neither refute nor confirm that the song was plagiarized from an earlier song by Brazilian composer Henrique Vogeler.

13. Tom Moon, "Elis Regina: The Feeling between the Notes," March 8, 2010, http://www .npr.org/templates/story/story.php?storyId=124357584.

14. See Pimentel (1995); Saraiva (2008).

15. Raimundo Fagner, interview by the author, December 21, 2011.

16. Ibid.

17. Fagner also recounts the incident in an interview in Regina Echeverria's book *Gon- zaguinha e gonzagão: Uma história brasileira* (2006, 271).

18. Ibid.

19. In her article "Palmilhando um chão sagrado: A construção da topografia nas can- ções do Pessoal do Ceará" (2007) linguist Maria das Dores Nogueira Mendes writes that the "discursive topography" of the Pessoal do Ceará helped position them in a larger Brazilian musical milieu.

20. Sunday, February 24, 2008, "Fagner—Cartaz de show—Orós—1977," *Música do Ceará*, http://musicadoceara.blogspot.com/2008/02/fagner-cartaz-de-show-ors-1977 .html.

21. Fagner interview.

22. Although Fagner is sometimes considered a singer of *brega*, a term that roughly translates to "tacky" and that typically refers to a genre of romantic schlock, his musician- ship, his schooled aesthetic, his hybridic approach to genre, and his nostalgic allusions to the Northeast place his work within the genre of MPB, which is how he understands it. (Some of his work, however, is also unmistakably *brega*.) In some contexts, Fagner's music has been described as *forrock* (a portmanteau of *forró* and rock), which is accurate in some ways but overdetermines Fagner's use of *forró*. Fagner, it should be noted, doesn't associate himself with *forróck*.

23. The Portuguese lyrics are "A seca sem chuva é ruim / mas a seca d'água é pior." The word *seca* (drought) in this case refers not to a lack of water but to a lack of agricultural productivity. Thus, a *seca sem chuva* is a bad crop due to a lack of rain, and a *seca d'água* is a bad crop due to too much rain.

24. "Chega de Mágoa," *Raimundo Fagner*, http://www.raimundofagner.com.br/chega_magoa.htm, accessed April 14, 2012.

25. "Súplica cearense" was written by Waldeck Artur de Macedo and Nelinho and was first released in 1967.

26. The Fagner Foundation also has a location in Fortaleza.

27. *Estados Anysios de Chico City*, "Fagner é o convidado de Alberto Roberto," directed by Cininha de Paula, Cassiano Filho, and Paulo Guelli, written by Eduardo Sidney. Rede Globo, aired 1991, date unknown.

28. In addition to his two houses in Orós, Fagner also owns a house along Rua Principal in Orós and another in a nearby town.

29. Meirismar Augusto Paulino, "Sob o céu de Orós," *Jornal o Povo*, May 30, 2003, http://www.opovo.com.br/app/opovo/vida-e-arte/2003/05/30/noticiavidaeartejornal,257035/sob-o-ceu-de-oros.shtml.

30. Ibid.

31. Ibid.

32. Ibid.

33. Fagner interview.

34. Alexander Dent describes covers of American songs by *música sertaneja* artists in São Paulo as "cross-cultural texts," arguing that they should not be seen as facile examples of cultural imperialism. He also calls for further study of "the dynamics of cultural exchange within a Hick Atlantic" (2005, 221). It is worth noting that according to Billboard Brasil, Mariah Carey's cover of "I Want to Know What Love Is" has the distinction of being the longest-running number-one hit. It was the number-one hit in Brazil from December 2009 until May 2010.

35. José Hilton Dantas, interview by the author, December 10, 2011.

36. "Entrevista com seu Dantas voz da liberdade 18 de junho de 2011," http://www.youtube.com/watch?v=qeSJoTJHNM4, accessed February 1, 2012.

Chapter 5. Real or Plastic *Forró*

1. Anuário Estatístico do Ceará (2014) "Demanda turistica via Fortaleza," accessed on February 25, 2018, http://www2.ipece.ce.gov.br/publicacoes/anuario/anuario2014/aspectosEconomicos/turismo/demanda_turistica.htm.

2. Ibid.

3. http://data.worldbank.org/country/brazil#cp_wdi, accessed January 12, 2016.

4. http://data.worldbank.org, accessed January 12, 2016.

5. Angela Lühning (2013) writes the opposite about the Brazilian city of Salvador in the same era. She claims that the municipal government supported some cultural practices but not others, ignoring the "cultural ecosystem" as a whole.

6. "Plano estadual da convivência com a seca," State Government of Ceará, February 2015, http://www.ipece.ce.gov.br/estudos_sociais/politicas_publicas/Plano_Convivencia_com_a_Seca_02_03_2015.pdf.

7. "Cantora Sylvinha Araújo, da jovem guarda, morre em SP," *G1*, June 26, 2008, http://g1.globo.com/Noticias/Brasil/0,mul614639–5598,00-cantora+sylvinha+araujo+da+jovem+guarda+morre+em+sp.html.

8. Fernando Sa, "'Mastruz com leite,' a indústria do forró," *Jornal o Povo*, February 20, 1992.

9. Ibid.

10. Christiane Viana, "Oxente, é Forró: O mercado cearense foi invadido por centenas de bandas e mais de 70 já gravaram disco," *Jornal o Povo*, June 25, 1994.

11. "Forró via satélite," *Jornal o Povo*, December 26, 1996.

12. "Megaempresário controla a noite," *Jornal o Povo*, September 19, 1993.

13. WikiLeaks, the online organization created in 2006 by activist Julian Assange that publishes classified documents, has been widely publicized in Brazil.

14. "WikiLeaks do forró na revista o globo," *Cabaré do Timpin*, March 27, 2011, http://musicaoriginalbrasileira.blogspot.com/2011/03/wikileaks-do-forro-na-revista-o-globo.html, accessed March 9, 2012.

15. "Rádio satélite vai levar Forró ao sul," *Jornal o Povo*, September 29, 1996.

16. "Conquista público e aire mercado no Ceará," *Jornal o Povo*, September 29, 1996.

17. "Que time é o teu, Mastruz?" *Jornal o Povo*, August 14, 1995.

18. "Conquista público"; Christiani Viana, "Indústria do Forró," *Jornal o Povo*, May 11, 1995.

19. João Fellet, "Consumo da classe C cresce sete vezes desde 2002, diz estudo," *BBC Brasil*, December 17, 2010, http://www.bbc.co.uk/portuguese/noticias/2010/12/101217_classec_consumo_jf.shtml, accessed March 8, 2012.

20. Wágner Gomes, "Classe C puxa consumo no Brasil," *Agência o Globo*, February 28, 2012, http://br.noticias.yahoo.com/classe-c-puxa-consumo-brasil-153727281.html, accessed March 8, 2012.

21. Adelson Viana, interview by the author, June 8, 2010.

22. Ibid.

23. Naiana Rodrigues, "Uma vida dedicada às tradições do forró," *Diário do Nordeste*, January 18, 2012.

24. Viana interview.

25. Glauco Araújo, "Chico César diz que não apoia banda de forró eletrônico no São João da PB," *G1*, April 20, 2011, http://g1.globo.com/pop-arte/noticia/2011/04/chico-cesar-diz-que-nao-apoia-banda-de-forro-eletronico-no-sao-joao-da-pb.html, accessed March 15, 2012.

26. Daniel Buarque, "Chico César tentar apagar polêmica do 'forró de plástico' no São João," *G1*, June 23, 2011, http://g1.globo.com/brasil/noticia/2011/06/chico-cesar-tentar--apagar-polemica-do-forro-de-plastico-no-sao-joao.html, accessed March 15, 2012.

27. "Quem paga o arrasta-pé no são joão?," *Jornal o Povo*, April 25, 2011.

28. Notes from a June 8, 2010, meeting.

29. "Férias em Fortaleza, a Capital da Alegria anima a alta estação," SETFOR, July 13,

2010, http://www.fortaleza.ce.gov.br/turismo/index.php?option=com_content&task
=view&id=150.

30. In Ceará the period between 1986 and 2002 is known as the Government of Changes
due to the sweeping reforms of Tasso Jereissati, who served as governor between 1987
and 1991 and again from 1995 to 2002.

31. Sara Maia, "Capital terá 718 mil turistas na Copa," *Jornal o Povo,* February 1, 2012,
http://www.opovo.com.br/app/opovo/economia/2012/02/01/noticiasjornalecon
omia,2776443/capital-tera-718-mil-turistas-na-copa.shtml.

32. To clarify, I am not arguing that the poor necessarily have a subjective preference
for noise. Rather, I am arguing that quiet is associated with wealth and economic development. As individuals gain status and wealth in Fortaleza, their ability to purchase sound
systems increases, as does their ability to seek recourse against acoustic disturbances.

33. Luana Lima, "60,8% das denúncias registradas na Semam são de poluição sonora,"
Diário do Nordeste, January 29, 2012.

34. Ibid.

35. http://www.cearaenoticia.com.br/2012/01/prefeitura-alerta-para-o-uso-ilegal-de
.html?m=1.

36. Alex Pimentel, "Paredões de som são apreendidos em Fortaleza neste final de semana," *Diário do Nordeste,* January 23, 2012.

Chapter 6. *Forró*, or Bread and Circuses

1. Mundano's widely publicized installation in California involved sculptures of *mandacaru* cacti, which he made from water pipes and fitted with temporarily running fau-
cets, into dry riverbeds and lakes, as well as ironic locations like a water park, to draw a
comparison between droughts in California and Brazil. His most famous project, called
Pimp My Carroça, involves the refurbishing and painting of hand-pulled trash carts and
a day of medical check-ups and pampering for the trash collectors and has taken place
on multiple occasions and in multiple cities.

2. The exchange rate between the U.S. dollar and the Brazilian real has varied significantly between 2004 and 2016, fluctuating between a low 1.5 reais to the dollar in 2008 and
an atypically high 4 reais to the dollar in 2016. Given this extreme variability, for the sake
of simplicity and clarity, I only include values in reais and not their conversion to dollars.

3. http://www1.folha.uol.com.br/cotidiano/2016/01/1730367-crise-economica-faz
-cidades-diminuirem-carnaval-pelo-pais.shtml?cmpid=facefolha.

4. Ibid.

5. Ibid.

6. http://www.theguardian.com/world/2016/jan/12/brazil-Carnival-economic-crisis
-recession.

7. In the days leading up to Carnival in 2016, the Zika virus, which caused microcephaly
in newborns of infected pregnant women, was often given as another reason for austerity.

8. http://www.al.ce.gov.br/index.php/clipping-o-estado/item/36900-deputados-classificam-como-%E2%80%9Cacertada%E2%80%9D-suspens%C3%A3o-de-verba.

9. Ibid.

10. http://www.brasil.gov.br/observatoriodaseca/.

11. http://blogdogecionevieira.blogspot.com/2016/01/prefeito-confirma-que-havera-carnaval.html.

12. http://diariodonordeste.verdesmares.com.br/cadernos/politica/parlamentar-denuncia-industria-da-seca-no-ce-1.1365290.

13. http://www.cidades.ibge.gov.br/painel/economia.php?lang=&codmun=231220&search=ceara|santa-quiteria|infogr%E1ficos:-despesas-e-receitas-or%E7ament%E1rias-e-pib.

14. http://politica.estadao.com.br/noticias/geral,sem-petrobras-e-com-economia-em-queda—nordeste-tera-sao-joao-da-crise,1698055

15. http://www.verdinha.com.br/microfone-aberto/2015/10/08/romarias-de-novembro-em-juazeiro-deve-agravar-ainda-mais-falta-dagua/

16. http://g1.globo.com/ceara/noticia/2014/02/juiz-proibe-uso-de-dinheiro-publico-no-carnaval-de-santa-quiteria-no-ce.html

17. http://www.revistaforum.com.br/2016/02/05/a-gestao-cultural-sob-ataque-crise-e-direitos-culturais-no-brasil/.

18. http://diariodonordeste.verdesmares.com.br/cadernos/caderno-3/impeachment-para-o-rei-momo-1.1480514.

Conclusion

1. See Liverman and Vilas (2006) for a nuanced understanding of neoliberalism's diverse—not exclusively negative—effects on environmental management in Latin America.

References

Abreu, João Capistrano de, and Arthur Brakel. 1997. *Chapters of Brazil's Colonial History, 1500–1800*. New York: Oxford University Press.

Aguiar, Pinto de. 1983. *Nordeste o drama das secas*. Rio de Janeiro: Civilização Brasileira.

Ahmed, Sara. 2008. "Open Forum Imaginary Prohibitions: Some Preliminary Remarks on the Founding Gestures of the 'New Materialism.'" *European Journal of Women's Studies* 15 (1): 23–39.

Albuquerque Júnior, Durval Muniz de. 1999. *A invenção do nordeste e outras artes*. Recife: Fundação Joaquim Nabuco, Editora Massangana.

Allen, Aaron. 2012. "Ecomusicology: Bridging the Sciences, Arts, and Humanities." In *Environmental Leadership: A Reference Handbook*, edited by Deborah Rigling Gallagher, 373–381. Thousand Oaks, CA: Sage Publications.

———. 2013. "Ecomusicology." *Grove Music Online. Oxford Music Online*. Oxford University Press, accessed October 7, 2017. http://www.oxfordmusiconline.com/subscriber/article/grove/music/A2240765.

Allen, Aaron S., and Kevin Dawe. 2016. *Current Directions in Ecomusicology: Music, Culture, Nature*. New York: Routledge.

Almeida, Custódio. 2003. "Ceará—Idéias." In *Bonito pra chover: Ensaios sobre a cultura cearense*, edited by Gilmar de Carvalho, 227–233. Fortaleza: Edições Demócrito Rocha.

Almeida, Moisés. 2009. "Imagens e memórias do Sertão." *Historien: Revista de história* 1:50–62.

Anderson, Mark D. 2011. *Disaster Writing: The Cultural Politics of Catastrophe in Latin America*. Charlottesville: University of Virginia Press. Andrade, Manuel Correia de Oliveira. 1985. *A seca: Realidade e mito*. Recife: Editora ASA Pernambuco.

Andrade, Mário de. (1928) 2008. *Macunaíma: O herói sem nenhum caráter*. Rio de Janeiro: Agir Editora.

Appert, Catherine. Forthcoming. In *Hop Hop Time: Popular Music and Social Change in Urban Senegal*. New York: Oxford University Press.

Aragão, Thais. 2013. "O triângulo e o biscoito fino para as massas: Reverberações culturais de uma prática ambulante." Conference proceedings of "O Gosto da Música: 90 Encontro Internacional de Música e Mídia." São Paulo: MUSIMID: Centro de Estudos em Música e Mídia.

Araújo, Paulo Cesar de. 2002. *Eu não sou cachorro, não: Música popular cafona e ditadura militar*. Rio de Janeiro: Editora Record.

Araújo, Samuel. 1988. "Brega: Music and Conflict in Urban Brazil." *Latin American Music Review / Revista de música latinoamericana* 9 (1): 50–89.

Archer, William Kay. 1964. "On the Ecology of Music." *Ethnomusicology* 8 (1): 28–33.

Arons, Nicholas Gabriel. 2004. *Waiting for Rain: The Politics and Poetry of Drought in Northeast Brazil*. Tucson: University of Arizona Press.

Attali, Jacques. (1985) 1992. *Noise: The Political Economy of Music*. Manchester: Manchester University Press.

Austregésilo, José Mario. 2012. *Luiz Gonzaga: O homem, sua terra e sua luta*. Recife: FASE Faculdade.

Azevedo, Miguel Ângelo de (Nirez). 1999. *O balanceio de Lauro Maia*. Belo Horizonte: Equatorial Produções.

———. 2012. *A história cantada no Brasil em 78 rotações*. Fortaleza: Universidade Federal do Ceará.

Baer, Hans, and Merrill Singer. 2016. *Anthropology of Climate Change*. New York: Routledge.

Bahiana, Ana Maria. 2006. *Nada será como antes: MPB anos 70–30 anos depois*. Rio de Janeiro: Senac.

Barad, Karen. 2003. "Posthumanist Performativity: Toward an Understanding of How Matter Comes to Matter." *Signs: Journal of Women in Culture and Society* 28 (3): 801–831.

Barbieri, Alisson F., Edson Domingues, Bernardo L. Queiroz, Ricardo M. Ruiz, José I. Rigotti, José A. M. Carvalho, and Marco F. Resende. 2010. "Climate Change and Population Migration in Brazil's Northeast: Scenarios for 2025–2050," *Population and Environment: A Journal of Interdisciplinary Studies* 31 (5): 344–370.

Barbosa, Ivone Cordeiro. 2007. "Entre a barbárie e a civilização: O lugar do sertão na literatura." In *Uma nova história do Ceará*, edited by Simone de Souza, 56–75. Fortaleza: Edições Demócrito Rocha.

Barkley, Ben, C. Rodríguez-Flores, C. Soberanes-González, and M. C. Arizmendi. 2012. "Laughing Falcon (*Herpetotheres cachinnans*)." In *Neotropical Birds Online*, edited by T. S. Schulenberg. Ithaca, NY: Cornell Lab of Ornithology. http://neotropical.birds. cornell.edu/portal/species/overview?p_p_spp=132596

Béhague, Gerard. 1980. "Brazilian Musical Values of the 1960s and 1970s: Popular Urban Music from Bossa Nova to Tropicalia." *Journal of Popular Culture* 14 (3): 437–452.

Bijsterveld, Karin. 2008. *Mechanical Sound: Technology, Culture, and Public Problems of Noise in the Twentieth Century*. Cambridge, MA: MIT Press.

Bishop, Elizabeth. 2011. *Prose*. London: Macmillan.

Bishop, John F. 2000. "Trem do Forró: Tourism, Musical Tradition and Transformation in Pernambuco, Brazil, 1945–2000." M.A. thesis, University of California, Los Angeles.

———. 2001. "Just as Sweet the Second Time Around: The Re-popularization of the Baião in Pernambuco, Brazil." *Studies in Latin American Popular Culture* 20:203–216.

———. 2004. "Who Are the Pirates? The Politics of Piracy, Poverty, and Greed in a Globalized Music Market." *Popular Music and Society* 27 (1): 101–106.

Blake, Stanley E. 2011. *The Vigorous Core of Our Nationality: Race and Regional Identity in Northeastern Brazil*. Pittsburgh, PA: University of Pittsburgh Press.

Bookchin, Murray. 1982. *The Ecology of Freedom: The Emergence and Dissolution of Hierarchy*. Palo Alto, CA: Cheshire Books.

Born, Georgina, ed. 2013. *Music, Sound and Space: Transformations of Public and Private Experience*. Cambridge: Cambridge University Press.Boym, Svetlana. 2002. *The Future of Nostalgia*. New York: Basic Books.

Brande, William Thomas. 1811. "An Account of a Vegetable Wax from Brazil." *Philosophical Transactions of the Royal Society of London* 101:261–268.

Bronfman, Alejandra, and Andrew Grant Wood. 2012. *Media, Sound, & Culture in Latin America and the Caribbean*. Pittsburgh, PA: University of Pittsburgh Press.

Buchanan, Donna Anne, ed. 2016. *Soundscapes from the Americas: Ethnomusicological Essays on the Power, Poetics, and Ontology of Performance*. London: Routledge.

Bull, Michael. 2004. "Thinking about Sound, Proximity, and Distance in Western Experience: The Case of Odysseus's Walkman." In *Hearing Cultures: Essays on Sound, Listening, and Modernity*, edited by Veit Erlmann, 173–190. Oxford: Berg.

Calvert, Peter, and Susan Calvert. 1999. *The South, the North, and the Environment*. London: A & C Black.

Capanema, Guilherme Schuch de, and Giacomo Raja Gabaglia. 2006. *A seca no Ceará*. Fortaleza: Museu do Ceará, Secretaria da Cultura do Estado do Ceará.

Cardim, Fernão. 1939. *Tratados da terra e gente do Brasil, introd. e notas de Batista Caetano, Capistrano de Abreu e Rodolfo Garcia*. São Paulo: Companhia Editora Nacional.

Cardoso, Leonardo. 2016. "The Politics of Noise Control in São Paulo." *Journal of Latin American Studies* 49 (4): 917–945.

Cascudo, Luís da Câmara. 1964. "A carnaúba." *Revista brasileira de geografia* 26 (2): 159–215.

———. 1986. *Contos tradicionais do Brasil*. São Paulo: Editora da Universidade de São Paulo.

———. 2012. *Dicionário do folclore brasileiro*. São Paulo: Global Editora.

Castro, Priscila Lima de. 2016. *Canto do Ceará: Os festivais de música do Ceará na cécada de 1960*. Fortaleza: Lumiar Comunicação e Consultoria.

Castro, Ruy. 2001. *A onda que se ergueu do mar: Novos mergulhos na bossa nova*. São Paulo: Companhia das Letras.

Castro, Ruy, and Julian Dibbell. 2012. *Bossa Nova: The Story of the Brazilian Music That Seduced the World*. Chicago: Chicago Review Press.

Castro, Wagner. 2008. *No tom da canção cearense: Do rádio e tv, dos lares e bares na era dos festivais (1963–1979)*. Fortaleza: Edições UFC.

References

Castro Neves, Frederico. 2002. "A seca e a cidade: A formação da pobreza urbana em Fortaleza (1800–1900)." In *Seca*, edited by Simone de Souza and Frederico de Castro Neves, 75–104. Fortaleza: Edições Demócrito Rocha.

———. 2007. "A seca na história do Ceará." In *Uma nova história do Ceará*, edited by S. de Souza, 76–102. Fortaleza: Edições Demócrito Rocha.

Catholic Church. 1961. *The Liber Usualis: With Introduction and Rubrics in English.* New York: Desclee Company.

Chandler, Billy Jaynes. (1978) 2000. *The Bandit King: Lampião of Brazil.* College Station: Texas A & M University Press.

Chianca, Luciana. 2007. "Devoção e diversão: Expressões contemporâneas de festas e santos católicos." *Revista anthropológicas* 18 (2): 2.

Cohen, Sara. 1997. "Identity, Place and the 'Liverpool Sound.'" In *Ethnicity, Identity and Music: The Musical Construction of Place*, edited by Martin Stokes, 117–134. Oxford: Berg.

Coopat, Carmen Maria Saenz, and Márcio Mattos, eds. 2012. *Agrupamentos da música tradicional do Cariri cearense.* Fortaleza: Quadricolor.

Corbin, Alain. 1998. *Village Bells: Sound and Meaning in the 19th-Century French Countryside.* New York: Columbia University Press.

Cordeiro, Nonato. 2009. "As transformações ocorridas no forró na década de 1990 em Fortaleza." Paper presented at "Relembrando Luíz Gonzaga," Centro Cultural Dragão do Mar, Fortaleza, Ceará, August 6.

Costa, Jean Henrique. 2011. "Luiz Gonzaga: Entre o mito da pureza musical e a indústria cultural." *Revista espaço acadêmico* 11 (130): 135–146.

Crook, Larry. 2009. *Focus: Music of Northeast Brazil.* New York: Routledge.

Crouch, David. 2006. "Tourism, Consumption and Rurality." In *Handbook of Rural Studies*, edited by Paul Cloke, Terry Marsden, and Patrick Mooney, 355–364. London: SAGE Publications.

Cruz, Danielle Maia, and Lea Carvalho Rodrigues. 2010. "Tempo de Carnaval: Políticas culturais e formulações identitárias em Fortaleza." *Revista proa* 2 (1): 1–32.

Cunha, Euclides da, and Leopoldo M. Bernucci. (1902) 2002. *Os sertões: Campanha de canudos.* São Paulo: Atelie Editorial.

Curran, Mark. 2011. *Retrato do Brasil em cordel.* São Paulo: Ateliê Editorial.

Curtis, James R. 1976. "Woody Guthrie and the Dust Bowl." *Places* 3 (2): 12–18.

Custódio, Leandro. 2009. "Afinal, o que é forró?" Paper presented at "Relembrando Luíz Gonzaga," Centro Cultural Dragão do Mar, Fortaleza, Ceará, August 6.

DaMatta, Roberto. 1991. *Carnivals, Rogues, and Heroes: An Interpretation of the Brazilian Dilemma.* Notre Dame, IN: University of Notre Dame Press.

Daughtry, J. Martin. 2015. *Listening to War: Sound, Music, Trauma and Survival in Wartime Iraq.* New York: Oxford University Press.

Dawe, Kevin. 2016. "Materials Matter: Towards a Political Ecology of Musical Instrument Making." In *Current Directions in Ecomusicology: Music, Culture, Nature*, edited by A. Allen and K. Dawe. New York: Routledge.

de Carvalho, Gilmar, ed. 2003. *Bonito pra chover: Ensaios sobre a cultura cearense.* Fortaleza: Edições Demócrito Rocha.

Della Cava, Ralph. 1970. *Miracle at Joaseiro.* New York: Columbia University Press.

De Marchi, Leonardo. 2015. "Structural Transformations of the Music Industry in Brazil 1999–2009: The Reorganization of the Record Market in the Digital Networks." In *Made in Brazil: Studies in Popular Music,* edited by Martha Tupinambá de Ulhôa, Cláudia Azevedo, and Felipe Trotta, 173–186. New York: Routledge.

de Melo Branco, Adélia. 2000. *Women of the Drought: Struggle and Visibility in the Face of a Disaster Situation.* João Pessoa, Brazil: Editora Universitária.

Denis, Jean Ferdinand, and César Famin. 1837. *Brésil.* Paris: Firmin-Didot Frères.

Denis, Pierre. 1910. *Le Brésil au XXe siècle.* Paris: A. Colin.

———. 1911. *Brazil.* New York: Chas. Scribner's Sons.

Dent, Alexander S. 2005. "Cross-Cultural 'Countries': Covers, Conjuncture, and the Whiff of Nashville in Música Sertaneja (Brazilian Commercial Country Music)." *Popular Music and Society* 28 (2): 207–227.

———. 2009. *River of Tears: Country Music, Memory, and Modernity in Brazil.* Durham, NC: Duke University Press.

———. 2012. "Piracy, Circulatory Legitimacy, and Neoliberal Subjectivity in Brazil." *Cultural Anthropology* 27 (1): 28–49.

de Oliveira, Francisco. 1977. *Elegia para uma re(li)gião: Sudene, Nordeste; Planejamento e conflitos de classes.* Rio de Janeiro: Paz e Terra.

Devine, Kyle. 2015. "Decomposed: A Political Ecology of Music." *Popular Music* 34 (3): 367–389.

Dibben, Nicola. 2009. "Nature and Nation: National Identity and Environmentalism in Icelandic Popular Music Video and Music Documentary." *Ethnomusicology Forum* 18 (1): 131–151.

Diplomatic and Consular Reports: Brazil; Report for the Years 1904–06 on the Trade of Bahia, no. 3901. 1907. London: Foreign Office and the Board of Trade.

Draper, Jack A., III. 2010. *Forró and Redemptive Regionalism from the Brazilian Northeast: Popular Music in a Culture of Migration.* New York: Peter Lang.

Dreyfus, Dominique. 1996. *Vida do viajante: A saga de Luiz Gonzaga.* São Paulo: Editora 34.

Dunn, Christopher. 2001. *Brutality Garden: Tropicália and the Emergence of a Brazilian Counterculture.* Chapel Hill: University of North Carolina Press.

Echeverria, Regina. 2006. *Gonzaguinha e gonzagão: Uma história brasileira.* Rio de Janeiro: Ediouro Publicações.

Eidsheim, Nina Sun. 2015. *Sensing Sound: Singing and Listening as Vibrational Practice.* Durham, NC: Duke University Press.

Erlmann, Veit, ed. 2004. *Hearing Cultures: Essays on Sound, Listening and Modernity.* Oxford: Berg.

Escobar, Arturo. 1999. "After Nature: Steps to an Antiessentialist Political Ecology." *Current Anthropology* 40 (1): 1–30.

————. 2006. "Difference and Conflict in the Struggle over Natural Resources: A Political Ecology Framework." *Development* 49 (3): 6–13.

Evans, David. 2006. "High Water Everywhere: Blues and Gospel Commentary on the 1927 Mississippi River Flood." In *Nobody Knows Where the Blues Come From: Lyrics and History*, edited by Robert Springer, 3–75. Jackson: University Press of Mississippi.

Fagner, Raimundo. 2003. *A música brasileira deste século por seus autores e intérpretes: Fagner*. São Paulo: SESC.

Fausto-Sterling, Ann. 2000. *Sexing the Body: Gender Politics and the Construction of Sexuality*. New York: Basic Books.

Favaretto, Celso Fernando. 2000. *Tropicália, alegoria, alegria*. São Paulo: Atelie Editorial.

Feld, Steven. (1982) 2012. *Sound and Sentiment: Birds, Weeping, Poetics, and Song in Kaluli Expression*. Durham, NC: Duke University Press.

————. 1996. "Waterfalls of Song: An Acoustemology of Place Resounding in Bosavi, Papua New Guinea." In *Senses of Place*, edited by Steven Feld and Keith H. Basso, 91–136. Santa Fe: School of American Research Press.

Feld, Steven, and Donald Brenneis. 2004. "Doing Anthropology in Sound." *American Ethnologist* 31 (4): 461–474.

Feldman-Bianco, Bela. 1992. "Multiple Layers of Time and Space: The Construction of Class, Ethnicity, and Nationalism among Portuguese Immigrants." *Annals of the New York Academy of Sciences* 645 (1): 145–174.

Fernandes, Adriana. 2005. "Music, Migrancy and Modernity: A Study of Brazilian Forró." Ph.D. dissertation, University of Illinois.

Ferretti, Mundicarmo. 2012. *Na batida do Baião, no balanço do Forró: Zedantas e Luiz Gonzaga*. Recife: Fundação Joaquim Nabuco, Editora Massangana.

Freyre, Gilberto. 1961. *Casa-grande & senzala: Formação da família brasileira sob o regime de economia patriarcal*. Rio de Janeiro: J. Olympio.

Frost, Samantha. 2016. *Biocultural Creatures: Toward a New Theory of the Human*. Durham, NC: Duke University Press.

Fox, Aaron A. 2004. *Real Country: Music and Language in Working-Class Culture*. Durham, NC: Duke University Press.

Franceschi, Humberto M. 1984. *Registro sonoro por meios mecânicos no Brasil*. Rio de Janeiro: Studio HMF.

————. 2002. *A Casa Edison e seu tempo*. Rio de Janeiro: PETROBRAS.

Frank, Andre Gunder. (1967) 2009. *Capitalism and Underdevelopment in Latin America: Historical Studies of Chile and Brazil*. New York: Monthly Review Press.

Garfield, Seth. 2010. "The Environment of Wartime Migration: Labor Transfers from the Brazilian Northeast to the Amazon during World War II." *Journal of Social History* 43 (4): 989–1019.

————. 2014. *In Search of the Amazon: Brazil, the United States, and the Nature of a Region*. Durham, NC: Duke University Press.

Garrard, Greg. 2004. *Ecocriticism*. New York: Routledge.

Giddens, Anthony. (1984) 2013. *The Constitution of Society: Outline of the Theory of Structuration*. Cambridge: Polity Press.

Gold, John R. 1998. "From 'Dust Storm Disaster' to 'Pastures of Plenty': Woody Guthrie and Landscapes of the American Depression." In *The Place of Music*, edited by Andrew Leyshon, David Matless, and George Revill, 249–268. London: Guiford Press.

Gondim, Linda M. P. 2007. "Os 'governos das mudanças' (1987–1994)." In *Uma nova história do Ceará*, edited by Simone de Souza, 409–424. Fortaleza: Edições Demócrito Rocha.

"Gramophone Wax." 1905. *Pharmaceutical Journal: A Weekly Record of Pharmacy and Allied Sciences* 74, 4th series, 20: 542.

Granata, Charles L. 2004. *Sessions with Sinatra: Frank Sinatra and the Art of Recording*. Chicago: Chicago Review Press.

Grant, Catherine. 2016. "Socio-economic Concerns of Young Musicians of Traditional Genres in Cambodia: Implications for Music Sustainability." *Ethnomusicology Forum* 25 (3): 306–325.

Gray, Lila Ellen. 2007. "Memories of Empire, Mythologies of the Soul: Fado Performance and the Shaping of *Saudade*." *Ethnomusicology* 51 (1): 106–130.

———. 2013. *Fado Resounding: Affective Politics and Urban Life*. Durham, NC: Duke University Press.

Greene, Paul D., and Thomas Porcello. 2010. *Wired for Sound: Engineering and Technologies in Sonic Cultures*. Middletown, CT: Wesleyan University Press.

Greenfield, Gerald. 2009. "Lampião, Luiz and Padim Ciço: Three Icons of the Brazilian Northeast." *Memory Studies* 2 (3): 393–410.

Greenough, Paul, and Anna Lowenhaupt Tsing. 2009. *Nature in the Global South: Environmental Projects in South and Southeast Asia*. Durham, NC: Duke University Press.

Guerra, Philippe. 1981. *A civilização da seca*. Fortaleza: DNOCS.

Guy, Nancy. 2009. "Flowing Memories: Taiwan's Tamsui River in the Performative Imagination." *Ethnomusicology* 53 (2): 218–248.

Hall, Anthony L. 1978. *Drought and Irrigation in North-East Brazil*. Cambridge: Cambridge University Press.

Haraway, Donna Jeanne. 2004. *The Haraway Reader*. New York: Routledge.

Hernández, Deborah Pacini. 1995. *Bachata: A Social History of Dominican Popular Music*. Philadelphia: Temple University Press.

Hertzman, Marc A. 2013. *Making Samba: A New History of Race and Music in Brazil*. Durham, NC: Duke University Press.

Hilty, Steven L. 2003. *Birds of Venezuela*. Princeton, NJ: Princeton University Press.

Hirschkind, Charles. 2006. *The Ethical Soundscape: Cassette Sermons and Islamic Counterpublics*. New York: Columbia University Press.

Impey, Angela. 2002. "Culture, Conservation and Community Reconstruction: Explorations in Advocacy Ethnomusicology and Participatory Action Research in Northern Kwazulu Natal." *Yearbook for Traditional Music* 34:9–24.

———. 2013. "Songs of Mobility and Belonging: Gender, Spatiality and the Local in Southern Africa's Transfrontier Conservation Development." *Interventions* 15 (2): 255–271.

Ingold, Tim. 2007. "Materials against Materiality." *Archaeological Dialogues* 14 (1): 1–16.

Ingram, David. 2008. "'My Dirty Stream': Pete Seeger, American Folk Music, and Environmental Protest." *Popular Music and Society* 31 (1): 21–36.

———. 2010. *The Jukebox in the Garden: Ecocriticism and American Popular Music since 1960.* Amsterdam: Editions Rodopi.

IPECE (Instituto de Pesquisa e Estratégia Econômica do Ceará). 2014. *Anuário estatístico do Ceará 2014.* Fortaleza: Secretário de Planejamento e Gestão (SEPLAG), Governo Estadual do Ceará. http://www2.ipece.ce.gov.br/publicacoes/anuario/anuario2014/creditos.htm.

Johnson, Dennis V. 1970. "The Carnaúba Wax Palm (*Copernicia prunifera*) and Its Role as an Economic Plant." M.A. thesis, University of California, Los Angeles.

———. 1972a. "Carnauba Wax Palm (*Copernicia prunifera*). I. Botany." *Principes* 16 (1): 16–19.

———. 1972b. "Carnauba Wax Palm (*Copernicia prunifera*). II. Geography." *Principes* 16 (2): 42–48.

———. 1972c. "Carnauba Wax Palm (*Copernicia prunifera*). III. Exploitation and Plantation Growth." *Principes* 16 (3): 111–114.

———. 1972d. "Carnauba Wax Palm (*Copernicia prunifera*). IV. Economic Uses." *Principes* 16 (4): 128–131.

Johnson, Herbert Fisk, Jr. 1936. *Carnaúba Expedition: The Story of a Scientific Adventure by Airplane to Study the Carnaúba Palm at Its Source in the Interior of Brazil.* With Arthur Dailey. Racine, WI: Western Printing and Lithographing Company.

Katz, Mark. 2004. *Capturing Sound: How Technology Has Changed Music.* Berkeley: University of California Press.

Kelman, Ari Y. 2010. "Rethinking the Soundscape: A Critical Genealogy of a Key Term in Sound Studies." *Senses & Society* 5 (2): 212–23.

Kennedy, Rick, and Ted Gioia. 2013. *Jelly Roll, Bix, and Hoagy: Gennett Records and the Rise of America's Musical Grassroots.* Bloomington: Indiana University Press.

Kenny, Mary Lorena. 2002. "Drought, Clientelism, Fatalism and Fear in Northeast Brazil." *Ethics, Place & Environment* 5 (2): 123–134.

Knaggs, Nelson S. 1944. "Carnauba—Brazil's Tree of Life." *Chemical & Engineering News* 22 (18): 1564–1569.

Krause, Bernard L. 2012. *The Great Animal Orchestra: Finding the Origins of Music in the World's Wild Places.* New York: Little, Brown.

Kun, Josh. 2005. *Audiotopia: Music, Race, and America.* Berkeley: University of California Press.

Lambert, Jacques. 1959. *Os dois Brasís.* Rio de Janeiro: INEP, Ministério da Educação e Cultura.

Lamen, Darien. 2014. "Sound Tracks of a Tropical Sexscape: Tropicalizing Northeastern

Brazil, Channeling Transnational Desires." In *Sun, Sea, and Sound: Music and Tourism in the Circum-Caribbean*, edited by Timothy Rommen and Daniel T. Neely, 267–288. New York: Oxford University Press.

Latour, Bruno. 2005. *Reassembling the Social: An Introduction to Actor-Network-Theory*. Oxford: Oxford University Press.

Latour, Bruno, and Catherine Porter. 2004. *Politics of Nature: How to Bring the Sciences into Democracy*. Cambridge, MA: Harvard University Press.

Lemos, Maria Carmen, Timothy J. Finan, Roger W. Fox, Donald R. Nelson, and Joanna Tucker. 2002. "The Use of Seasonal Climate Forecasting in Policymaking: Lessons from Northeast Brazil." *Climatic Change* 55 (4): 479–507.

Levin, Theodore. 2006. *Where Rivers and Mountains Sing: Sound, Music, and Nomadism in Tuva and Beyond*. Bloomington: Indiana University Press.

Lima, Maria Érica de Oliveira. 2007. "For All, folkmídia e a indústria cultural regional." *Razón y palabra* 60. http://www.razonypalabra.org.mx/anteriores/n60/oliveiralima.htm.

Lion, Jean Pierre. 2005. *Bix: The Definitive Biography of a Jazz Legend, Leon "Bix" Beiderbecke (1903–1931)*. New York: Continuum.

Liverman, Diana M., and Silvina Vilas. 2006. "Neoliberalism and the Environment in Latin America." *Annual Review of Environmental Resources* 31:327–363.

Lookingbill, Brad. 1994. "Dusty Apocalypse and Socialist Salvation: A Study of Woody Guthrie's Dust Bowl Imagery." *Chronicles of Oklahoma* 72 (4): 397–413.

Loveless, Megwen. 2010. "The Invented Tradition of Forró: A 'Routes' Ethnography of Brazilian Musical 'Roots.'" Ph.D. dissertation, Harvard University.

———. 2012. "Between the Folds of Luiz Gonzaga's Sanfona: Forró Music in Brazil." In *The Accordion in the Americas*, edited by Helena Simonett, 268–294. Urbana: University of Illinois Press.

Lühning, Angela. 2013. "Sustentabilidade de patrimônios musicais e políticas públicas a partir de experiências e vivências musicais em bairros populares." *Música e cultura: Revista da ABET* 8 (1): 44–58.

Lyra, Augusto Tavares de. 1912. *O Rio Grande do Norte, 1911*. Rio de Janeiro: Typ. do Journal do Commercio, de Rodrigues.

Madrid, Alejandro L., and Robin D. Moore. 2013. *Danzón: Circum-Caribbean Dialogues in Music and Dance*. New York: Oxford University Press.

Maia, Emy. 2009. "Sintonizando: Para uma 'história cultural' de rádio em Fortaleza, 1924–1944." Paper presented at Museu de Imagem e Som, Fortaleza, Ceará, July 18.

Mark, Andrew. 2014. "Refining Uranium: Bob Wiseman's Ecomusicological Puppetry." *Environmental Humanities* 4 (1): 69–93.

Martín-Barbero, Jesús. 1993. *Communication, Culture and Hegemony*. London: Sage.

———. 2006. "A Latin American Perspective on Communication / Cultural Mediation." *Global Media and Communication* 2 (3): 279–297.

Matos, Cláudia Neiva de. 2007. "Namora & briga, as artes do forró: Auto-retrato de um baile popular brasileiro." In *O charme dessa nação: Música popular, discurso e sociedade brasileira*, edited by N. B. da Costa, 421–444. Fortaleza: Expressão Gráfica e Editora.

McCann, Bryan. 2004. *Hello, Hello Brazil: Popular Music and the Making of Modern Brazil.* Durham, NC: Duke University Press.

Mellers, Wilfrid. 2001. *Singing in the Wilderness: Music and Ecology in the Twentieth Century.* Urbana: University of Illinois Press.

Mendes, Maria das Dores Nogueira. 2007. "Palmilhando um chão sagrado: A construção da topografia nas canções do pessoal do Ceará." In *O charme dessa nação: Música popular, discurso e sociedade brasileira,* edited by N. Costa, 401–420. Fortaleza: Expressão Gráfica e Editora.

Merriam, Alan. 1964. *The Anthropology of Music.* Evanston, IL: Northwestern University Press.

Moehn, Frederick. 2007. "Music, Citizenship, and Violence in Postdictatorship Brazil." *Latin American Music Review* 28 (2): 181–219.

———. 2011. "'We Live Daily in Two Countries': Audiotopias of Postdictatorship in Brazil." In *Brazilian Popular Music and Citizenship,* edited by Idelber Avelar and Christopher Dunn, 109–130. Durham, NC: Duke University Press.

Morais Filho, Melo. (1888) 2002. *Festas e tradicoes populares do Brasil.* Brasília: Senado Federal, Conselho Editorial.

Morcom, Anna. 2015. "Landscape, Urbanization, and Capitalist Modernity: Exploring the 'Great Transformation' of Tibet through Its Songs." *Yearbook for Traditional Music* 47:161–189.

Moreira, Nicolau Joaquim. 1875. *Agricultural Instructions for Those Who May Emigrate to Brazil.* Rio de Janeiro: Imperial Instituto Artistico.

Morelli, Rita de Cássia Lahoz. 2009. *Indústria fonográfica: Um estudo antropológico.* Campinas: Editora Unicamp.

Morris, Mitchell. 1998. "Ecotopian Sound or the Music of John Luther Adams and Strong Environmentalism." In *Crosscurrents and Counterpoints: Offerings in Honor of Bengt Hambraeus at 70,* edited by P. F. Broman, N. A. Engebretnen, and B. Alphonce, 129–141. Gothenburg: University of Gothenburg Press.

Murphy, John P. 1997. "The 'Rabeca' and Its Music, Old and New, in Pernambuco, Brazil." *Latin American Music Review / Revista de música latinoamericana* 18 (2): 147–172.

———. 2006. *Music in Brazil: Experiencing Music, Expressing Culture.* New York: Oxford University Press.

Murray, Sean. 2009. "Pianos, Ivory, and Empire." *American Music Review* 38 (2): 1, 4–5, 13–14.

Nelson, Donald R., and Timothy J. Finan. 2009. "Praying for Drought: Persistent Vulnerability and the Politics of Patronage in Ceará, Northeast Brazil." *American Anthropologist* 111 (3): 302–316.

Neuman, Daniel M. 1990. *The Life of Music in North India: The Organization of an Artistic Tradition.* Chicago: University of Chicago Press.

Ochoa Gautier, Ana María. 2006. "Sonic Transculturation, Epistemologies of Purification and the Aural Public Sphere in Latin America." *Social Identities* 12 (6): 803–825.

References

———. 2014. *Aurality: Listening and Knowledge in Nineteenth-Century Colombia.* Durham, NC: Duke University Press.

———. 2016. "Acoustic Multinaturalism, the Value of Nature, and the Nature of Music in Ecomusicology." *boundary 2* 43 (1): 107–141.

Oliveira Pinto, Tiago de. 2001. "Som e música: Questões de uma antropologia sonora." *Revista de Antropologia* 44 (1): 222–286.

Olivenor, José. 2002. "'Metrópole da fome': A cidade de Fortaleza na seca de 1877–1879." In *Seca*, edited by Simone de Souza and Frederico de Castro Neves, 49–74. Fortaleza: Edições Demócrito Rocha.

Oosterbaan, Martijn. 2008. "Spiritual Attunement Pentecostal Radio in the Soundscape of a Favela in Rio de Janeiro." *Social Text* 26 (3[96]): 123–145.

Paiva, Flávio. 2014. *Invocado: Um jeito brasileiro de ser musical.* Fortaleza: Armazém da Cultura.

Paz, Ermelinda A. 2002. *O modalismo na música brasileira.* Brasília: Editora MUSIMED.

Pedelty, Mark. 2012. *Ecomusicology: Rock, Folk, and the Environment.* Philadelphia: Temple University Press.

———. 2016. *A Song to Save the Salish Sea: Musical Performance as Environmental Activism.* Bloomington: Indiana University Press.

Pedroza, Ciro José Peixoto. 2001. "Mastruz com Leite for all: Folk-comunicação ou uma nova indústria cultural do Nordeste Brasileiro." In *Anais da XXIV Congresso Brasileiro de Comunicação.* Campo Grande: INTERCOM.

Pennesi, Karen. 2007. "The Predicament of Prediction: Rain Prophets and Meteorologists in Northeast Brazil." Ph.D. dissertation, University of Arizona.

Pennesi, Karen, and Carla Renata Braga de Souza. 2012. "O encontro anual dos profetas da chuva em Quixadá, Ceará: A circulação de discursos na invenção de uma tradição." *Horizontes Antropológicos* 18 (38): 159–186.

Perrone, Charles A. 2017. "Backlands Bards: From Fine Folk Verse to Lofty Lapidary Lyric." *Review: Literature and Arts of the Americas* 49 (1–2): 35–42.

Peterson, Marina. 2012. *Sound, space, and the city: civic performance in downtown Los Angeles.* Philadelphia, Pa: University of Pennsylvania Press.

Pimentel, Mary. 1995. *Terral dos sonhos: O Cearense na música popular brasileira.* Fortaleza: Banco do Nordeste do Brasil / Gráfica e Editora Arte Brasil.

Pires, Antônio. 1988. "Carta do Padre Antônio Pires de Pernambuco de 5 de junho de 1552." In *Cartas avulsas (1550–1568): Azpilcueta Navarro e outros.* Belo Horizonte: Editora Itatiaia.

Post, Jennifer C. 2007. "'I Take My Dombra and Sing to Remember My Homeland': Identity, Landscape and Music in Kazakh Communities of Western Mongolia." *Ethnomusicology Forum* 16 (1): 45–69.

Queiroz, Rachel de. (1930) 2000. *O quinze.* São Paulo: Editora Siciliano.

Ramalho, Elba Braga. 1997. "Luiz Gonzaga: His Life and His Music." Ph.D. dissertation, University of Liverpool.

———. 2000. *Luiz Gonzaga: A síntese poética e musical do Sertão*. São Paulo: Terceira Margem.

Ramnarine, Tina K. 2009. "Acoustemology, Indigeneity, and Joik in Valkeapää's Symphonic Activism: Views from Europe's Arctic Fringes for Environmental Ethnomusicology." *Ethnomusicology* 53 (2): 187–217.

Ramos, Graciliano, and Evandro Teixeira. (1938) 2008. *Vidas secas: 70 anos*. Rio de Janeiro: Record.

Rees, Helen. 2016. "Environmental Crisis, Culture Loss, and a New Musical Aesthetic: China's 'Original Ecology Folksongs' in Theory and Practice." *Ethnomusicology* 60 (1): 53–88.

Rehding, Alexander. 2002. "Eco-musicology." *Journal of the Royal Musical Association* 127 (2): 305–320.

———. 2011. "Ecomusicology between Apocalypse and Nostalgia." *Journal of the American Musicological Society* 64 (2): 409–414.

Reily, Suzel Ana. 1997. "Macunaíma's Music: National Identity and Ethnomusicological Research in Brazil." In *Ethnicity, Identity and Music: The Musical Construction of Place*, edited by Martin Stokes, 71–96. New York: Berg Publishers.

———. 2002. *Voices of the Magi: Enchanted Journeys in Southeast Brazil*. Chicago: University of Chicago Press.

Ribot, Jesse C. 2014. "Cause and Response: Vulnerability and Climate in the Anthropocene." *Journal of Peasant Studies* 41 (5): 667–705.

Rice, Timothy. 2014. "Ethnomusicology in Times of Trouble." *Yearbook for Traditional Music* 46:191–209.

Rios, Kênia Sousa. 2002. "A cidade cercada: Festa e isolamento na seca de 1932." In *Seca*, edited by Simone de Souza and Frederico de Castro Neves, 105–129. Fortaleza: Edições Demócrito Rocha.

———. 2003. "O tempo por escrito: Sobre lunários e almanaques." In *Bonito pra chover: Ensaios sobre a cultura cearense*, edited by Gilmar de Carvalho, 79–89. Fortaleza: Edições Demócrito Rocha.

Roda, P. Allen. 2014. "Tabla Tuning on the Workshop Stage: Toward a Materialist Musical Ethnography." In *Ethnomusicology Forum* 23 (3): 360–382.

Rodrigues, Francisca I. F., and Erotilde Honório Silva. 2009. "A popularização do rádio no Ceará na década de 1940." In *História da Mídia Sonora: Experiências, memórias e afetos do Norte a Sul do Brasil*, edited by Luciano Klöckner and Nair Prata, 106–129. Porto Alegre: EDIPUCRS.

Rogério, Pedro. 2008. *Pessoal do Ceará: Habitus e campo musical na década de 1970*. Fortaleza: UFC Edições.

Rogers, Thomas D. 2010. *The Deepest Wounds: A Labor and Environmental History of Sugar in Northeastern Brazil*. Chapel Hill: University of North Carolina Press.

Roseman, Marina. 1991. *Healing Sounds from the Malaysian Rainforest: Temiar Music and Medicine*. Berkeley: University of California Press.

References

Ryan, Robin. 2013. "Not Really a Musical Instrument? Locating the Gumleaf as Acoustic Actant and Environmental Icon." *Societies* 3 (2): 224–242.

———. 2015. "'Didjeri-doos' and 'Didjeri-don'ts': Confronting Sustainability Issues." *Journal of Music Research Online 6.*

Sakakeeny, Matt. 2010. "Under the Bridge: An Orientation to Soundscapes in New Orleans." *Ethnomusicology* 54 (1): 1–27.

Samuels, David W., Louise Meintjes, Ana Maria Ochoa, and Thomas Porcello. 2010. "Soundscapes: Toward a Sounded Anthropology." *Annual Review of Anthropology* 39:329–345.

Sant'Anna, Affonso Romano de. 1978. *Música popular e moderna poesia brasileira.* Petrópolis: Vozes.

Santos, José Américo. 1983. *As secas do Norte do Brasil.* Rio de Janeiro: Tip. de Machado & Cia.

Santos, José Farias dos. 2002. *Luiz Gonzaga: A música como expressão do Nordeste.* São Paulo: IBRASA—Instituição Brasileira de Difusão Cultural Ltda.

Santos, Martha S. 2012. *Cleansing Honor with Blood Masculinity, Violence, and Power in the Backlands Of Northeast Brazil, 1845–1889.* Stanford, CA: Stanford University Press.

Saraiva, José Américo Bezerra. 2008. "Pessoal do Ceará: A identidade de um percurso e o percurso de uma identidade." Ph.D. dissertation, Universidade Federal do Ceará.

Schafer, R. Murray. (1977) 1994. *The Soundscape: Our Sonic Environment and the Tuning of the World.* Rochester, VT: Destiny Books.

Schama, Simon. 1995. *Landscape and Memory.* New York: Alfred A. Knopf.

Scheper-Hughes, Nancy. 1992. *Death without Weeping: The Violence of Everyday Life in Brazil.* Berkeley: University of California Press.

Schippers, Huib. 2010. "Three Journeys, Five Recollections, Seven Voices: Operationalizing Sustainability in Music." In *Applied Ethnomusicology: Historical and Contemporary Approaches,* edited by Klisala Harrison, Elizabeth Mackinlay, and Svanibor Pettan, 150–160. Newcastle upon Tyne: Cambridge Scholars.

Schippers, Huib, and Catherine Grant, eds. 2016. *Sustainable Futures for Music Cultures: An Ecological Perspective.* New York: Oxford University Press.

Schreiner, Claus. 1993. *Música Brasileira: A History of Popular Music and the People of Brazil.* New York: Marion Boyars Publishers.

Seeger, Anthony. 2004. *Why Suyá Sing.* Chicago: University of Illinois Press.

———. 2015. "Natural Species, Sounds, and Humans in Lowland South America: The Kĩsêdjê/Suyá, Their World, and the Nature of Their Musical Experience." In *Current Directions in Ecomusicology: Music, Culture, Nature,* edited by Aaron Allen and Kevin Dawe, 89–98. New York: Routledge.

Seemann, Jörn. 2008. "From Candle Wax to E 903: Commodity Geographies of the Carnaúba Palm (*Copernicia cerifera*) from Northeastern Brazil." Paper presented at the Ninth International Congress of the Brazilian Studies Association, New Orleans, March 27–29.

Severiano, Jairo. 2013. *Uma história da música popular brasileira das origens à modernidade.* São Paulo: Editora 34.

Sharp, Daniel B. 2014. *Between Nostalgia and Apocalypse: Popular Music and the Staging of Brazil.* Middletown, CT: Wesleyan University Press.

Siegel, B. 1971. "Migration Dynamics in the Interior of Ceará, Brazil." *Southwestern Journal of Anthropology* 27 (3): 234–258.

Silva, Erotilde Honório. 2006. *O despertar da memória: As narrativas dos excluídos da terra na construção do Açude Orós.* Fortaleza: Secult.

Silva, Expedito L. 2003. *Forró no asfalto: Mercado e identidade sociocultural.* São Paulo: Annablume/Fapesp.

Simonett, Helena. 2014. "Envisioned, Ensounded, Enacted: Sacred Ecology and Indigenous Musical Experience in Yoreme Ceremonies of Northwest Mexico." *Ethnomusicology* 58 (1): 110–132.

Skidmore, Thomas E. 1974. *Black into White: Race and Nationality in Brazilian Thought.* New York: Oxford University Press.

———. 2010. *Brazil: Five Centuries of Change.* New York: Oxford University Press.

Slater, Candace. 1982. "Cordel and Canção in Today's Brazil." *Latin American Research Review* 17 (3): 29–53.

Smith, T. Lynn. 1944. *Brazil: People and Institutions.* Baton Rouge: Louisiana State University Press.

"The Social Dimensions of Climate Change: Discussion Draft." 2011. United Nations Task Team on Social Dimensions of Climate Change, New York.

Solomon, Thomas James. 2000. "Dueling Landscapes: Singing Places and Identities in Highland Bolivia." *Ethnomusicology* 44 (2): 257–280.

Stahl, Matthew. 2002. "Authentic Boy Bands on TV? Performers and Impresarios in the Monkees and Making the Band." *Popular Music* 21 (3): 307–329.

Sterne, Jonathan. 1997. "Sounds Like the Mall of America: Programmed Music and the Architectonics of Commercial Space." *Ethnomusicology* 41 (1): 22–50.

Stewart, Kathleen. 1988. "Nostalgia—a Polemic." *Cultural Anthropology* 3 (3): 227–241.

Stimeling, Travis D. 2012. "Music, Place, and Identity in the Central Appalachian Mountaintop Removal Mining Debate." *American Music* 30 (1): 1–29.

Stobart, Henry. 2006. *Music and the Poetics of Production in the Bolivian Andes.* Burlington, VT: Ashgate.

Stokes, Martin. 1997. "Introduction: Ethnicity, Identity and Music." In *Ethnicity, Identity and Music: The Musical Construction of Place,* edited by Martin Stokes, 1–28. New York: Berg Publishers.

Sugar, Piassava Fiber, Carnauba Wax, and Ipecac. U.S. Bureau of Foreign and Domestic Commerce, vol. 3. Washington, DC: Government Printing Office, 1921.

Sutton, Allan. 2010. *A Phonograph in Every Home: The Evolution of the American Recording Industry, 1900–19.* Denver: Mainspring Press.

Taddei, Renzo. 2006. "Oráculos da chuva em tempos modernos: Mídia, desenvolvimento econômico, e as transformações na identidade social dos profetas do sertão." In *Os profetas da chuva*, edited by Karla Martins, 161–170. Fortaleza: Tempo d'Imagem.

———. 2017. *Metereologistas e profetas da chuva: Conhecimentos, práticas e políticas da atmosfera*. São Paulo: Terceiro Nome.

Tainter, Charles Sumner. 1887. "Tablet for Use in Graphophones." U.S. Patent 393,190.

Taube, Edward. 1952. "Carnauba Wax—Product of a Brazilian Palm." *Economic Botany* 6 (4): 379–401.

Taylor, Timothy D. 2002. "Music and the Rise of Radio in 1920s America: Technological Imperialism, Socialization, and the Transformation of Intimacy." *Historical Journal of Film, Radio and Television* 22 (4): 425–443.

Tester, Keith. 2002. *The Life and Times of Post-modernity*. New York: Routledge.

Thompson, Emily Ann. 2002. *The Soundscape of Modernity: Architectural Acoustics and the Culture of Listening in America, 1900–1933*. Cambridge, MA: MIT Press.

Titon, Jeff Todd. 2009. "Music and Sustainability: An Ecological Viewpoint." *World of Music* 51 (1): 119–137.

Toliver, Brooks. 2004. "Eco-ing in the Canyon: Ferde Grofé's *Grand Canyon Suite* and the Transformation of Wilderness." *Journal of the American Musicological Society* 57 (2): 325–368.

Travassos, Elizabeth. 2000. "Ethics in the Sung Duels of Northeastern Brazil: Collective Memory and Contemporary Practice." *British Journal of Ethnomusicology* 9 (1): 61–94.

Trotta, Felipe. 2009. "Música popular, moral e sexualidade: Reflexões sobre o forró contemporânea." *Revisa Contracampo* 20:132–146.

Trotta, Felipe, and Márcio Monteiro. 2008. "O novo mainstream da música regional: Axé, brega, reggae e forró eletrônico no Nordeste." *E-compós* 11 (2): 1–15.

Truax, Barry. 1984. *Acoustic Communication*. Norwood, NJ: Ablex.

Tsing, Anna Lowenhaupt. 2011. *Friction: An Ethnography of Global Connection*. Princeton, NJ: Princeton University Press.

U.S. Government Printing Office. 1932. "Carnauba Wax." *Trade Information Bulletin*, no. 801–825.

Van Perlo, Ber. 2009. *A Field Guide to the Birds of Brazil*. New York: Oxford University Press.

Vasconcelos Solon, Daniel. 2006. "O eco dos Alto-Falantes: Memória das amplificadoras e sociabilidades na Teresina de meados do século XX." M.A. thesis, Universidade Federal do Piauí.

Veiga, Manuel. 2013. "Sustentabilidade e música: Uma visão enviesada." *Música e Cultura: Revista da ABET* 8 (1): 19–33.

Vianna, Hermano. 2011. "Technobrega, Forró, Lambadão: The Parallel Music of Brazil." In *Brazilian Popular Music and Citizenship*, edited by Idelber Avelar and Christopher Dunn, 240–249. Durham, NC: Duke University Press.

Vianna, Letícia. 2001. "O rei do meu baião: Mediação e invenção musical." In *Mediação, cultura, politica*, edited by Gilberto Velho, 61–88. São Paulo: Aeroplano Editora.

Vieira, Sulamita. 2000. *O sertão em movimento: A dinâmica da produção cultural.* São Paulo: Annablume.

Vieira, Tanísio. 2002. "Seca, disciplina e urbanização: Fortaleza—1865/1879." In *Seca,* edited by Simone de Souza and Frederico de Castro Neves, 17–48. Fortaleza: Edições Demócrito Rocha.

Waxer, Lise. 2002. *The City of Musical Memory: Salsa, Record Grooves, and Popular Culture in Cali, Colombia.* Middletown, CT: Wesleyan University Press.

Wetherell, James. 1860. *Brazil. Stray Notes from Bahia: Being Extracts from Letters, etc., During a Residence of Fifteen Years.* N.p.: Webb and Hunt.

Whelden, Schuyler. 2017. "More Courage Than Man: Performative Interpretation in Brazilian Protest Song." Paper presented at the Society for Ethnomusicology 62nd Annual Meeting, Denver, Colorado, October 28.

Williams, Raymond. 1973. *The Country and the City.* New York: Oxford University Press.

———. (1977) 2009. *Marxism and Literature.* Oxford: Oxford University Press.

Wisnik, José Miguel. 1977. *O coro dos contrários: A música em torno da Semana de 22.* São Paulo: Livraria Duas Cidades.

Wong, Deborah. 2014. "Sound, Silence, Music: Power." *Ethnomusicology* 58 (2): 347–353.

"The Woods of Brazil." 1897. *United States Congressional Serial Set* 3,540: 659–660.

Wrazen, Louise. 2007. "Relocating the Tatras: Place and Music in Górale Identity and Imagination." *Ethnomusicology* 51 (2): 185–204.

Index

Index

Index

Index

Index

MICHAEL B. SILVERS is an assistant professor of musicology at the University of Illinois at Urbana-Champaign.

The University of Illinois Press
is a founding member of the
Association of American University Presses.

University of Illinois Press
1325 South Oak Street
Champaign, IL 61820-6903
www.press.uillinois.edu

Songbook
Luiz Gonzaga
Volume 1 by Almir Chediak
978-8574074177

Volume 2
978-8574074184